Warm wishes Nicky S x

THE MIND

VOLUME 1 OF *THE HUMAN GARAGE* TRILOGY

Published by Snazell Publishing

Cromwell House
Wolseley Bridge
Stafford
Staffordshire
ST17 0XS
NickyS@painreliefclinic.co.uk

ISBN: 978-0-9931678-1-2

Paperback Edition 10th November 2015

THE
MIND

VOLUME 1 OF *THE HUMAN GARAGE* TRILOGY

BY

NICKY SNAZELL

Snazell Publishing

Also Available From Nicky Snazell

The 4 Keys To Health

Coming Soon From Nicky Snazell

The Body (The Human Garage Part 2)

The Soul (The Human Garage Part 3)

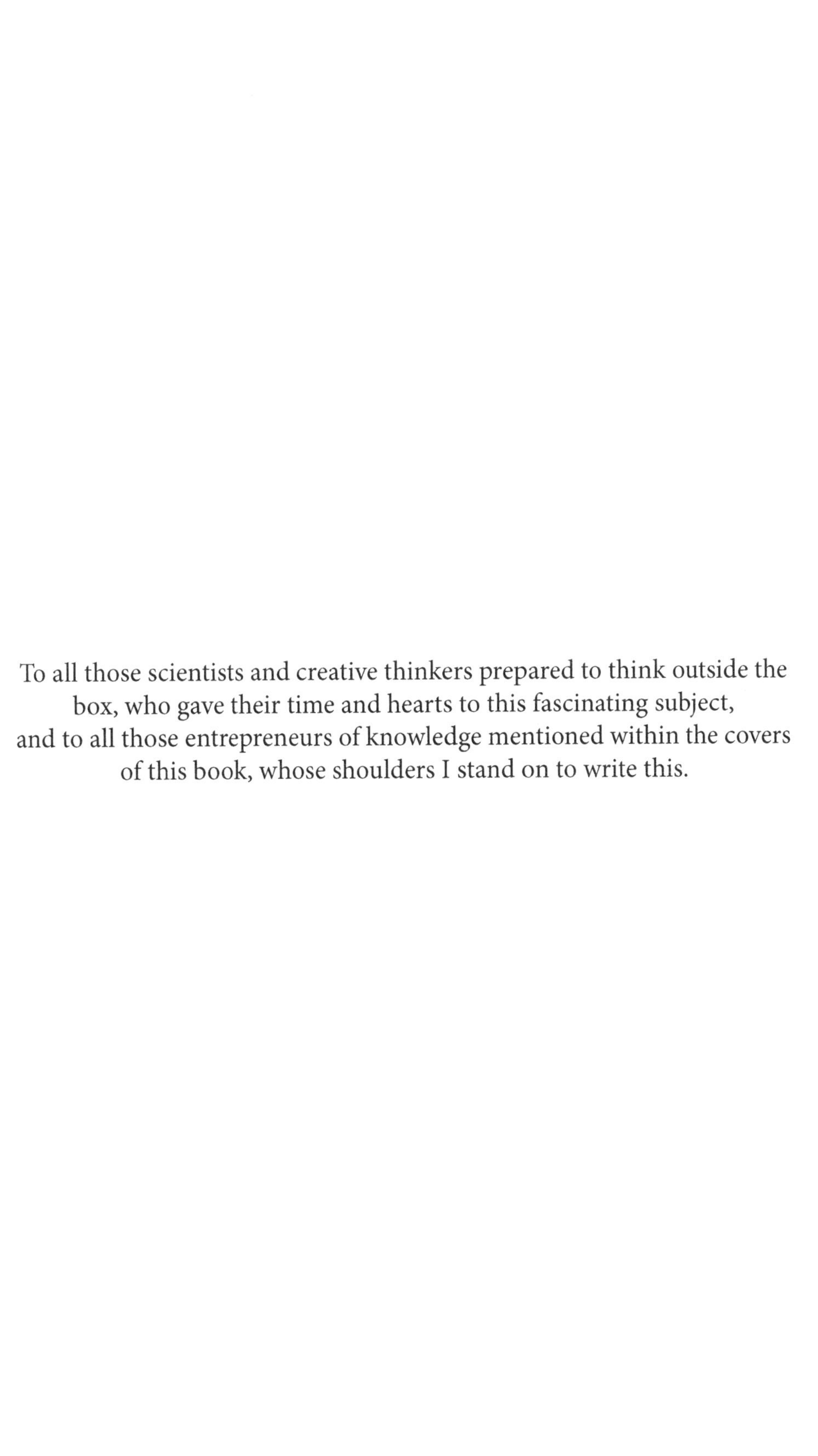

To all those scientists and creative thinkers prepared to think outside the box, who gave their time and hearts to this fascinating subject, and to all those entrepreneurs of knowledge mentioned within the covers of this book, whose shoulders I stand on to write this.

Praise for THE MIND

VOLUME 1 OF THE HUMAN GARAGE TRILOGY
BY NICKY SNAZELL

"It has been long said that we humans don't come with an owner's manual, and Nicky Snazell has taken on the challenge to right that oversight. Her witty yet practical approach to delivering some pretty complex concepts and information makes it both user friendly, useable and fun. Read it, use it, benefit big."

– *Joseph McClendon III, PhD.*

"Nicky Snazell's guide to comprehending and harnessing the power of your mind will astound you and change the way you live."

- *Carol E. Wyer, author of* Grumpy Old Menopause.

CONTENTS

FOREWORD

There must be more to life than this. How often have you heard those words spoken? How often have you spoken those words? The answer to the question is, "Yes, life does have more to offer, a great deal more."

I have always felt that humans are cursed with a compulsion to fetter themselves with all kinds of restrictions, mostly self-created. There are of course those who through illness and infirmities have restrictions forced upon them but all too often they allow those conditions to define who they are. Most restrictions are, however, created in the mind and generally it is because people do not have sufficient self-belief to fulfil their true potential.

So how are these restrictions to be overcome? There is a key, available to all, to unlock the fetters and that key is my friend Nicky.

I have known Nicky for a great many years and in all those years she has been driven by one ambition and that is to help people find a better life whether it be through overcoming illness or through achieving their true potential. She has a very strong belief in the goodness of people and believes that they deserve to be helped to find a life that they can enjoy and take pride in. She was born with abilities and understanding that most will never achieve in their lifetime but even so she has dedicated herself to improving her skills and knowledge. All with one purpose, and that is to aid others.

Nicky uses the analogy of a garage and cars to illustrate her arguments. Make her the key to switching on your life and starting your journey towards the future that was intended for you.

Kenneth Douglas, Esquire, M.B.E.

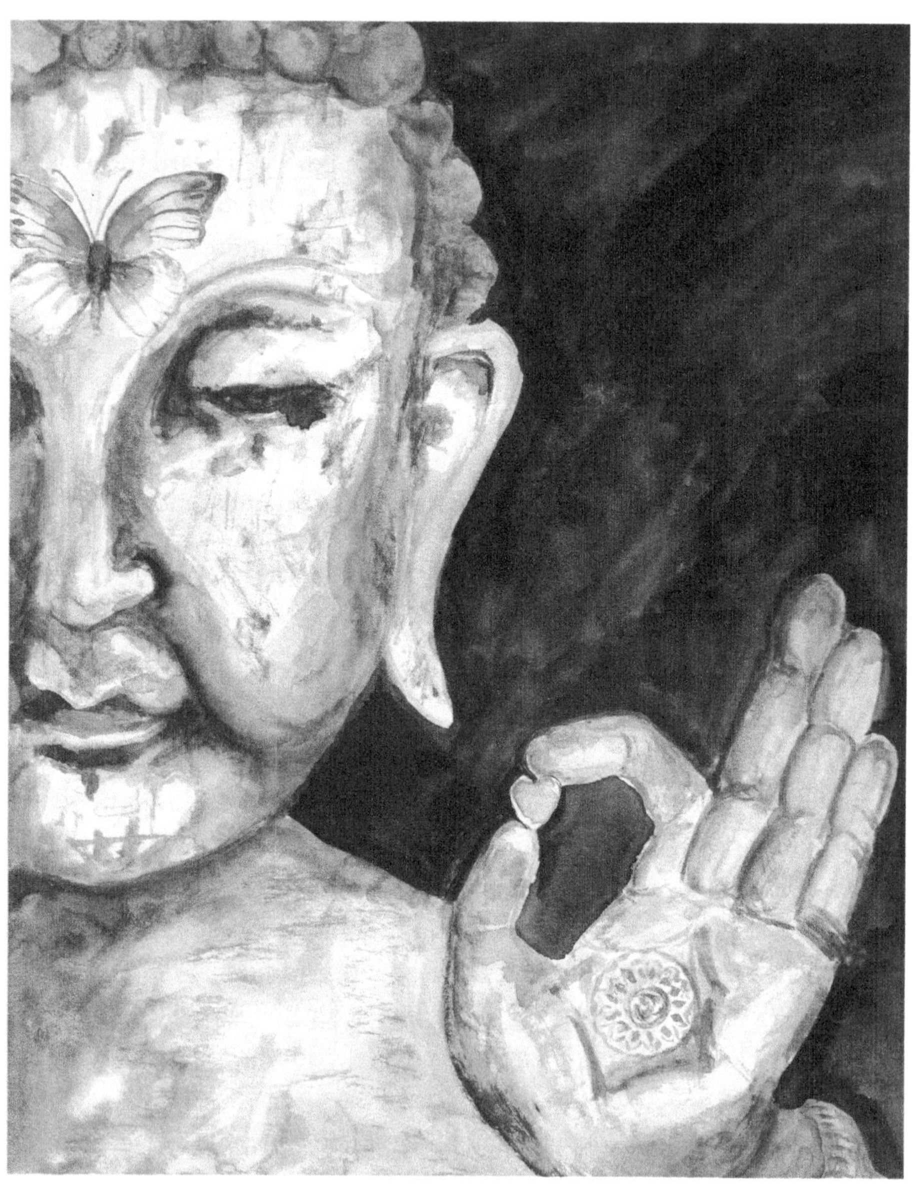

Buddha, by Shirley Harvey Bates

Introduction To Trilogy

"If we did all the things we are capable of, we would literally astound ourselves."

Thomas Edison

I'm fortunate enough to run a pain relief practice in Staffordshire that I've filled with wonderful, knowledgeable people, and I'm pleased to say that these staff members are now my friends as well. They come to the practice already armed with an abundance of knowledge: nursing, physiotherapy, sports therapy, and orthopaedic medical and surgical qualifications, as well as in some cases, reiki training. They are both mechanics and healers, ready to improve the health of our patients.

Once here, they start studying and applying my integrative approach to health – we so often work in the illness industry, not the wellness industry, and I try and keep that in mind when I'm treating my patients, as well as teaching my staff. In my clinics (as I now have a second one in Yorkshire), we utilise all the hard work researchers have put in to be able to create the latest technology. For example, Quadscan can scientifically calculate how healthy our cells are, with its cellular health analysis measuring nutrients, fat, water, bone, and muscle ratios. HeartMath can measure heart rate variance (HRV), as well as evaluating our mindset and the ability to create the correct mind state for healing, instead of stressing. We can assess fitness, such as how well our lungs and heart cope with exercise, and how flexible and strong we are, and there's also a way of looking at how pressure moves up through our feet and body as we run and walk, using gait scanning and biomechanical assessment. This shows us how we can improve posture and reduce joint wear.

Then, by carrying out several detailed assessments involving physiotherapy, neuropathic and psychosocial pain evaluation, and magnetic resonance, we can prescribe tailor-made treatment plans for our patients. These can involve mind state and nutrition advice, massage, manipulation, acupuncture, revolutionary IMS for nerve pain, exercise prescription for life, electrotherapy such as shockwave, laser and ultrasound, and healing where appropriate. Then, once we're happy that we've got the patient as close to optimum health as is now possible for them, we integrate their treatment with revolutionary technology: magnetic resonance (or MRT), that pushes back the hands of time. That's right – never before have we had the capability at our fingertips to regrow cartilage and bone cells at an accelerated rate, which otherwise wouldn't regenerate due to aging. Never before have we gone this far within physical medicine, and it's exciting that we get to see its amazing results in our patients. This Star Trek-like technology is slowly emerging as the new science of today, and most importantly, modern practitioners are being more accepting of the mind-body link.

With my background in shamanic reiki healing, neurolinguistics programming and psychology, I am very aware of the power of the mind and I feel privileged to be in the driving seat of the physical medicine of tomorrow. I strongly feel that analysis of any 'block' a patient is experiencing – which is stopping them from healing – is extremely important. Keeping accurate records and applying both an intuitive and scientific approach to health will give a broader understanding, something that is vital as we pave the way forward for healing future generations.

Throughout this series of books, I am going to give you my recipes of integrated medicine for physical health. Through sharing true stories of some of my current patients (these have been composited from several sources and some details changed to protect their privacy), my aim is to get you to be able to walk in their shoes, feel their pain, and hear their stories and beliefs about suffering, so you can relate their experiences to your own. Only by getting those light-bulb moments – those ah ah's! – will you be in a good place to heal. I want to open up an awareness in you about the stories you tell yourself and how self-destructive they can be. A lady said to me only this week, "If my suffering helps another soul then I can bear it more easily."

My patients are too shy to be on stage, so when I do live shows, I came up with the idea of having puppets made and dressed up to represent them. It is my way of carrying these troubled souls into the room for you, and to get their message across in a clear – and fun! – way.

Have you got hidden beliefs/tragic memories locked into a place in your body? Then let me help you discover them, and consequently, heal from them.

We all tell ourselves a story about our bodies and our health. I know I certainly do – for every injury or operation I've had, I have a story, and I have to be careful how I replay that story. Memory is fluid (it's not like a DVD that plays the same thing over and over again without changing), and whenever we recall something, we create and mould a new version of it.

So, let's rewrite your story about your life, starting today. Read on, and remember that you – and you alone – are the author of your life. You are in charge, and it's time to take charge right now.

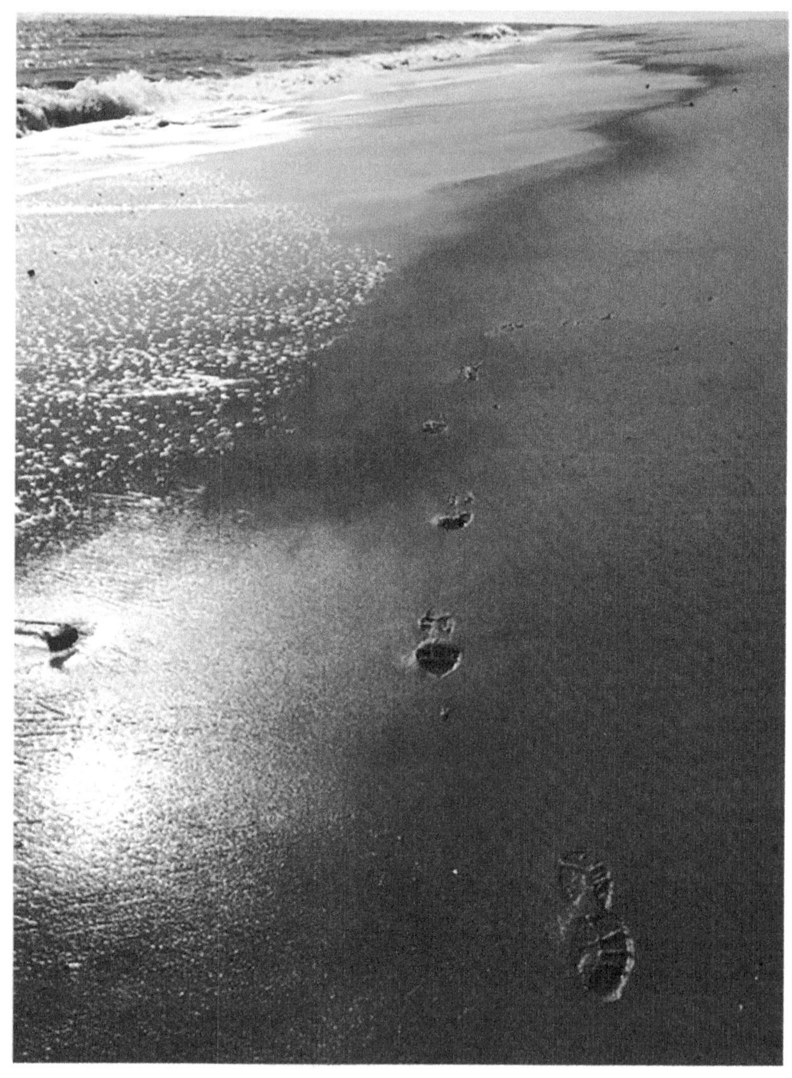

Footprints in the sand. A Norfolk Beach.

Introduction To Mind

"The scientists of today think deeply instead of clearly. One must be sane to think clearly, but one can think deeply and be quite insane."

Nikola Tesla

When I think of the mind, I think of a million different things. I spent so long in my art room, playing with various themes and colours, trying to depict the mind – thinking of the spark of brain cells and car engines idling in an eerie garage – that it all looked like something out of a science fiction book. How on earth do you go about illustrating a book cover about something as amazing and complex as the mind?

Then, when I was on my windy Norfolk beach, watching my footprints wash away as the waves broke on the shore, bam! It came to me: our thoughts, actions, and lives are ever-changing. Thoughts in particular are formed and disappear so fast that they are exactly like my imprints in the sand – coming and going within seconds.

I yearn to leave something important behind on this planet, beyond the day when my carbon unit will just be dust particles. Don't you? After all, we need to give a greater meaning to our existence. All those thoughts that we hold – just for seconds, some of them – are ever-changing, as that is all they can ever be. Those thoughts, built on top of each other, create our health and future, and we alone are responsible for them.

You are the author of your life; you are constantly walking through your life, and while there will only ever be your footprints behind you, you can carry everyone else's footprints in your heart. What do I mean by this? Well, as you walk through life and beyond, you can choose to take others' words and meaningful stories and pass them on – whether by word of mouth like in the olden days, or through paperbacks and ebooks like today.

As I was thinking about my footprints on the sand, I also started thinking of painting (a hobby I love when I have the time). I thought of the imagery of waves, and then I started thinking of my own painting, The

Mind's Eye, as after researching all of the material for this book, I see things differently through the mind's eye. So, at the last moment, I chose the painting as the cover for this book, as I think it encapsulates what I'm trying to say in these pages.

This volume is all about brain structure, about how the mind creates transient thoughts and how it actually controls and repairs your body. This, the first in the trilogy, contains six chapters, all featuring keys themes regarding your health. They have been broken down into easy to read subheadings, and you can use the comprehensive contents to locate specific topics – just run your finger down the contents page and select a subject that calls to you.

As you read, keep a notepad near so you can do your homework – only then will you get the most out of this book. Do not rush to distil what has been a quarter of a century of experiences, instead meditate on any meanings that come to you. I have written this in a multi-dimensional way, so that it can be read at different depths of perception, depending on where you are in life. This is my story. It only represents a tiny fragment of human consciousness.

Whilst writing this, I have studied many, many papers, books, videos and the highlights of both scientific and spiritual conferences to include the most up to date research for you. *The Human Garage* – volumes 1 to 3 – is a written account of the methods I've used over the last 25 to 30 years in my relentless endeavour to 'mend' my patients. The analogy of the *Human Garage* is an interesting one. It came to me time and again, after thousands of weary souls hobbled into my office, slamming their car keys on my desk and using expressions like, "I need an MOT, a service, and a few spare parts, not to mention some WD40 for a few rusty joints, and a jump start for the old battery!"

This got me thinking, and it is from this analogy that my expanding ideas grew. I knew I had to explain that humans have to stop treating their bodies like their cars; cars cannot love you back, or feel empathy or create. If the world of nanorobotics is truly not too distant in the future, we need mindfulness to reset our awareness of the compassionate, spiritual side of human nature. We drive our fragile carbon units recklessly, on an even more fragile and neglected planet. We rely on navigation systems to tell us how to get somewhere, just as we lazily rely on subconscious programs to drive us, while our chattering monkey brain imbeds little memory to a meaningless journey of getting to some destination. How often do we realise that we can't remember where we are, or how we got there? An unfocused, undisciplined mind is as disastrous as a badly programmed CPU (the central processing unit in a car) and yet we all drive one, don't we?

We need to awaken our consciousness to the greater plan and be aware of how the moral and spiritual essence of our being needs to shine through. Especially in a world that allows poverty and violence to live alongside extreme wealth. We have to question certain facts about lifespans. For example, in America – which has the world's leading hospitals and medical care – why is the life expectancy steadily decreasing?

I liked the parable about human consciousness that was forwarded to me recently by Fazila, (who as an aside kindly organised the Z factor event last year, so thank you, Faz). It was a short clip of a book by Anand Giridharadas, about a little-known shooting in a Texan mall 10 days after 9/11. In brief, American vigilante Mark Stroman (a violent man with a cruel childhood) killed two people and deliberately shot a Bangladeshi immigrant in the head. This man was Raisuddin "Rais" Bhuiyan, and although he survived the shooting, he lost the sight in one of his eyes. Bhuiyan was a good, innocent man, an officer in the Bangladesh Air Force, shot because he was a Muslim. He was simply caught in a cycle of vengeance between humans of different worlds.

The incredible ending of the parable was that years later, Rais fought to stop Stroman – who at that point was on death row – from being executed via lethal injection. Stroman knew of this, and through counselling and love, was a changed man before he was executed. This illustrates the power of the human mind, and just goes to show how our minds can shape the way we look at our lives.

This man – before the interjection of one of his victims – was lost, and with all the mixed emotions and twisted belief systems instilled in our human existence, it is little wonder that we miss the signposts and therefore get lost on our way. We coast through life, waking up months or years later saying, "Why am I in this financial mess?" or," Why am I in this dead end, meaningless job?" or, "Why am I with a partner I can't talk to anymore?" I am confident that if you read this book, you can avoid a lot of these pit falls; you just have to get in the right mindset from the start.

In this set of books, I share with you for the first time everything I do clinically, intuitively, mechanically, and psychologically within my own *Human Garage.* I have written and presented on health and pain around the world over many years, but my talks only ever touch on tiny parts of what I've created in my clinics. These volumes are about why and when I use and teach certain techniques, as well as where I sourced them in the world, and from whom I've learnt to hone these skills. Drawing on nearly 30 years of clinical experience, I have included brief stories of true cases, so you can share in their experience (these have been heavily disguised by cutting and pasting the patients' details to protect their privacy).

My first book – *The 4 Keys To Health* – was the foundation to these volumes, for without gaining four green keys (using my traffic light approach to health), healing will be far less tenable. Four red keys may mean it would be foolhardy to even start many of these techniques and treatments which need the body to step up and start healing. This is especially relevant when it comes to cellular regeneration with magnetic resonance treatment (MRT). Over recent years I have had the privilege of helping to introduce MRT, originally known as MBST, to the UK, extending physical medicine into the realms of quantum science. This allows the re-growth of cartilage, tendon and bone tissue in worn, tired joints, reigniting the joys of painless activity and sport. I have battled with the same scepticism that met my late uncle, when he was getting one of the first scanning machines into the Q.E in Birmingham. This has been exhaustingly frustrating due to archaic belief systems and a lack of knowledge on behalf of the medical profession. There will be more about this journey in the next volume, The Body.

I decided to divide *The Human Garage* into three volumes, and this book is my first volume of the trilogy Mind, Body and Soul. Some of you will have a yearning to read up on the mind, while others will be more interested in the physical body and my treatments. Finally, there will also be those of you who gain comfort from energy medicine. These books will appeal to those of you who perhaps already have ailments, and who also have a deep interest in learning more about physical medicine and healing. Moreover, friends who attend my seminars and courses can use them as reference tools. For my colleagues – surgeons, doctors, physiotherapists, sports therapists, acupuncturists, osteopaths, chiropractors, reiki healers, masseurs, and nurses whom have never met me – Hello. May my books offer an insight into how I think and what I do, and may they also help you with your own journey and truths.

Let us get on now and I can explain why the mind is the first volume in this trilogy. What has the mind got to do with illness or injury, you ask? Everything, I reply.

Recently, there has been a lot more research into using mindfulness training to empower the brain. However clever we are, the unconscious brain is still far too slow to react at the speed of modern machines and computer programs, but we can program computers to do tasks our physical flesh cannot. With our vehicles we have a CPU (central processing unit), which I call the car brain. Just like our reptilian unconscious brain, the car brain responds to programs such as anti-braking programs for survival.

Our conscious brain and motor circuits (which move our muscles) could simply not react fast enough in an emergency, such as preventing the wheels from locking in order to maintain control. For instance, the task of pressing our foot off and on the brake pedal hundreds of times a minute – with the correct amount of pressure to adjust for slippery surfaces – is impossible, however, the car brain can do this for us easily. We humans programmed the car brain to do this, as we cannot physically do it ourselves.

Now, how about traction control? The latest motorbike brains can cope with extreme demands of braking when at great angles of lean, no matter what speed the bike is travelling at. This involves adjusting to the amount of force and grip needed, by in part involving a 3D gyroscope and different terrains of changing friction. The bike brain is programmed with a launch control program, whilst the human conscious mind makes unskilled mistakes.

It is our unconscious lizard brain that tells us to swerve out of the way of another car, as our conscious brain is too slow to react, and relying on this would be fatal. The unconscious brain processes a million bits of information to one bit of conscious information. Isn't it interesting that we program computers with an intelligence to calculate and carry out programs, in a time frame that our human conscious brain cannot even begin to match?

Our culture is so infused with technology that our social evolution is now enveloped with computer programs. We are at risk of heading towards being part human, part machine – and even perhaps totally robotic. Technology is great, however, mindfulness training is needed in our children, to hang onto the human spirit and consciousness, as well as our ethical, moral way of being. We need to remember how to communicate with each other, how to listen and how to feel compassion.

This book is about how to reach inside your brain and regain control of your thoughts. To take responsibility for your own happiness, integrity and intuition. My aim is to whet your taste buds regarding how you can use your new-found knowledge about your brain to make your life more enriching, more focused and more purposeful. I will teach you how to drive your mind, to make your body more youthful and healthy. You will find within these pages the secrets of my craft, helping your mind find purpose, happiness, contentment and self-love. You can then use this to empower positive brain states that will help heal both yourself and others.

I find the brain both fascinating and confusing, and for this book I have combined my personal and clinical experiences with the latest research. I hope that the analogies, simple explanations and homework woven within the tapestry of this book will give you enough tools to change your life and those souls closest to you. Please select whatever aspect of this book calls to you, meditate on the words and most importantly – DO YOUR HOMEWORK. It can be very useful to keep your own journal on how you change. I would love for you to come and tell me the results at one of my talks, or on the internet via my websites, Facebook, Twitter or email.

Also, if there is anything you'd like me to include in my next books, please tell me and then you too could be woven into the fabric of this legacy.

If you take nothing else away from this book, please understand that: taking THE RESPONSIBILITY of making THE FIRST small step to change your mind, WILL change your life. Now, let's delve into the brilliant and complex subject that is the human mind.

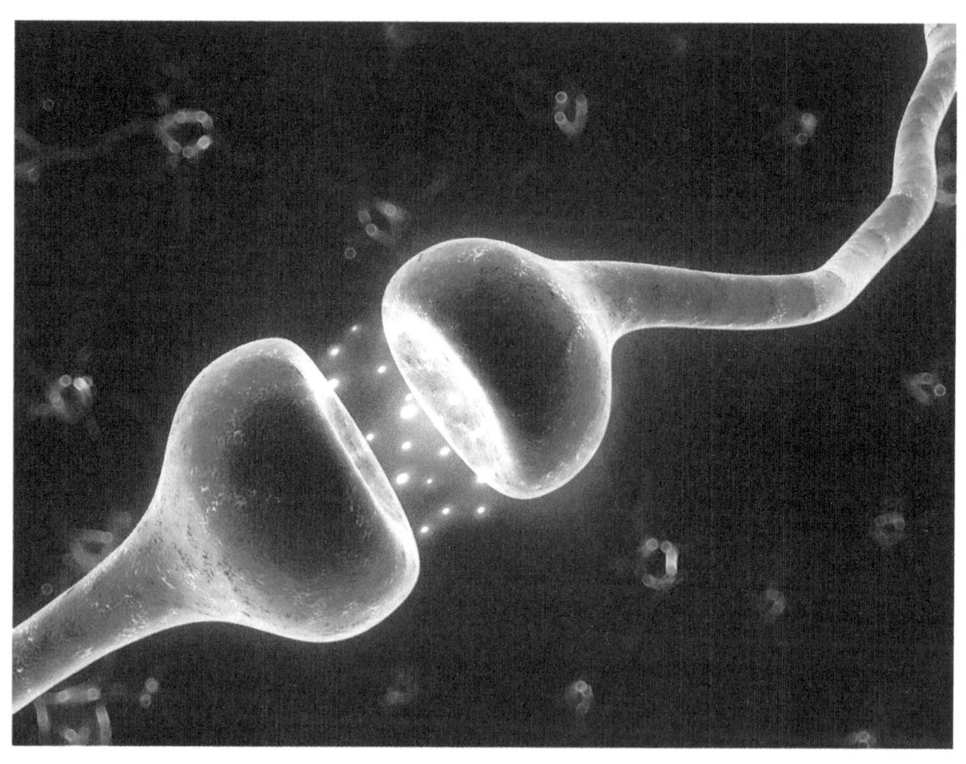

A Synapse

Chapter One

"When the first transhuman intelligence is created and launches itself into recursive self-improvement, a fundamental discontinuity is likely to occur, the likes of which I can't even begin to predict."

Michael Anissimov

YOUR BRAIN IS LITERALLY A TRILLION TINY NUTS AND BOLTS

So, let's think about the brain. Is it full of sugar and spice and all things nice…? Well no, not quite.

I want you to visualise what your brain is made up of biologically. How often do you travel inside your head and focus on how your thoughts are actually made? Do you ever consider what they are made up of? Do you ever stop to think who – and what – exactly you are?

How about these questions: What makes you unique? How do you know you are human? Who told you that you are a separate being with your own unique identity? Who is it inside of you that thinks your thoughts? Where does your soul reside: is it inside or outside of you? Do you have a calling or a purpose to your life? When your body perishes, is that the end of you? Like footprints in the sand, will the sea wash them out, leaving no imprint on humanity? Will you leave deep footprints on people's hearts and minds with your actions? Where is your innate understanding about connectedness and collective consciousness?

If an ingenuous entity or alien was to look at human life forms, what would he discover about the way we live our lives? How easy would it be to copy human consciousness into robotic forms? While we're on this subject, what are your thoughts about nanorobotics? This may seem like a strange question, but it is already part of our lives, and it is likely to have a much bigger role in the future.

Even now we rely heavily on computers, cars, phones and yes, robots, to think and function for us. We allow televisions to brainwash us with constant subliminal messages about how we should act and think. Do you not find that you generally think more clearly when you're away from television and media input? I know I do.

So what gives us the right to say we are special and that we are excellent guardians of the earth, sharing compassion, intelligence, healing, and love? You will discover that this book is a mosaic of memories, scientific papers, and excerpts from many international experts on the mind. My constant questioning is to awaken you to how you need to drive your mind away from weakness, powerlessness, and ill health. You are the author of your life, and you can rewrite it with the help of this book.

3LB OF FAT

Who am I? Who's thinking these thoughts? What medium do I create my thoughts in? Well, if we look at my brain, you'll find that it is 3lb of fat, a sobering thought! It is made up of 1.1 trillion cells and 100 billion building blocks called neurons, with each of these having 5,000 connections called synapses, so there are lots of little nuts and bolts in this head of mine. These neurons are told whether they should fire or not, according to chemical messengers called neurotransmitters.

This is my brain, this vast, complex central processing unit (CPU), much like a vast universe housed in a small ball of fat. I have a vivid memory of staring down into a human brain during my studies, feeling both disbelief and amazement. Is this where my soul is? Is this unattractive, fatty lump the evolutionary pinnacle of biological intelligence on earth? I found it amazing then, and I still do today.

HOMEWORK:

If someone – say, an alien from outer space – asked you who you are, how would you reply? Write it down.

Did you write: 'I am a colony of trillions of cells and I am responsible for all of them?' I thought not. Now don't be shy; what did you write?

'HEAVY' NEUROPHYSIOLOGY FOR BRAINY GEEKS

I think it is important for those brainy geeks out there to understand where brain science is going, especially with the ongoing evolution of computers and robots. As I've said, the brain communicates through many – well, 100 billion if you're counting – little nuts and bolt-like structures, which are called neurons, and these nuts communicate by chemical, electrical discharges through tentacle-like structures. They each fire about 5 to 50 times a second, which is a lot faster than a human hand could fire a gun. Like a computer, the brain transfers and stores bytes of information. However, much more impressive than a computer (which makes me feel better), the human brain has 100 billion unique patterns. This means that the nuts (neurons) have 10 to the millionth power chances of firing, and that means an incredible number of different states of the brain. Atoms in the universe are only 10 to the 18th power. Impressed? You should be – imagine designing this monster! I can just imagine calling out our friendly clever I.T. geek Lee to find a programming fault at so many pounds a minute. It would be expensive to say the least!

Now, try to wrap your head around this: millions of neurons must fire in unison to create even a tiny thought. If I'd realised this much effort was involved, I would have concentrated on having more intelligent thoughts in the past and less naughty ones!

Did you know that we can never experience exactly the same thought or fragment twice? So I guess we always have a chance to airbrush a thought. The brain is too fluid to hold a static thought for any time; we can only imbed similar ones by repeating a similar thought or action time and again, in order to reinforce a behaviour or skill. In fact, we have to do this to develop any kind of skill at all. The reason I know this is because with modern technology, we can actually measure the brain's explosive waves of activity that occur when we sense the environment, something that sculptures the architecture of the brain. This could be fun with certain adventurous sensory activities. I giggle to myself when I imagine wearing a helmet of wires feeding back to techno goof equipment, or lying in an fMRI scanner, having naughty thoughts and causing the electrical activity to go off the scale! Well, you have to have a little fun sometimes.

BRAIN CELL OR MEDUSA?

The brain cell is very interesting to look at: it has its own head called a cell body, a snake-like body called an axon, a tail, and then rather strange-looking tentacles; it always reminds me of the mythical creature Medusa, with snakes around her head. The switch part of the neuron (the head) is called the cell body, and the dendrites that stick out of it collect information on inhibitory or excitatory signals. It is the Hamlet of brain cells – 'To fire, or not to fire, that is the question!' These switches make up the 'grey matter' in the brain, while its snake-like body, the axon, is white brain matter. The axon ends in more dendrites that boss the other neurons about.

WHAT'S THIS FUNNY FIRING THING?

Let's consider one neuron on its own. When it fires, it releases bubbles (vesicles) of happy juice (serotonin) through tendrils (dendrites) into the switch of a neighbouring neuron, and each neuron has 200 bubbles (Robinson, 2007). When it fires, it sends an electrochemical wave rippling down the snake-like body (axon) from its head (the cell body switch) to its fluffy tail, and it uses 10 bubbles of ammunition per fire. They need refilling, otherwise you can end up firing a dud, and in that case you are effectively a nut with a vasectomy. All clever stuff, eh? It is much like having to take your car to a petrol station – constant refilling is needed. The signal reaches another neuron through its tail, with the synapses oozing neurotransmitters, and once the signal is read, the necessary action can take place. Computer simulations of neural networks show permanence to the complex neural networks that aid survival, while the less useful ones fade. In other words, thoughts that aid survival stick like Velcro, and thoughts that do not slide like Teflon.

Consciousness to me is like waves crashing on the beach. Every thought is so transitory that it dissolves fast to give way to the next, much like my footsteps in the wet sand on the shore edge. Hence, there are constant changes in the synapses, and these brain cells start to spark (Atmanspacher and Graben, 2007). The stream of consciousness ebbs and flows with actions, desires, and sensations formed by cascades of fleeting neural assemblies that dissolve in a second (Dehaene, Sergent and Changeaux, 2003; Thompson and Varela, 2003) exactly like the tide on my seashore.

WARNING SENSORS ON THE DASHBOARD

The brain works hard to keep all of my snazzy systems in balance, and believe me, for me to ever be considered balanced is a tall order indeed! Sensors, just like car sensors, send signals – windscreen wash low, oil low, traction needed – and these signals relay to regulators in order to restore the balance. Specific signals bubble up when action needs to be taken; I certainly know when my hands are cold, or when I'm hungry or thirsty, or if my muscles are too full of lactic acid (which are all very common occurrences!).

A CUT ABOVE THE REST

Now, I'd like to take you on a little journey to the dissection labs at the Q.E. Medical School, where I'll give you a whistle stop tour of the fat in our head. So, what does the brain actually look like? I can remember thinking, whilst doing repeated brain dissections, that it was strangely unimpressive. I still remember getting on the narrow coffin-shaped lifts up to the dissection labs – something I always found morbidly fitting in the circumstances. I remember when visiting a handful of universities that all of the dissection labs initially repulsed me, then gradually, the repeated visits became easier to stomach, with them ultimately shaping my appreciation of anatomy.

The lift door to the labs would open, and there in front of my eyes would be rows of the dead, in various stages of dissection. The spark of life was long gone, and once my nose adjusted to the smell of formalin – not to mention the sight – I was fine, and luckily still upright. Dissection labs could not be avoided with the subjects I chose: biology and psychology, then physiotherapy before going on to teach anatomy. The thought of it was worse than it really was, and the 3D imagery was necessary to understand the architecture of the human body.

This was further enhanced when teaching anatomy to postgrad docs, surgeons, and physios, where their recreation would consist of me dragging them around an exhibition that came to Europe, featuring artistically arranged dissected humans. Well, what can I say, there was nothing much on at the cinema! Then the kids – er, I mean adult medics and physios – were released to local bars and restaurants, if their appetite had survived the exhibition. Personally, seeing all this dead meat did help me stick with having no red meat in my diet!

DO YOU DIG UP YOUR DEAD?

Many years ago in the last century, surgeons would pay grave robbers to dig up bodies so they could dissect them, and a few premature deaths are said to have occurred as well. I've never had the urge to do this, so don't worry: there are no secret doors to the backs of my clinics. In the past, doctors – like Jekyll and Hyde – would have a consulting room in the front, and a smelly, ghoulish dissecting lab in the back.

Next, let's describe what's in my hands: we are now going to concentrate on the brain. So get ready – I am now inside your head.

IS THAT LARGE SLIMY WALNUT REALLY MY BRAIN?

For those of you not familiar with handling brains, how would I describe it? Well, it's like holding a coconut-sized walnut, one made of a firm, greyish-brown jelly. The two hemispheres look like old, grey, wrinkly tissue, and they house the highly evolved human cortex. Brains have evolved upwards, bottom up – so to speak – and inside out, with the oldest, most primitive bit at the base, along the neuroaxis (Lewis and Todd, 2007; Tucker, Derryberry and Luu, 2000).

IN THE ATTIC OF THE BRAIN LIES THE LOFTY HUMAN

If we look down on the top part of the brain, each half of the cerebrum has four main areas, which are called lobes. The frontal lobes house the cortex, which is Latin for 'bark' and which does the thinking, the planning, and which experiences the conscious emotions. This cortex also includes the prefrontal cortex (PFC), the cingulate and insula, and these guys are the executors of organisation, future plans, values, self-monitoring, and self-control. If this area is small in your own brain, you will lead a wilder, more irresponsible, monkey brain-led life... sounds like fun!

At the back of the top bit of the brain are the occipital lobes, one of the four main areas and the one that is concerned with vision; light and dark are processed and pictures are put together through memory. Around the ears is another key area, the temporal lobes, which are used for sound, speech, and memory. This surround sound system also has visual memories, holding the areas of meaning making as well as the hippocampus (the library of explicit memories), and the fire alarm monkey brain, the amygdala. Then we have the parietal lobe, dealing with perception, movement, and recognition. The parietal left lobe establishes that the body is different from the environment, and the right parietal lobe compares the body to features in the environment. For example, 'I am not a tree or a cloud, I am separate and independent. Who am I in space? I do not walk on water, I do not fly...' It is literally an in-built TomTom, but without the dodgy signal issues and stupid maps.

The cortex also includes sensory and motor strips that stretch from ear to ear, and as I run my finger along this part of my head, I think about how this area conveys sensations and movements. Sitting at the back of the brain – like it's under a tail – is the older mammalian cerebellum. It is needed in movement, and it reminds me of a small cauliflower.

CUTTING IN TWO TO GET TO THE MONKEY BRAIN

When I cut the brain in two, there are many lumpy, bumpy bits and various different chambers. A curved band of white tissue – called the corpus callosum – is a bridge, moving information throughout the brain, and allowing both sides of it to talk to each other. Roughly speaking, the right half of the brain is the more intuitive, creative, funny, and musical part, as well as being a memory of who you are. The left is concerned with logic, planning, fact, and vocabulary retrieval and usage; it is a list maker, and the author of your life script. Left-sided businessmen can be boring with Asperger-like symptoms, as they concentrate on one thing at a time and everything else goes to hell. They can be excellent at staring at a computer screen for hours, as this autistic quality doesn't allow life, emotion, or people to get in the way. I know someone like this… My own brain is more right-sided, as finance, maths, logical data, and research bores the pants off me. Painting, music, healing, spiritualism, and writing, however, all inspire me. So what are you inspired by? Are you more right or left brain dominant?

Underneath the bridge in your brain, the mammalian emotional limbic system sits. This is an older part of the brain and is your 'Say it how it is and f**k up the situation' monkey personality of your brain, generating knee-jerk reactions, as well as emotional, alarmist, and protective behaviour. It is always feeding information up into the conscious lofty cortex above, constantly sending emotional urges and appetites. Basically put, it is the Grand Central Station of emotion. It includes the amygdala, the basal ganglia (which is broken with Parkinson's disease and a lack of dopamine juice), and the hippocampus. The hippocampus (your library) holds long-term memory, and very importantly, the amygdala is our fear centre.

Interestingly, the limbic part of the brain is more evolved then the closely linked diencephalon. This part of the brain consists of the thalamus – the central switchboard for sensory information, also known as a router or relay station – and the hypothalamus, which is the director of the autonomic nervous system, and is in charge of endocrine (hormones) in the pituitary. This little guy decides if you feel sweaty and horny, or cool as a cucumber; it drives the need for thirst, sex, and food, and also feels terror, rage, and lust.

SNAKE BRAIN

Looking beneath the monkey brain, we travel back in time to our most primitive part of the brain – the reptilian brain stem. Formed from nerves coming up from brain stem, this part of our brain has an important lifesaving job: looking after our breathing, heart rate, blood pressure, and alertness. This is our subconscious lifesaver, as this ancient brain reacts very fast to danger. The instinct in us to survive is so strong that our conscious brain is barely aware as we jump from danger or swerve the car to avoid an accident.

The ancient brain stem sends 'brain juices' (neuromodulators) such as norepinephrine and dopamine up into the brain to energise and motivate goals decided by the highly evolved cortex, and in a rather manipulative way, it anchors successful outcomes with rewards.

These brain areas – the lofty cortex, the middle earth limbic system, the diencephalon, and at the basement, the snake-like brain stem – work together to keep us motivated, and they are integrated up and down the neuroaxis. The more primitive lower levels keep us orientated and energised, motivating the upper levels, which guide, regulate, and inhibit them right back. You could say that the lower levels are more hardwired and responsible for bodily physiological functions for survival. They have a direct control over our flesh, well, most of the time…

WHERE DO YOU OPERATE FROM? SNAKE, MONKEY OR HUMAN?

HOMEWORK:
Where do you operate from, and does it depend on the situation?

The snake personality is about non-emotional, non-moral, ruthless survival, and it is often depicted in business transactions or at times of extreme danger. A drowning man often drowns his rescuer – I used to be a lifeguard, so I know you have to be very strong. The monkey brain personality is about fear, emotion, being needy, herding instincts, and being reactive to environmental cues in order to save the lives of itself and family. It is reactive without logical, strategic, higher-processing thought. The human brain is more highly evolved, with complex computer-like analytical thought, accessing memories to judge how to react to a situation, thinking in the past, present, and future, being emotional, and at times, moral and caring. We operate with all these aspects of the brain working together.

I find it fun to pick a subject and decide – in terms of approximate percentages – where MY main drivers come from for that situation or activity. I think you'll find that it will depend on your mind state at that moment: whether you are fighting for your life and survival, if you are ill, or if you are completely content, safe, and rested. Furthermore, your incredible brain will know if you need to run a subconscious program for fast, efficient, accurate skills or a slower, ponderous, more conscious program.

Sportsmen – especially with events like world superbike – rely on subconscious programs to survive and win. I am proud to boost our patients who won last year; the snake in them came out and grabbed the prize. You can take the meaning of that last sentence any way you want – it was metaphorical, honestly!

LET ME DESCRIBE BRAIN FUNCTION LIKE A CAR FACTORY

At university, I struggled (with my scatty mind) to understand brain neuroanatomy. I like to learn with metaphors and pictures, and what I'm learning needs to hold meanings for me, otherwise I don't remember the details, but here goes: the upper evolved lofty human lobes are like MDs (managing directors) of car companies. They are less directly involved in the lives of the shop floor managers and factory workers making the parts, and they have the authority and the freedom to change policies and procedures, as well as creating and forecasting the financial business plans for the future. They have 'neuroplasticity', the capacity to change the way the cars are built, according to experience.

Further down the employment ranks (the neuroaxis), the monkey and reptilian departments get things done and constantly monitor for danger and competence. Car fitters need to assemble parts accurately according to instructions, specifications, and the speed of the assembly line. All these integrated strategies work together to produce – in this analogy – the cars. The finished products are built to a high, reliable, and safe standard according to the information available, and human existence relies on this analogy of cars being safely built.

Unlike the specific timing of the assembly line, time is more flexible behind the desk. Up in the lofty MD human office, pondering is possible, as well as evaluating improvements with intellect. Below in the monkey-snake factory, the workmanship from the workforce is clearly visible and rewarding to the boss. Their time is controlled, automatic, and work is often speedy with cost-saving initiatives being put in place. Successfully-made cars are highly visible, and this rewarding information is passed up, reinforcing certain decisions for the future.

Human, monkey, and snake are all essential to the analogy of the car; none can survive without the other, and in principle, none are more important than each other. If snake forgets to tell lungs to breathe, or monkey that the engine is about to blow up, the importance of the calculus of profit is meaningless.

Pause for a moment and think about your job and how your brain works. Does your job best suit where you predominately think from? Will your personality be sculptured differently if you change jobs? For better or for worse, you bet it will. What would have happened to the assembly line if snake or monkey had run it?

HOMEWORK:

Where are you operating from and where do you *want* to operate from? Is it mostly from the lofty human brain, with its computer banks? The reactive, emotional mammalian brain? Or the primitive, ruthless reptilian brain?

WHAT DRUMBEAT DO YOU DANCE TO?

Let's poke around a bit more in this jellyfish lookalike frontal cortex (Lewis and Todd, 2007), and let's go back to my car factory analogy to help me explain what can be a very dull and complex subject. Here we go: the snazzy brain neurophysiology model. We are inside the brain now, as depicted by another car factory analogy – after all, this series of books is called *The Human Garage*. This analogy is important, as with an evolving world of nanorobotics, we need to feel the essence of the human spirit. Too many weary souls come to my clinics, slam their car keys on my desk, and like robots, ask to have their broken part fixed, or an overhaul and MOT certificate. There is no appreciation of health and responsibility, or the importance of shamanic connectedness and love, or of healing beyond a pill or surgery, needle or manipulation. If the mind (soul) is not driving the body, there is no healing, as like a jellyfish, the brain's tentacles feel life through every limb, every touch, and every movement.

When I work in my unusual way with shamanic reiki healing, adding in the mechanics of dry needling, laser and manipulation, and magnetic resonance treatment (the likes of which are explored in my next two volumes), I can feel when the soul ignites. Once the mind believes it can heal the body, peace, contentment, and connection with healing is possible. If the spark plugs are not ignited, the body may be repaired in the correct way with an excellent mechanic, however the life force cannot rekindle life and so suffering ensues.

Let's return to the garage analogy of the brain. Up in the lofty prefrontal cortex is a working memory space, and here we have plans of how we do things. This is right next to a motor workshop, where we get things moving, and that is right next to the main office. Now, here sits the first of two hubs, or let's call them hub managers, Mr ACC. In terms of my clinic, my husband Alan Cramphorn (as financial strategy director) is the equivalent of Mr ACC in the garage. Mr ACC is sitting at his big desk in the lofty prefrontal cortex, and once he has the information gathered together, with the plans drawn up and actions noted, a transformation in activity starts. I like to imagine a Catherine wheel with sparklers, as Mr ACC starts pulsing in a gamma frequency of 30 to 80 Hz a second. It takes a human child three to six years to get to a developmental stage where they can light up this hub of sparklers. Therefore, you have to be over six years old to run a company and be very bossy.

Mr ACC will then send a signal about specific, purposeful, controlled, and measured actions towards a goal in building the cars, and he will also flag up any conflicts. This wheel hub of sparklers reaches out to other departments – to the emotional workers called the amygdala, the hippocampus, and the hypothalamus. Here the workers think and feel (Lewis, 2005), bringing heartfelt, warm emotion to logical thought. This hub – Mr ACC – is the keystone to the information passed from the evolved top part to the bottom, delivering measured, reasoned motivations.

The passionate, warm, motivated manager Mr Amygdala (or Mr Attwood, to relate it to my practice manager, Dean Attwood) is a very different kettle of fish. He is the second motivational hub, and he works bottom up with reactive, passionate motivation. This hub judges what is unpleasant or a threat, as well as the intentions of others, and also gives a fast appraisal of the situation. When the factory workforce feels motivated, this guy is motivating by synchronising his frequency with the rest of the limbic brain and the reptilian brain stem workforce. He operates at 4 to 7 times a second, which is theta frequency (Lewis, 2005; Kocsis and Vertes, 1994), in a relaxing, dreamlike mode.

Mr ACC, who is cool as a cucumber, is the head of the factory and his deputy manager, Mr Amygdala, is the heart of the factory. The feedback loop phase locks their rhythms together to exchange meaningful information and create focused motivation. If you can imagine this factory in your head, are you a head manager or more of a 'from the heart' manager with your decisions? Are you aware of your decision-making processes and drivers?

CAN YOU CHILL AT WORK?

This skill is honed with meditation. It is tough to change beliefs, so if you believe work is stressful, it will be. The unconscious is a million times more powerful than the conscious – it has to be: imagine if we consciously had to remember to replace damaged cells, or to keep our temperature, BP, heart rate, oxygen, and pH all at the right levels. I have enough problems filling my hot tub full of chemicals, and keeping my tropical fish tanks at the optimum setting. We would be keeling over everywhere if we had a dress down Friday where our conscious minds looked after our physiology; just think how many minutes we would survive – it wouldn't be many.

HOMEWORK:
Think about how incredible the human body really is.

The HeartMath research out in California is very relevant to this, and it is discussed more in-depth elsewhere in this book. It can be difficult to grab a few moments with HeartMarth (a device that allows you to measure your health and stress levels), but it is less problematic than sitting cross-legged at work with a joss stick for half an hour; especially in the middle of a crisis, as this could be seen as a reason for a disciplinary procedure! If anyone asks, just blame my book.

HRV (heart rate variability) is the gold standard for stress (find out more at www.heartmath.com), and Doc Childre's work on practising a few minutes of coherence at work every day is clever in that it helps stress, anger, and stress-induced illnesses. Coherence is a measure of a regular, rhythmical heartbeat, strengthened and encouraged by the practice of deeper, slower breathing, connecting with the heart, and positive thoughts in mindfulness practice. Poor coherence (with a read-out of erratic short cycles of heartbeats) is a physiological indicator of stress. I discuss in *The 4 Keys To Health* how I have presented on this abroad.

I have a device on my desk, which is always red at work (showing I'm stressed), as I'm absorbing all the negative emotions of my patients who are in pain.

So, let's have a quick recap. Shift the focus to your heart by thinking of an emotionally empowering thought, and hold onto these grateful, loving thoughts as you breathe steadily through your heart. This fires up and connects those brain cells to your heart, helping you to lessen the physiological damage from chronic stress.

So why chill? Nurturing good intentions helps visceral reactions. It's a good thing to digest without pain, and it is so important to calm the nervous system, as these thought frequencies ripple up and down the neuroaxis affecting every organ in the body. Tibetan monks are the gurus of relaxation and of harnessing the healing powers of the subconscious mind. Whilst these monks are meditating, with clever, modern-day technology, scientists can demonstrate that large areas of the brain are in the gamma brainwave state, between 30 to 80 Hz (Lutz et al, 2004). We are now finally understanding the power of harnessing a relaxed mind state. That's why learning skills to calm the often troubled brain is so important to health. More about this later.

The frustrating thing with the human brain is that we are wired for survival, and relaxation is not seen as being high on the priority list. Survival strategies for genes work better in more simplistic animal brains, but when it comes to humans, there's a lot more to think about: the evolved human mind suffers more, we worry about future actions, we worry about what past actions did to us, we get frustrated, disappointed, and angry when in pain, and we can feel sad by simply replaying old thoughts. The good news is that the more we understand the human part of our brain, the more empowered we become. Think about how and why your emotions change. You may not have an actual tiger hunting you down – thankfully – but feel your stomach jump in response to stimuli and your heart suddenly race… are you aware of the trigger? What mindfulness and awareness skills would you now use to think outside the box? You will have lots by the time you've read this book.

NORFOLK SNAKE

Don't worry, this is not 50 Shades of Snazzy…

I was walking along the dunes near my Norfolk beach with my mother one summer morning, the same dunes I have run over ever since I could just about waddle along in a large nappy. I know this because I have seen the cine films, and we are talking a *huge* nappy, by the way…

Anyway, this morning – having grown out of nappies – my eyes were scanning the beautiful sky and undulating dunes, which were covered in green marram grass, when I spotted a slithery object near my feet, and my brain started computing a response at light speed. Visually, the light bouncing off this thing was sent into the occiput of my cortex, telling me that I have seen a slithery object that looks like a wobbly stick. The occiput then put together an image and posted it out, down to the hippocampus (the library of memories) for a fear evaluation, and at the same time it was sent into head office (PFC) and other lofty parts of my brain for time-consuming decisions on that image. The filing cabinets were emptied out to search for any long-term memories of a wobbly, slithery-moving, stick-like object, considering both its location and whether it should be there or not.

In the meantime, my good old reliable older brain, the hippocampus – nothing to do with hippos – which is supposedly seen as more stupid but by God is needed in a crisis, checks its short list of scary, relevant memories. The response it comes up with is: jump first, think later, as it's likely to be a killer SNAKE. It screams at the office boy in my brain and sounds a car horn in the amygdala. The warning ricochets around my brain, and a fast track message goes to the fight/flight neural and hormonal systems to get my body ready for action (Rasia-Filho, Londero and Achaval, 2000).

I jumped up in the air, putting my flip-flops back on in mid-flight, and pulled my mother violently away, shouting like a woman possessed, "Snake! Help!" and basically making a complete prat of myself. It was at that moment that my slow PFC office brushed the dust off a file called harmless Norfolk grass snakes versus poisonous adders. I think my older limbic brain was wiser, as I had no intention of getting closer to the snake to see if it was poisonous, and even worse, in a bad mood. As it turned out, it was indeed an angry viper.

As an aside, its interesting to note that even with the current computer technology we have, where we can throw out older computers to update incompatible hardware and software, our brains fused millions of years of upgrades into seamless communication networks, just so I could leap out of the way of a slithery creature.

In case you're interested, the story had a happy ending – the snake was unhurt; I stepped over it carefully. More importantly – in case you didn't ask – I was fine too.

LEFT AND RIGHT SIDE OF BRAIN

There is a lot of controversy about the left and right sides of the brain and their activities, and the fast communication system makes the whole effect seem seamless. However, I was taught that the left was more about sequential processing, calculating, planning, language, numbers, and data orientation. The right is more visual and concerned with spatial processing, like knowing where to pot your snooker ball, which street to drive down, and putting the toilet seat down after a man has peed. The right brain is also holistic, sensitive, artistic, and musical. I have written more about which side of the brain men and women use later on in this chapter.

HOMEWORK:
Write down your best skill and how you do it, and decide which part of the brain you use to achieve it. Don't cheat and read the bit on male and female brains first.

As an aside, I was interested in which side the brain damage occurred in my stroke patients. Those with a right-sided clot or bleed meant that they might not know the outside from the inside of their pyjamas, and a left-sided problem often affected speech and logic, which makes sense from the location of where we find spatial orientation, as well as speech and logic centres. My left-sided brain stroke patients were more prone to pathological crying, and had no drive, goals, or perseverance. Let's think about this: with a right-sided stroke, you may suffer from pathological laughing, like Batman's Joker, and with a left-sided stroke, you may start crying uncontrollably. I think I'd favour having one on the right; I think I might be happier with the laughing over the weeping.

MEMORY – CAN WE REMEMBER WHERE IT IS STORED?

Memory is stored all over the place, and its elusive location has been chased a lot over the years. Generally with an aging brain, short-term memory gets poorer, whereas long-term memory gets better, and researchers say that this loss is slowed down by exercise. Snazzy's helpful tip: if you can't remember where you left your car keys, start moving about more. So, your mind builds with what is called implicit memories of living, and these building blocks sculpture who we are and how we relate to others. The problem with our need to survive is that we store many more negative memories than we do positive ones, and even just one episode of depression can reshape circuits to make its recurrence more likely (Maletic et al, 2007). We also favour storing negative facts over others as we are wired for survival, not happy, indulging thoughts. This makes us miserable and grumpy, especially when we replay unhappy or fearful memories.

I bet you didn't remember me telling you this, but your memory is fluid and changes when replayed, something lawyers can play on in court by the descriptive way they ask questions of their witnesses. I remember being told a true story about a car crash case, and the word 'smashed' was used falsely, deliberately, and manipulatively by the barrister. The witness innocently invented broken glass in the evidence by linking a false memory of what the word smashed indicated, with no idea they were making it up.

Some time ago, I had a conversation with part of my old marketing team in Yorkshire along the lines of how unreliable memory is, and they told me there were American researchers looking into memory and law. They told me that in order for critical memory to be considered reliable in relaying evidence, there should only be a short time between the event and the recall of the event. That recall evidence should be kept to a minimum, something that makes sense to me; every time I re-tell the snake story, he gets longer and bigger in size, and the one I recently came across in the clinic car park grew at least a foot every time I recalled it.

Another interesting fact is that true memories are not stored like they are in a computer; the brain actually draws on simulating capacities to fill in missing details, regenerating the memory (Paré, Collins and Pelletier, 2002). When you remember something, neurons assemble to form a pattern, and if there is a strongly emotional situation going on as you are recalling a memory, there is the possibility that this could flavour the newly constructed prototype of the original memory. The memory will also be coloured more with this emotional tone if it happens repeatedly, hence counsellors need to be aware of this.

Getting patients to laugh and smile during treatment results in a potent, positive association to treatment, even though it can be painful. The body is better wired to move towards healing and has a better memory of the experience of healing. Norman Cousins and Patch Adams drew my attention to this many years ago, when being a clown was frowned upon whilst on duty in hospital… still, it never stopped me!

SNAZZY'S EVOLUTION EXHIBITION, WHERE THE BRAIN BEGAN

Back in the late 80's I remember thoroughly enjoying the act of filling a whole biology lab with my anthropology exhibition on evolution. I had all sorts of skull, skeletons, and stuffed creatures on display, and I still have the photos to this day – I could be nerdy and show you some time over a cup of tea and a biscuit… I found it fascinating how the brain evolved and collected new parts, without getting rid of earlier designs and by simply connecting new specialisations.

As the brain evolved from reptilian creatures, we just kept adding new bits to it, while still keeping the old bits in there – unlike computers – hence the early primitive reptilian brain became linked with the more evolved monkey brain, then the highly evolved (or, some say, evolving) human brain. The human brain's evolution was believed to be a big step: from eating fish – which supplied key protein-making amino acids – to transforming the prefrontal cortex.

THE STUFFED TRAMP

Talking of stuffing things, I remember that around that time – in the 80's – I was told a rumour that a rather eccentric artist carried out a taxidermy procedure on a tramp, as he was frustrated that he hadn't finished painting him when he died. He lived on Plymouth Hoe, near where my late nana lived, and at the time she was not impressed; I remember hearing her whisper to my mother about this old tramp getting stuffed late one Saturday night, and I have to say, I thought she meant something else… Of course, stuffing your friends isn't really in vogue now, and I didn't add him to my exhibition then, although I did ponder if he had a smile on his face…

Anyway, where was I? Ah yes, I found evolution and then anthropology fascinating, as I loved looking at God's creatures. It's incredible to think that life began 3.5 million years ago, and that invisible microbes began 3 billion years ago. That's a long time if you look at the overall timescale; we humans are changing very slowly.

HOMO ERECTUS (THE TESCO BANANA EFFECT)

Talking of change, I have a little confession about my anthropology project: I did have to change one rather large drawing, as I got into trouble with my Homo Erectus holding a club in his hand, proudly jutting up from his groin. I still remember the slide (in the presentation I did that held key marks towards my degree) and the horrified expressions on the professors' faces, while I couldn't speak for laughing; I was always apologising for my wicked sense of humour.

LIFE BEGAN SWIMMINGLY

Anyway, back to the brain's evolutionary path: it began in water, with jellyfish developing neural tissue, then fish developing a nerve tube at the top of the spine, with neural clumps starting to specialise into smelling, vision, and movement. That was the start of everything.

SPEAKING WITH FORKED TONGUE, SNAKE BRAIN

This primitive unconscious brain was instinctive, seeking out food, shelter, and a mate – sound familiar? Do you know anyone like this? If a snake eats a mouse, it would not stop to consider anything about that mouse: whether or not it had left a family behind, or if it had just had its feet in dog shit.

SCALES TURN INTO WOOL AND FUR

Then these early reptilian unconscious brains developed further into the mammalian ones, which house the reptilian core, and which have a more elaborate social and behavioural response to life. The names of this part of the brain are: the thalamus, like a router, using sight, smell and vision together; the almond-shaped amygdala, our fear alarm; the hippocampus, our crude memory; and the hypothalamus, translating a reactional response – such as, "HELP!!!!" – into a physiological change. This complemented the instinctual reptilian responses with behaviours to give more choice of action. Emotions gave a more specialised, highly developed way to store information and communicate it to each other in a group or herd, and the cortex evolved into a mammalian consciousness that then went on to form a more complex cortex.

WE WERE ALL MERMAIDS?

Hence, intellect rose out of instinctual behaviour. In the modern human brain, instinct, emotion, and intellect flow and integrate seemingly smoothly. 3 million years ago, an earlier brain – a third of the size of mine – was found in our early hominid ancestors who were called Australopithecus Africanus. Early hominids were thought to have a long aquatic period, and they would have had hairless skin, a hooded nose, and sebaceous glands – that would explain my appearance in the pool! These ancestors then walked on two legs as long as 4 million years ago, and walking freed up limbs to use tools, which further allowed the environment to continue to sculpture the brain.

FISH FOR BRAIN FOOD

Then, 1.5 million years ago, mankind leapt forward with a bigger brain, possibly due to eating fish and absorbing more amino acids, though the missing link is still shrouded in mystery. 10,000 years ago, with the end of the last ice age when lots of brain-rich food became available, the prefrontal cortex began to stir. 7,000 years ago, Neolithic man had cattle, harvested crops of grain, and navigated canoes for hundreds of miles by the stars. Slowly, the new brain's software evolved with DHA (docosahexaenoic acid) rich food, largely found in molluscs and fish.

MITOCHONDRIA, THE POWERHOUSE OF OUR CELLS

This is a little offbeat, but very interesting to me; as a biologist I see mitochondria as the squatter that brought the gift of fire. Eons ago, a bacteria now called the powerhouse (mitochondria) sneaked into our cells, but these are only maternally inherited. Mitochondria are the conductors of the genetic orchestra, having a say in which gene is on and off, and if dysfunction and cancer threatens our survival, they are the bodyguard to stop the cell turning into a baddie. Its job is to literally shoot the cell – get the cell to commit suicide – if it starts to become faulty, in order to save the body from replicating faulty cells (like cancer). It is so incredible to think that a chance encounter – literally a squatter – is now responsible for our lives. Mitochondria provide the fuel for new neural networks, and nerves firing together in patterns create actions.

WHAT STATE ARE YOU IN?

Talking of taking action, the brain is constantly working in different states, the frequencies of which can be measured. When human brains are young, they stay predominately in certain states, and even the foetus is now known to respond to the mother's thoughts and chemistry, especially with emotions such as fear or happiness. Up until a person is seven years old, the brain is likened to a digital recorder, and as it has a delta brain wave pattern, it is akin to an adult when asleep; at two to six years old, the brain functions in delta frequency, the imaginative dreamlike state of an adult. As a teenager, the alpha and beta frequencies take the child out of its trance-like state, and at this point, the digital recordings are now more difficult to get, as the interfering neocortex is logically filtering and reasoning the data input. Between seven and sixteen years old we change a lot, and the brain digitally prunes out 80% of our neuron interconnections, which shortens all the collection of data into hardwired beliefs about fear, safety, pain, love, punishment, the meaning of life, the planet, relationships, and so on. The anchoring sets out how we see the world and how we interact with it emotionally.

HOMEWORK:
What do you think your anchors are?

I will specifically explore emotions in another chapter, as right now I need to describe how our brain function evolved to the point where we could even have emotions.

THE MODERN TRIUNE BRAIN

Simply speaking, the modern brain is three distinct evolutionary steps through from animal evolution. In the top part are the modern, computer-like, conscious, complex, conceptual, and intelligent bits, the middle houses our more ancient mammalian herding – emotional and motivationally intense – and at the base, we have our reptilian, primitive, survival-wired, unconscious brain.

Over millions of years, our ancestors developed three main strategies for creating boundaries between them and the world, as well as between mind states: maintaining balance (homeostasis), and the stability of mental and bodily physiological systems; avoiding threats and death; and moving towards opportunities for reproduction – offspring, food and a better lifestyle. When these strategies were failing and threatening future genes, neural networks evolved to create pain and suffering as a survival strategy.

Now, let's look closer at these three adult brains (the triune brain), which work together in different situations, such as when going on a date and choosing a mate.

IS YOUR COMPANION A SNAKE, MONKEY OR HUMAN? OR PERHAPS YOU WOULD PREFER TO DATE A ROBOT?

I revisited Paul MacLean's triune model of the brain whilst reading Peter Levine's *Waking The Tiger*. MacLean was an American neuroscientist in the 1950's, and he suggested that we had three distinct evolutionary neurocomputers, each with its own intelligence and each with its own sense of time, space, and taste of the world and life. It's a very generalised, simplified model of what really happens, but quite frankly, reading through all my old brain anatomy and physiology notes was far too f**king boring to include in this book. So a simple version will do for me, if that's okay with you.

SNAKE HEAD, SPEAKETH WITH FORKED TONGUE

The oldest brain is the snake brain, the cold-blooded, business-like, unemotional, uncuddly, lifesaving old git. However, we would die quickly without it, as it regulates our heart rate, breathing, and body temperature, and is also involved in flight or fight actions. The snake senses a vibration, it knows it needs to feed, and it attacks a small mouse for instant gratification. It does not stop to think that the baby mouse may have parents nearby, that it could be carrying a disease or poison, that is was a living, intelligent creature, or how many calories there are in a bite. The snake kills, the snake lives. This is why if you find yourself stranded on a desert island, you should choose a mate with a predominately reptilian-centred brain if you want to live.

Mind you, once your reptilian mate has taught you how to hunt, fish, or eat veggies, and build a shelter and find water, his company will no longer be necessary, and quite frankly, boring and unpleasant. Once living on a desert island is safe, you could do with trading him in for a mate with a focus on a more evolved part of the brain – this will be much better for conversation.

The mammalian brain is instinctive in an emotional, social sort of way. Remember when we were dissecting the brain? We were looking at the limbic part of it, and within it there was the amygdala, the hypothalamus, and the hippocampus. This evolving brain survived the dinosaur's reptilian brain, and as the dinosaurs became extinct, the mammals flourished. This brain can distinguish colour and what it means to survive. If you have a friend who functions mostly from this part of the brain, he is the one to be stranded on a desert island with – and leave your Bridget Jones knickers at home. All defensive strategies are genetically programmed into a highly effective survival brain. Rhythmical cycles of rituals are repeated over and over again, and these control behaviour with no emotion or moral interaction.

HOMEWORK:
So which part of the brain do you predominately operate from?

The triune brain is always at play at the dinner table. When going out on a raunchy dinner date – although sadly, in my case, I have to go to my dusty archives to think about this type of scenario – the reptilian part of my brain is deciding if he is on the menu. What can I say? I'm hungry.

THE SEAHORSE IN MY SOUP

The mammalian part of the brain has four questions due to four fundamental programs, called the 4 F's: Fear, Feed, Fight and F**k. Is this dinner date safe to be out with? Is he going to hurry up and choose from the menu so I can eat? Will he turn out to be aggressive or a ruthless business partner? And is he good in bed? These thoughts should not be happening all at the same time, so it's no wonder that we get in such a mess!

Now, how does my mammalian brain do all this? How does it sense and take part in how the brain processes information and acts? I don't think we really know, however here are some evolving ideas. The hippocampus is found deep in the temporal lobes, and it was given its name by 16th century Italian anatomist Aranzi, who noted its resemblance to a seahorse and therefore gave it the Greek name for the creature. This seahorse operates like a digital camera, processing stills and videos; these 'pictures' are likened to facts, and can be spoken or recalled, and are called declarative memory. 'Videos' are more complex and record spatial and temporal events, which lead to episodic memory. So, Mr Seahorse acts as a way station, gathering data from the five senses, memorising it in different forms, and then processing the bits and sending them on. If the dinner guest is seen as a threat, the pics go straight on to the amygdala, as well as other non-threatening data, such as how good-looking and well dressed he is, whether he's spilt food down his shirt, and so on – all that info goes straight to the highly evolved human cerebral cortex.

Mr Seahorse is very sensitive to stress, and MRI (magnetic resonance imaging) shows up the rot – I mean, deteriation – that stress causes. Too much stress and school is over; we cannot process information through the higher centres, and so genuine feelings stop, alongside our ability to show healthy emotion. Sadly, this is seen diagnostically as the earliest signs of dementia. Now, this is too depressing – instead, read my *4 Keys To Health* book and reboot. Save Mr Seahorse.

MR ALMOND SLICE

We shall call the amygdala 'Mr Almond', as this is the Greek word for it, due to its shape. Incidentally, I've always had a thing about almonds; like a squirrel, I store them away and forget where I've put them. You will always find some in my drawers – steady now, I mean desk drawers. They are a great healthy snack, although not so healthy once in marzipan… I'm hungry now… At this point, my reptilian brain is telling me to stop writing and go and find an F: food, in this case. Sorry, we're talking about our alarm amygdala in the mammalian brain, not its namesake, the almond.

The amygdala is our unconscious guard, which refers to perceived or real threats: Mr Fear. He doesn't know the difference between a movie, a video game, a tiger, or a boss, and the latter is difficult to know sometimes. The point is we act unconsciously, immediately, and reflexively to escape danger, and in our modern lifestyle, constant and unnecessary stress is toxic and promotes chronic illness. I will go into more details of stress in another chapter about mind states and emotions.

RIPPLE AND SHIMMY LIKE A DEER

Think of a herd of deer – I love watching them by my clinic, and it is their limbic brain that allows them to smell danger, communicate it, and move as a herd in one emotional body. This paves the way to a more rational brain in more highly evolved mammals, and this formation of herding for protection, as well as this effective communication regarding danger, was one of the keys to outwitting the dinosaurs, those small-brained, large-arsed reptiles. It's a bit like with first dates; we feel safer near other people, especially if he's a bit ugly!

In order to get rid of the body's chemically-induced fear juices, these clever herds of deer have rhythmical muscle rippling. Humans can't do this, so we swear, get stressed out, and get an acid stomach. I suggest to my surgeon/GP/physio friends to jump up and down between patients, or dance just for a minute, to dissipate the stressful chemistry. I don't suggest you actually do it in front of the patients, however, as it could be misinterpreted as inappropriate behaviour; saying, "You're stressing me out so I'm in a lifesaving mode, rippling my muscles," would not go down too well, especially when your patient needs you to be in your neo and prefrontal cortex, to give empathy with a correct diagnosis. You certainly could not do this between courses on your dinner date, unless you go to the little girl's room, of course.

Mammals can also employ the freeze response at the point of capture and near death. This switches off pain, and may fool the predator into thinking he's looking at stale, old prey, and is therefore safe to leave it unguarded, meaning that escape is now possible. Of course, it's not always a good thing – just think of the old rabbit in the headlights: when the bunny freezes in the middle of the road, it isn't such a useful evolutionary thing when faced with oncoming cars.

PLAYING DEAD ON SNAZZY'S COUCH

My patients play dead when they're hoping I will forget to give them the dry needling treatment. My hippocampus reminds me where they are – on my couch, not too difficult – and how deep the needle must go, as well as reminding me where the problem is. Soft music helps to still the panic building in the amygdala, and to lessen the impulses about fear going through the hippocampus to the cortex. Memories remind my patient that we've been here before on Snazzy's couch and that we did not die, so stand down all alarm systems; there is no need to run. The thalamus sends through the messages from my mammalian brain with sensations of needle pricks from my sensory cortex, and I also get rhythmical surges upwards from the reptilian brain, to control fear and to adjust breathing and heart rate according to the feedback loop and pain levels.

Underneath the 'relay station' (the thalamus) is the hypothalamus, and this constantly adjusts the body, along with the pituitary, to keep it optimally adapted to the environment, as well as gathering information and sending out inhibitory and excitatory impulses.

The 500 million year old git – the reptilian brain – is formed from clumps of glial cells that glue the structure together, and like amplifiers, they amplify or synchronise electrical activity within the brain. They do not help me to soothe patients when they have heightened nerve pain such as sciatica; they are exciting neurons that transmit pain. The brain stem is formed from the nerves that run up the body through the spinal column, an area I have spent so many years treating. There will be more of this in volume 2.

ENCOUNTERING A FRIEND IN ANOTHER COUNTRY

So, the reptilian and mammalian parts of your brain know if their therapist, therapy room, or home is friendly. They know how far away your home is – like a TomTom – and how far away predators and prey are. They clearly understand boundaries between their terrority and others, and recognise their species, family, and other people. They embrace boundaries and isolation, them and us, bad guys and good guys, and determine this with emotion. They know which side of their boundary they are on and why. You know that feeling when you meet a patient in the supermarket and you can't think of their name because they're in a different place? Or you bump into a close friend or relative in another country and you don't recognise them to start with? That's when you need your higher brain to help.

This happened to me with a friend and colleague, Pam, when we were both in America for a few days, unbeknown to each other. She lived and worked in Spain at that time and myself in the UK, so when we ran into each other in the States, we didn't know what to do. After first thinking, 'this can't be', we said hello, thinking that it looks like my buddy, and sounds like her, but we're in America! Then I said bye and walked off, before thinking, hang on, we've bumped into each other by chance and have no way of contacting each other, as the human modern bit of my brain (the neocortex) was being lazy. We might as well have been a couple of deer or mice meeting – talk about not engaging our brains! We met up again many months later.

THE NEW BRAIN, THE NEOCORTEX

The New Brain is called the neocortex, which is well developed in higher mammals, and in humans it is responsible for such activities as intellectual thought, writing, and speech. They say that higher advanced neocortical thinking and true appreciation of death does not kick in until you're about 40 years old. The thalamus is a router in effect, as it relays the 4 F's about our dinner guest to this part of the brain, with the sensory information needed for reflection, and hopefully appropriate – or if not, enjoyably inappropriate – behaviour. Here in the neocortex, we are capable of selfless actions and thought, as well as reasonable, logical, passionate, artistic thoughts, and the ability to enjoy music and think of future events. This evolutionary adaption enabled us to plant crops, store winter crops, and see to animals. It also allowed us to understand cycles of nature, time, and soil nutrition, and to be able to build safe dwellings in a close-knit social community. Planning can predict consequences of actions and give moral judgements.

Now, back to the dinner date. If we've enjoyed a nice glass of wine and are feeing philosophical, we could employ our prefrontal cortex with our dinner guest and hope that he also has one. Here we think creatively, inventing and discovering science, music, and God. Here we could discuss marriage, kids, career, and travel. The neocortex is believed to house our sense of self, the unique aspects of our character, our chiselled wisdom of the self.

A quick word of warning here: if you're out on a lusty dinner date and are communicating with your date from the neocortex – or worse still from the prefrontal – and your guest is wrestling with the 4 F's in his reptilian, mammalian connections, you will not be very aligned to receive the forth F at the end of night. You probably won't see each other again for some time, whilst he runs off and over the hills.

Our instinctive primitive brain gave a firm grounding to our intellect, thoughts, language, and choices. Our sense of self was evolving, and as to our soulfulness – where can this critter be hiding out?

WHERE IN THE BRAIN DO WE FIND THE SOUL?

Where did the idea of the soul come from? And where in the brain do we find our consciousness, our sense of self? Which animals possess this sense of self, and in essence, a 'soul' fragment? Is all of nature connected through a web of energy?

HOMEWORK:
Find out the answers to these questions and drop me a line before I finish volume 3!

Here's a scientific answer. The ancient, primitive, survival-driven brain allowed glimpses of consciousness to be built on neural systems, and these symbolised biological values that then developed into motivational, emotional systems. These neural systems are now housed in the middle of the primitive brain stem and extend into the cortical zones of the limbic system. Here we have a profound sense of self, or what the scientists would call, 'the conception of the soul'.

The periaqueductal grey area (PAG) of the midbrain is very dense and ancient, and it is now known to produce emotional behaviour in both animals and humans. This PAG lies close to the four twins part of the ancient brain stem that integrates a sensory map of the world, which is a multimodal integration of touch, hearing, and vision. This, integrated with emotion and the motor map of the body, allows a physical orientation to stimuli and hence a primal soul – a simple archetypal life force of vertebrates and all mammals upon which the more complex neural structures evolved (Damasio et al, 2000; Panksepp, 1998).

When you and I see an object or speak the name of it, the information enters an assembly line, traversing the brain. This mostly consists of subconsciously gathering emotional data, memories, and coordinating with the muscle activation area (motor), before constructing a meaning for it and an action schema. The brain then selects a few assembly lines to bring into consciousness, all of which offer useful interactions. For example, a glass of water represents a vessel to carry fluid to the mouth, but the hand needs to lift the glass to get it there.

HOMEWORK:

So who are you? Take a moment now and say out loud: I am… let's see, the visible public body, character, job, family member, thoughts, feelings, values and beliefs, place in society… and so on. The trouble is, if we are a collection of all these things that keep changing as our bodies replace cells as we grow older, fitter, and lazier, and as we change weight, jobs, partners and locations, what makes us individual and gives us our sense of being a unique, essential self? We as Homo sapiens hold the belief that we have an actual place where consciousness lives. When we move an object, we know it is us who moved it. We know that we exist on different days and times, i.e. we know that tomorrow when we wake up, we will be the same essential self as today.

So now we've had a whistle stop tour of the brain and its evolution, where does the mind fit into this? Where is the spirit in the machine? Here lies the controversy.

WHERE IS THE SPIRIT IN THE MACHINE?

Is our mental or spiritual experience just a by-product of the brain's activity? "Healing the soul – not medicating the brain – is the root meaning and true purpose of psychiatry. Through a relationship in which we can feel what we truly feel and so become who we truly are" [Frattaroli, 2001). Dr Frattaroli, in his *Healing The Soul* book, went on to cite several key scientists' opinions about the brain-mind link being purely brain functions.

In 1998, Eric Kandel – a neuroscientist – took a very scientific robot-like stance, saying that all mental processes, even the most complex psychological processes, derive operations from the brain. The central tenet of this view is that what we commonly call the 'mind' is actually a range of functions carried out by the brain (Kandel, 1998). The philosopher John Searle echoed the opinion that every sensory emotional experience was just brain processes (Searle, 1995).
The noble biochemist Francis Crick once said, "You're nothing but a pack of neurons," – not a very inspiring phrase, I have to say (Crick, 1994). Crick believed that our emotional responses, beliefs, and free will were yet again just brain processes. Antonio Damasio, the brain researcher, stated that the mind did indeed come from brain processes, though he also added that we should look deeper into why neurons behaved in a thoughtful way (Damasio, 1994), while Lewis Judd suggested more of an awareness of how a damaged brain can create a disordered mind (Judd, 1990).

David Satcher, surgeon general, maintained that mental illness was caused by chemical imbalances in the brain and physical changes, so he did not venture into the mind theory, just the physical brain changes (Satcher, 1999). I could not find any hard evidence or research to back up these claims one way or the other, as it's a very difficult subject; 'the mind' or 'soul' is a very emotional, questionable, spiritual puzzle, and one that will come to light more with the movement of nanorobotics. I will share with you my spiritual journey in the third volume of this series and there I will share my soul experiences.

EVIDENCE THE BRAIN AND MIND ARE SEPARATE

Dr Bruce Greyson talked about near death experience in a discussion I heard that was recorded at the United Nations conference at the University of Virginia (Greyson, 2011). Dr Greyson talked about the mind and the brain being scientifically classed as the same thing, however, in extreme circumstances there appeared to be a split. He related this to Newtonian physics; working in everyday life but in extremely fast actions, the model breaks down and quantum physics principles explain the rest. There is documented evidence of patients recovering after clinical death to describe clear thinking at times of extreme brain dysfunction, as well as gathering information from dead relatives they did not know about. Food for thought that a mind or soul – separate from the brain – exists and records information, even whilst the brain is shut down.

Here's a couple of nice spiritual quotes:

- "Language and culture sculpture our minds from birth" (Han and North, 2008).
- "Our human minds are attracted to other loving souls and our energies align with theirs" (Siegal, 2007).

Dr Michael Newton's work into hypnotism and past life regression shares many cases of man discussing the soul's needs and the journey beyond the human brain (Newton, 2002). Again, there will be more about this in book 3.

A MACHINE WON THE WAR FOR US (ENIGMA CODE)

I recently watched a moving film called *The Imitation Game*, which is based on a true story and which features the brilliant Benedict Cumberbatch in the lead role. The story is both tragic and enlightening regarding the human mind, looking at one man's emotional fragility, his beliefs, and his unrelenting drive. It shows that the life changing impact of a powerfully creative force within the human mind is capable of building a machine to solve complex problems at a speed beyond the evolutionary boundaries of our biological brain.

The film was based on the true story of Alan Turing during World War II, in the darkest hour of devastation and loss of life, when it looked like we were losing. He was a brilliant, emotionally tortured, unsung war hero, and the exceptional mathematician who built the first computer to crack the enigma code and, in turn, win the war for us. Millions of variations had to be calculated in just 24 hours – something beyond the ability of the human mind. Alan's machine cracked it, and by using information from the machine regarding where the Germans would strike, England won the war. Many people lived thanks to this marriage between man and machine.

The story flows deep. The computer was named after Alan's childhood sweetheart, Christopher, who died at age 18, breaking his heart. Alan was gay, and by giving his machine the name of his former love, Christopher's spirit lived on within it. Homosexuality was still against the law in those days, and Alan avoided being imprisoned by accepting the punishment of being injected by dangerous female hormones, which caused tremors, depression, and brain dysfunction. He killed himself aged just 42. Had he lived, imagine what other miracles his mind could have come up with. It was such a shame – brilliance being stamped out by bigoted, soulless, 'human' behaviour.

Yet again we have a story about how someone with special gifts, was – essentially – murdered by a lack of tolerance in the human mind. Jesus was a healer, and he was placed on a cross to die. Humans in general are very capable of brutal punishment and intolerance; this race has a lot of disappointing history to answer for.

If we want to hang onto our precious consciousness, perhaps we should take a long, hard look at what it is we are hanging onto, before we're held accountable and questioned as to why the human race should be saved.

SO WHAT DO ROBOTS THINK ABOUT?

If we leap forward in time from the first computer in the 1940's to the 1990's, we can see that the world of 'Nanorobotics' has been biting at our heels. As far back as 1996, the head honcho of the Al research project at the London Imperial College, Mr Alexander, believed he had endowed a robot with an aspect of consciousness. Its electronic circuitry replicated neural mechanisms, which gave rise to a sense of self-awareness. The robot learned by using its body in the same way a human does.

By building a 'self' into a machine, you make the information it receives meaningful and emotional, so how far can artificial intelligence mimic biological consciousness?

Remember the robot that NASA sent to Mars, to be aware and take in sensory info from the environment? Well, the stupid idiot got stuck behind a rock, which was quite embarrassing – going all that way and spending all that money for it just to get stuck! But why did this happen? The robot rover didn't have any awareness of self programmed into it, so he didn't know his boundary, or that the rocks were separate from him.

My patients are now more frequently coming into my office with excitement about implants of all kinds: for Parkinson's, cochlear implants for hearing, retinal-visual, and robotic limbs. This fascinating area of neuroscience involves studying brain code, teasing out brain messages and mimicking them with algorithms. Then, wireless communications are sent back to the brain to signal an activity. Historically implanted electrodes get attacked by the immune system, however nowadays the coating in growth hormone and soft hydrogels allows neurotransmitters to grow connections with little damage to brain tissue. In the case of the eyes, genetically manipulated neurons respond to signals from specific light frequencies, and with the neuron recognising the manufactured signal, it fires.

By 2050, scientists believe we will have robot brains that can deal with 100 trillion instructions per second (Moravec, 2009), and the time is rapidly approaching when robotic brains could potentially be billions of times more powerful than an unaided biological human brain – very thought-provoking. If you're interested in this subject, futurist Raymond Kurzweil wrote about such ideas in his book, *The Singularity Is Near* (Viking, 2005).

Today, in 2015, robots are at about age seven, and are still lacking equivalent common sense; their meaning making of outcomes is technical and laborious. Haven't we already relinquished so many tasks to machines? Just think about it: cars, navigation, computers carrying our dairies, calculating, and keeping memory for us, emails communicating for us... Are we not slowly just becoming the energy that switches on the machine? A company at the moment is building a personal robot that can keep your home secure, remind you of appointments, provide extensive data in meetings, read to you, give you recipes, order shopping, and so on. Sounds like a good alternative to having a grumpy human in the house!

New research headed up by the physicist Majewski, and carried out by the neuroscientist Brefczynski-Lewis, was presented at the society for neuroscience in Washington D.C. in November 2013, and it involved testing a portable P.E.T scanner worn as a helmet whilst the subject went about their everyday activities. The idea was to explore different brain activities in normal and brain damaged subjects. This is an example of technology being helpful to gain a better understanding of healthy brain function and dysfunction. However, I get teased enough wearing my head torch; I think adding a helmet would really freak out my patients! I'll wait until they come out with a smaller, more discreet model.

At the time of editing this book, there is a series on television called *Humans*, which explores robots with consciousness integrating with our lives. The reality of this happening is not far away.

Specialists in artificial intelligence suggest that by 2019, a $1000 computer will match the processing power of the human brain. By 2029, once the software of intelligence is in place, the computer will match 1000 human brains.

Heard of smart dust? No, me neither; it sounds like a Harry Potter invention. Well, at Berkeley in the USA, the University of California created flying robots the size of a grain of sand that can sense, compute, and communicate.

By 2030, nanorobot technology will be viable. Nanobots are the size of a human blood cell. They are being created to scan inside the brain and be wirelessly driven, allowing the secrets of the brain to be downloaded.

COULD ELECTRONIC BRAIN CELL NETWORKS SEAMLESSLY CONNECT AND WORK WITH BIOLOGICAL NEURONS?

A company called Hedco Neurosciences (Ted Berger) built integrated circuits that match digital and analogue information processes of neurons. Carver Mead (Caltech) have also built integrated circuits that emulate digital analogue characteristics of mammalian neural circuits.

The San Diego Institute for Nonlinear Science looked at electronic neurons emulating biological ones. Neurons are an example of chaotic computing; a network of neurons initially reacts in a frenzy of chaotic computing. When a signal is received, the initial frenzy of random signals settles down into a stable pattern which means a decision has been made. If the task is pattern recognition – believed to be 95% of human brain activity – the emergent pattern is a conclusion of recognition.

So can electronic neurons engage in this dance with biological ones? Yes, biological and electronic networks can. In San Diego, spiny lobsters did just this, and many such experiments are happening right now with human neuron clusters.

Ray Kurzweil discusses the pros and cons of robotic evolution with his critics in his book, *Are We Spiritual Machines?* (Discovery Institute, 2002). Whether we like it or not, we have a formidable combination happening, with human pattern recognition, high resolution brain scans, reverse engineering with knowledge sharing, and the speed and memory of non-biological intelligence.

The *Robocop* movie is happening for real. If we keep the old carbon unit body, it can be enhanced with biotechnology of gene enhancement and replacement and nanotechnology, controlled by a formidably intelligent brain. Or perhaps because robotic bodies and brains will be more intelligent and symptom free, there could be a real danger that a superior race is being born to supersede us.

MEMES DRIVE OUR EVOLUTION

Talking of artificial systems mimicking human consciousness, central to this is the subjectivity of the sense of self I keep banging on about. Memes are pieces of information that pass between humans and that shape our social evolution. In a sense, our persisting perception of who we are moment by moment is a memeplex.

I am drawn back to my early biology days and Dawkins' 1976 book, *The Selfish Gene* (Oxford University Press, 1999). I was 12 when this came out – for those of you thinking I'm writing this from a nursing home! Dawkins argued that replicators of information are a driving force of social and cultural evolution, and he called these MEMES. These are tunes, ideas, fashion, catch phrases, engineering, architecture, pottery, cooking, TV, radio, and so on. Every song and every story I've heard, repeated, and passed on is a meme. My designer running gear, the car I drive, and the shorthand phrases I use get passed on like sneezes – they go viral. Memes can create false dogmas, false beliefs, and can also create governing bodies to drive laws and rules. As our language gets more complex, we describe ourselves in more complex ways, through our plans, desires, free will, and decisions. Human consciousness is a self-plex, created by a human meme machine (Blackmore, 1999).

MEMES AND GENES

It seems that memes are a vehicle to grasp the reins of cultural evolution, and to pick the direction we're going in. A mind virus spreads by communication, and once created, it has an independent life, a secret code of behaviour. It is the key to Pandora's Box. These little nuts and bolts of internal knowledge can manipulate human behaviour. Billions of years ago, viruses appeared in biology – in plants, animals, and humans – and started carrying diseases. The second world is in computers, in electronic form, while the third world is the mind of culture.

So where does the idea of the soul fit in? Is it a programmed collection of genes and memes or a divine spark? Memes, like biological viruses, are self-serving. In a weak individual they can challenge beliefs, lay down new ones, and allow unjust events to happen en masse. Biological viruses inject new instructions into the cell about copying themselves, and cell death is often (though not always) needed for the virus to spread. Viruses need to make many, many copies with no further effort on behalf of the creator.

So many memes control our lives – for example, sex laws. Only a hundred years ago, women were limited due to memes: they should stay at home, not have a vote, get less significant jobs than men and get paid less. Speaking of which, let's look at money – what a manmade illusion of value! Kids get programmed for success or failure according to repeated messages about their ability, and advertising drives our perception of 'having stuff', get my drift?

We hang onto our memes, which constitute our belief systems. If people are confused rather than steadfast in their beliefs, then institutions can program people with self-serving means. These are often detrimental mind viruses. They penetrate minds easily due to a thirst to learn, then spread their prescribed chain of events and actions by communication between minds. Designer viruses can damage happiness through their selfish needs.

If we could recognise viruses, we could tame their power. If we seize the reins, we could pick the direction of cultural evolution. The mind virus is in effect a secret key to behaviour and not necessarily the best: monkey see monkey do, just take a look at what's on the TV!

HOMEWORK:
Sit down with your family and question your beliefs and where they come from. This is especially important – and especially eye-opening – with teenagers.

We talked about the 4 F's and how powerful they are in our primitive brain circuitry, and how important they are to the survival of our genes. These genetic drivers steal conscious behaviour; we are wired to be alert and listen out for any sexual, threatening, fearful, lustful, hungry, or angry messages, and *Newsnight*, newspapers, and fiction novels all know this. They pull at the prehistoric wiring for gene replication.

Once we've paid attention to any needs of the 4 F's – avoiding fearful actions, satisfying lust, and anger and hunger – we can go into the loft of our brains and look to human consciousness. The second order of needs are many and include: belonging to our tribe, distinguishing our self from others, being cared for and caring for others, obeying rules and authority, seeking approval and faith, and missionary and self-perpetuating traditions. Memes that are familiar and easy to understand generate a good feeling and get many more replications, because communicating them to others feels good and is easy to do.

MEMES DICTATE OUR FAMILY LIFE

I remember my reproductive professor spelling out the sexist roles for us before showing us explicit footage of third year research, which was basically people copulating in various positions. All the secretaries brought in coffee and popcorn to watch the footage, and no I wasn't in it; I was very shy in those days.

Sex-centred roles are good examples of memes: woman does this, man does that. About a hundred years ago, men were seen as the head of the household and much more capable of intelligent decision-making and thinking, as well as being able to vote. This was all fabricated through memes. Men selectively earnt more money and were employed in more positions of status and power than women. Those at the top of the hierarchy enjoyed the company of several women, spread their genes with many litters, and could ensure their kids were financially secure and fit to propagate successful genes in grandchildren – say no more. They liked attractive, younger women whom neither challenged them intellectually nor financially. They could grow ugly and obese, and they got away with it, on the whole. Those men in a less status dominant position may have had a plainer wife at home to protect his genes, and she was less likely to go off with a choosy alpha male. He felt safer knowing that his small number of infants would have a mother around them, and he would stay with them, as he couldn't afford too many litters to move between.

Women were programmed by memes in a very different way: to be second class citizens, to look beautiful and slim, to cook, to clean, to nest build, to breed, to rear young and only to possess 'useful' opinions, ones that were deemed useful to men and to their child rearing activities. Women were programmed to be attractive to men and to be excellent mothers. Women needed time to gestate a child, to feed it and care for it, and to crave security and a safe, comfortable dwelling in which it can grow. However, women were – and still are – attracted to roughly two types of men: shall we say alpha and beta. Alpha for their good looks, muscular bodies, power, dominant hierarchical positions, and good genes. This type of man would shoot sturdy, powerful, successful sperm, and with many different women, just because he can. Women would crave his sexy attentions, and were driven to do so by his caveman wiring. I remember looking down the microscope at many different sperm samples (in my early days of research, not just for fun), and there was a hell of a difference between sperm, from big, fast, beefy ones, to the slower, wobblier, skinnier ones!

Anyway, back to the woman's dilemma. She wants both Mr Alpha's babies and Mr Beta's trustworthy company, and so the complexities of families continues into modern day living. Regarding Mr Beta, women are not so physically attracted to him, but are more mentally and consciously drawn to his company. The woman stands a good chance of not having to share this man with other women's litters, and she will think that even if he is having affairs, he will more than likely hang around. His genes are poorer, but he helps with child rearing and is a pleasant companion. Get my drift, ladies? TV soaps still drive these memes, don't they? Go on, take a moment to think of your favourite one.

Marketing forces make computer programs to create designer memes, the motivation being for financial gain, selling, or power. It is basically legal brainwashing.

HOMEWORK:
Say you decided to launch a scientific revolution in your home or school, to disinfect it against meme viruses. How would you behave? In its place, what memes would you be spreading? Take a moment to write down your thoughts; make a note of how quickly the family engage in a computer, TV, or iPad, before interacting with each other. How is the meal time conducted at home, and what is the conversation dialogue about? How many memes are there?

HOMEWORK:
What if you wanted to launch a meme? What would it be about? What is its mission? How fast could it spread? Is it simple and clear enough? And is it loaded with the 4 F stimuli?

HOMEWORK:
How did you spend your day? How many hours were spent in front of computers, where you analysed data and facts, then duplicated ideas? How many emails loaded with info did you send out? When you read newspapers and hear the news, how many were loaded with 4 F stimulating words?

Wasted time spent on negative information, upon which you cannot CHANGE, is etching away at your happiness, your vision, and your life's purpose. Instead, melt away your time to make your impact on the world in a profoundly exciting, life changing, healing way. Do you want to reach out for a higher purpose, for a calling? Then read on.

WANT TO HAVE A HIGHER CALLING?

In meditation, you start understanding about your primitive wiring, about how the 4 F's are helping you survive, building on intellect, learning, teaching, rationalising, politics, art, law, and so on. There can be a time in your life, however, when everything can become stiflingly boring and repetitive. Some of us climb over that mental barrier, throw off our comfort blanket and ask uncomfortable questions about the bigger picture. We then have to face emotionally painful issues and be prepared to have a more isolated life. Have meaningful relationships, not convenient ones. Chase goals and projects only for the greater good, especially ones that are meaningful and that change others' lives as well as our own. Here, a few of us transcend into the third level of consciousness, the only place we can grow into fulfilling our true life's purpose.

I had my darling wise friends and mentors in hypnosis, NLP, reiki, and spiritual healing to guide me at my most frustrating times in life. To work and converse at this level for the greater good is blissful.

HOMEWORK:
Pick a purpose and create your future you. Come on, write it out NOW.

MALE AND FEMALE BRAINS

Let's look at some differences in male and female brains. For instance, fMRIs show that women have 14 to 16 areas of the brain for evaluating others' behaviours, whereas men have four to six. Women's brains are also better organised for multi-tasking. The hypothalamic nucleus is responsible for typical sexual behaviour in males and is 2.5 times bigger in men's brains than in women's. The corpus callosum, an interface cable, is where the hemispheres communicate, and ladies, of course ours is bigger: there are 30% more connections, and we also have an anterior commissure, an unconscious link.

This could explain the more intuitive emotional aspect of women. We pull sides of the brain into play with a task, whereas men only use the most appropriate parts and have to focus more. Men have fewer connecting fibres, and are wired to work within compartments, to specialise more and have the need to focus without distractions. You can't talk and watch TV or stroke the cat at same time, can you? If you can, you could be like *Little Britain*, 'the only gay in the village'. Men work on single, focused tasks, don't you, guys? Admit it.

Women, on the other hand, are better at detecting lies when face-to-face with someone because of their ability to interpret both verbal and body language. Women are also better at reading relationships than men when in a room full of people, and they are better at identifying different emotional cries from kids. Their superior sensory abilities win every time; a woman will weigh up how people feel and recognise these feelings first.

Men will look for exits, what needs fixing, building construction, and any enemies or familiar faces. If you want a guy to crash a car, ring him up and talk to him – it's a form of manslaughter for Grumpies. Women struggle with night vision driving, as well as with spatial awareness (how close the car is to the curb or another car, and the direction of approach).

Men's hunter instincts and better right-sided spatial night brain handles night vision much better. With computers, men's natural long-sightedness leads to more eyestrain than women for close up work. The left side of the brain develops faster with girls, making speech and learning a foreign language easier. With boys it is the right: they are generally better at maths, buildings, puzzles, perceptual problems, and problem solving. Men have a specific place for direction, and women for speech. Men can see architectural drawings in 3D, women generally can't. With aging, we ladies lose memory and spatial organisation from the hippocampus. Men lose tissue mass from their frontal and temporal lobes, losing thinking and feeling, which leads to irritability and personality changes. I.e. 'Grumpiness'.

As an aside, if you directly stimulate the temporal lobes in both men and women you can induce an orgasm. I wonder where the point is? Just out of scientific interest, you understand. Women have receptors in the skin 10 times more receptive, fired up by oxytocin. Women hug and touch more. We have better taste receptors as well, and have especially sweet taste. Women sniff men's immune systems for attraction, and we have a better sense of smell overall.

When it comes to sex and love, men can more easily experience both separately; there is not the strongly connected wiring in the hypothalamus that women have. According to some books, men easily have multiple affairs with good physical relationships without concerning themselves with the emotion of love. For women, the emotional aspect of sex is more entwined (Pease, 2001).

BORN GAY

Let's talk about getting pregnant. About eight weeks after making love, you have a small foetus growing inside you. The foetus is sexless at first, but then if the foetus is XY (a genetic boy), it develops cells that release male juices (hormones) like testosterone, to grow balls and configure a male brain. Say, however, that the correct dosage is not delivered. This means that the baby can have a male body and a predominately female brain, and at puberty the boy will be homosexual. A baby girl (XX) should get female hormones to form a female body and brain, but if she receives male hormones she develops a male brain, and will at puberty be gay.

The chances for a body brain mismatch are believed to be 10% to 15% in men, and 10 % in women. Do you know anyone like this? Luckily for me I have a body brain match; it must be so hard for folks who don't, and years ago, same sex relations were punished by imprisonment.

Gay men can be very different as there are two centres in the brain: the mating centre and the behaviour centre. The mating centre is in the hypothalamus and decides which sex we are attracted to according to the levels of sex hormones. The behavioural centre again will depend on the amount of hormones received, hence gay men can be butch or effeminate and attracted to another man. It is the same for lesbians: the mating centre determines the gender she is attracted to, while the behavioural centre will determine the characteristics she adopts. She can either be a feminine or a butch woman, attracted to other women.

GAY MEN'S BRAINS ALIGN MORE WITH WOMEN'S

In 1991, the journal *Science* announced that gay men's brains were different to straight men's brains; the corpus callusum is bigger, while the hypothalamus is smaller (Le Vay, 1991). In 1994, Dean Hamer at the institute for Health in Washington discovered a gene that was carried on the maternal side that affected male sexuality. In 2008, Swedish scientists used P.E.T scanning to show same sized hemispheres for gay men and women, however in straight men the right was slightly larger (Savic et al, 2008).

ELITE ATHLETES TRAINED WITH MONKEY, HUMAN AND COMPUTER BRAIN MODEL

So we are intelligent, emotional, sexual adult Homo sapiens. Our complex integrated brain structure houses the human and computer-like structures, and then the monkey, which is reactive, emotional, and compulsive, and which is fired up every time we perceive a situation to be dangerous. Our built-in survival response checks the computer banks of memories and values – in effect its MEMES – to see if there is any data on this specific incident. If the answer is NO, then the 'monkey brain' reacts. If the situation is unique and not life threatening or intimidating, the human cortex slowly works out a way to respond. If the parietal lobes have pre-programmed circuitry to this specific event, then the program runs at speed, and if it is a good, productive program, it is to the benefit of man, especially as slow, conscious thought is not involved and the response is played out about 20 times faster.

Professor Steve Peters (who looked at the chimp paradox in 2012) has helped to bring 12 Olympic medals home, encouraging elite athletes to understand intelligently the way we can control our conscious and unconscious programs. He worked on a slightly different brain model to Levine, and his model excludes discussions on the snake brain; instead of discussing the triune brain in a biologist's terms of snake, monkey and human, Prof Peters looked at it from a psychiatrist's point of view, instead looking to the parietal lobes where we store programs based on experience and values. He called this the computer, so his model was monkey, human, and computer.

'If the chimp or computer are relaxed and are not worried, then you will automatically work with the computer, which means you can perform routine daily tasks without conscious effort, as your computer works according to an automatic program. However, if any danger or unusual circumstances appear, then the chimp or human will wake up and take over' (Peters, 2012). This has so much relevance to elite sportsmen who can, under stress, turn a subconscious skill back into a conscious one with dire consequences, hence a honed, skilful, fast program is interfered with.

It's known that sportsmen mentally run through their event before physically doing it. I recently saw a clip on an NLP website, where Richard Bandler interviewed gold medallist, Iwan Thomas. In summary, he had honed his skills at sitting quietly before a race and going through a life size movie, looking at the upcoming run through his eyes and seeing himself win. He said he imagined himself running with an imaginary stopwatch. He listened to positive voices only, and his fuel was little positive things people had said to him in the past.

So, run your life as if in a movie and make your life how you want it to be. I'm always teaching patients to move their body in their head before they actually do it, and if appropriate, with laughter or music.

In a recent article about motorcycle racing in MCN magazine (July 22, 2015) it was discussed how Marc Márquez and Valentino Rossi's racing totally changed with psychological training: they said that riders needed complete self-belief, as just a tiny amount of doubt could cause their skills to disappear. Having treated world leaders in world superbike and MotoGP, I can see why. Their lack of fear about their injuries is mind-blowing, and their recovery rate is exceptional. In Moto this year they discussed how psychology training transformed the championships.

FACIAL, VERBAL AND NON-VERBAL BODY LANGUAGE

Darwin gets a mention here due to his interest in body language (his book was like a bible to me at University, much to the horror of deeply religious students). Since his time, almost a million nonverbal cues have been noted in our body language. Back in the 50's, Albert Mehrabian said that we communicated 7% with verbal words, 38% with the intonation of our words, and that 55% of our communications were completely non-verbal (Wiener and Mehrabian, 1968). In fact, we recognise 250,000 facial expressions, and talk for only about 12 minutes a day, with each sentence over in 2.5 seconds. With face-to-face communications, 60 to 80% of the impact of the message is non-verbal. As Homo sapiens we are a hairless ape, our origins steeped in ancient biology. We communicate non-verbally with the emotional tones of our story, and women can interpret these communications much more accurately than men.

I learnt a lot more about all this presenting and being videoed after friends injected my face with Botox; they were setting up a new clinic and needed a model, and I was fascinated by how actors looked so young in front of the cameras. It was an interesting experience, although not one I intend to repeat, as there are natural ways to fire up facial muscles rather than paralysing them. Just after this Botox experience, I was up on stage in Spain when I realised that the translators had no idea if I was laughing or crying – it felt like part of my soul was missing, along with any wrinkles. The camera and sound crew explained everything, and even the best technology cannot, as yet, transmit the speed and the tiny flutters of these muscles. No doubt one day technology will catch up, and I wonder if the need for live performances will dry up at that point. Anyway, I soon had my 'natural' old face back again.

Facial expressions that convey emotion are called micro-expressions, and they last for less than a quarter of a second. These muscle patterns convey congruency about what you are communicating and account for at least half of that communication. When the video man slowed down YouTube videos, my face looked so weird, as the expressions suddenly jumped out at me. Our voice intonation is also very important in conveying emotion; a faster speech will alert our mammalian brain to send 'wake up' juices, and matching intonation calms this part of the brain. Slow, steady, quiet speech will help to get the message across and help the computer to make recordings. However, you need to change the volume and speed at times to wake up the sleeping human or audience!

My rather tactless but funny American presenter Ronnie once said to me, "If you insist on having your face au natural in the future, how about a Brazilian bum lift? It's all the rage in Hollywood." Well, you will be pleased to know that me, myself, and my regular arse got back up on stage. There'll be no adding in airbags there, thank you very much; I have my own! My pupils would have gone to pinpoints at that comment.

Once on stage, I tend to talk with my hands quite a lot and move around. Except, that is, when I have them up my puppets' bums… but my puppet show is another story; when doing Z Factor with Joseph McClendon, I have my hand up his puppet's arse, which is called Little Jo. Anyway, back to body language: the body conveys our brain's emotions by fast and slow, open and closed positions. Everywhere I move on stage paces out my story; funny stories are always in one part of the stage, I move forward when talking about the future, and step back for the past. Upright and open for fearless or funny, slow and hunched-up for depressed or frozen, and fleeing for fearful.

The words we use have emotional tags. To convey this, I link members of the audience up to HeartMath equipment, which registers heart rate variance and stress levels. With this device I can find out which ones are dead or asleep. Just one word – that's right, one word – will change the colour on the screen. The brain attaches meaning to a word by thorough data retrievals and values, and checks congruency and any associated danger before acting accordingly, either staying in an unconscious program or in a conscious human state, or diving into a monkey-driven fear state. In the latter case, the brain wave state changes, digestion stops, cell division also stops and the body goes into a full alert drill, even if motionless. There will be more about this in the next chapter.

I remember being linked up to HeartMath (again, there will be more on this later in the book) at one of Patrick Holford's events. I was still feeling really rough, having been knocked about by a flu virus I'd picked up flying back from presenting two weeks previously. I remember turning round to see my erratic readings up on a large screen, showing burnout to the audience, and Patrick gleefully giving me his book on stress and fatigue. It was a little embarrassing, but also enlightening. I, in turn, used this device on John Parker – a truly talented meditation teacher – up on stage in Switzerland, where I successfully demonstrated John's powerful meditation on his mind state. Thankfully, mine was green after we'd enjoyed driving to the event over the beautiful, soul-enriching Swiss Alps – lovely scenery is very healing.

For now, hold onto the thought that your mind controls your response to disease, and in the next chapter, I will look more in depth at how our emotions affect our health.

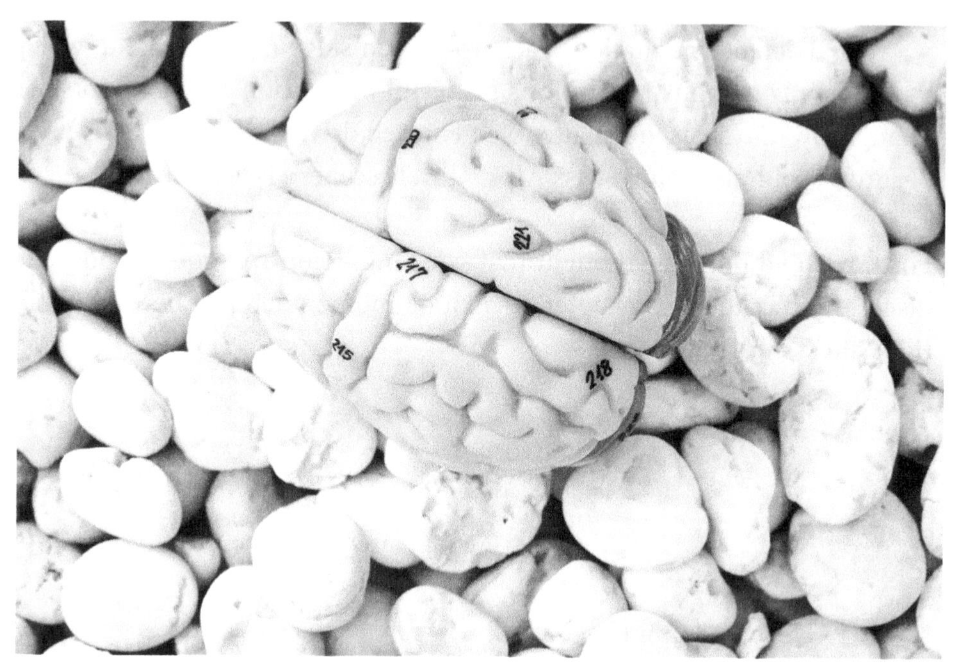

Mind on the beach

Chapter Two

"Somewhere, something incredible
is waiting to be known."

Carl Sagan

EMOTIONS AND BELIEFS ABOUT AGING IMPACT OUR HEALTH MORE THAN GENES

This is so true, hence the old saying: 'As you sow so shall you reap'. In other words, what you think, you become. One of my favourite speakers is Dr Northrup, an American gynaecologist, holistic author, and presenter in America, and she is well known for saying in her seminars that our emotions and beliefs are very important predictors of our health and our aging process. I have quoted some studies she brought to my attention in this section.

Mario Martinez, a clinical neuroscientist, discussed how 'cultural portals' are the most powerful predictors of our biological age, unless we live ageless lives. So, blow out a few candles on your cake if you've read my *4 Keys To Health* book. Do not act 20, 40, or 60 years old. Marketing folks will fire a lot of memes at folks over 50, as 70% of their money is disposable income, with 66% going on new cars and 50% on computers. You must buy this and do that at this age... However, at 77, John Glenn didn't worry about his age when he had to get fit for space with the help of Joan Vernikos, former director of NASA. She would talk about the constant need to stay active in old age and to experience the gravitational flow.

Harvard professor Ellen Langer recounts her research in her classic book, *Mindfulness* (De Capo Press, 1989), and she conducted a study featuring 70 to 80 year old men. One group were immersed in 1950's music, films and so on – a time period when they were at their peak – while the second group lived in the current time. Medical tests pre and post the experiment showed a dramatic improvement in the former group, with their body language and gait depicting men who were ten years younger (Langer, 1997). They did not, however, comment on their abilities as lovers of the ladies, I did check.

The OSLAR (Ohio longitudinal study of aging and retirement – what a mouthful) by B. Levy stated that you could live another 7.5 years simply by having healthy beliefs about aging (Levy et al., 2002), as well as naughty thoughts. No, actually, I made up the last bit.

Another study looked at two groups of people aged 60 to 80 and timed their cadence – the time their foot was off the ground whilst walking. Just whilst walking, no other activity! In my clinic this is an indication of pain, knee and hip osteoarthritis, age, and uncertainty of balance. The first group in the study had subliminal messages in computer games of words such as wise, astute, accomplished, and so on. The second group, however, had words like senile, dependent, diseased, and silly arse... just kidding on the last comment! Yes, you guessed it; the subconscious was listening and took smaller steps to improve balance in the second group, like an older person does (Hausdorff, 1999). Hence the old saying: you are what you think. If you look at the word 'e…motion', the way you walk says a lot about your mindset. I watch my patients walk down the path to my clinic, and by the time they reach the door, I have a pretty good idea how the interview will start.

When you're growing old, it can be an invaluable time to fill your memory (the hippocampus) with unrushed neural connections of wisdom, competence, and value. A life well lived, disappointments understood, imperfections tolerated, patience, and understanding. Wisdom can only unfold in the goodness of time, when it is meant to, and the mindfulness approach discussed in this book really will help to keep you healthier as you age.

Again, Dr Northrup brought to my attention a study involving nuns and Alzheimer's, and the point of the study was to show that the way we looked at our life stopped a damaging pathology from expressing itself. The study in Minnesota began in 1986, looking at nuns in their twenties to see if they could distinguish why some nuns showed Alzheimer's symptoms when in their eighties (and why others did not). They did this by using brain plaques, which are a way of depicting brain damage. Fascinatingly, at death, autopsies showed the same amount of brain plaques, and yet the symptoms were only shown in some of these nuns. The link was clearly their perception of life, the evidence of boring autobiographies written about life in their twenties related to 80% of these nuns showing Alzheimer-like symptoms. With the autobiographies featuring creative, inspiring, energetic, linguistic flourishes and complex language structure, only 10% showed symptoms (Riley et al., 2005). The lesson here is to get writing an inspiring essay or journal about your life's purpose in a colourful way to avoid brain rot, NOW!

You know the ol' middle-aged spread? Well, did you know that too much stress can put pounds on you, even in a day? This is due firstly to water retention, then fatty tissue, and it is actually the body reacting to stress juices, increasing our weight and reducing our metabolism. They say excessive empathy makes you fat, so beware, healers. Colette Baron-Reid wrote about this in her book about weight loss for people who feel too much (Colette Baron-Reid, 2010).

YOU alone are the author of your life story, and even if you forget everything else in this book, don't forget this. It is emphasised in the relatively new science of epigenetics: this is the science of how our lifestyle switches genes on and off, and it was really in its infancy when I was in biology research labs. This theory gathered a lot more momentum when Bruce Lipton – an infamous American research biologist – wrote the *The Biology of Belief* (Lipton, 2008). This wonderful book looks to many factors, including emotion and belief and how they affect gene expression, again confirming that the way we live our lives affects our genes, hence long-term health really does have a lot to do with our emotions and beliefs. Dr Lipton's work also went deeper into our beliefs and where they came from; he looked into the hardwiring that occurs in the foetus brain according to the mother's mindstate, and her response to the environment – for example, whether she found life stressful and fear-provoking.

HOMEWORK:
When you get a pain or an illness, ask your subconscious mind: what is going on in my life right now? What are my beliefs about this and how do they relate to this? Most importantly, how do I fix it once I've learnt what I need to do from this suffering? What is my soul lesson?

When I'm feeling creative, I do this by using a prop such as a dowser, with each direction it turns meaning yes, maybe, or no, and then I ask my subconscious some questions. It works in the same way kinesiology does. Another favourite of my authors is Deepak Chopra. An eminent oncologist (a cancer specialist), he is responsible for yet another huge pile of books on my desk. Deepak also discussed, on numerous occasions, how at least around 50% of our emotional responses are hardwired by our mother before birth, including our happiness markers. Hell, how do we address a problem created before we were born, you may well ask? Both these eminent speakers/ authors agree that trans meditation is the only possible doorway to change these hardwired neural networks.

Dr Daniel Keown is an inspiring medic and speaker. I heard a quick lecture from him just a couple of months back, and have delved into his thoroughly enjoyable and deep book on acupuncture and embryology to add a couple of quotes of his: 'Personality has an enormous effect on genes, but genes only partly explain people's personalities' and 'Genetic twins with the same genes, the exact same genotype, can end up very different in personalities' (Keown, 2014).

I treat a few twins and they seesaw up and down in mood, health, and weight according to their lifestyle and often look 10 years older/younger than each other. This again explains why some people inherit or catch diseases and others don't, being more to do with how they interact with their genetic code. Many studies show that the state of mind is linked to health, and our health is only partly determined by our genes. Our thoughts shape our personality and the choices we make about how we live our lives, which then affects our genes. Dr Keown also states in his book, 'Studies describe lifestyle but it could easily be personality' (Keown, 2014).

HELP ME SHAPE UP THE HAPPINESS OF CHILDREN

It warms my heart to know that mindfulness ideas are creeping into our children's school curriculums; neuroscientists, cognitive psychologists, and educators have all recorded improvements in happiness, optimism, attention to lessons, and a reduction in distracting and bullying behaviour. A special lady and actor Goldie Hawn is deeply involved in this rewarding work.

HOMEWORK:
For all you teachers, parents, uncles, aunts, and grandparents, here are some of the mindfulness things I do with my nephews, Rafael and Reuben, and my niece Skyla, all of whom are under five years old at the time of writing this:

HEARTFELT PLAY

HOMEWORK:
Get the children into pairs, or if it's a single child, you be the partner yourself. Let them hold a piece of lego in their hand, with their eyes closed, and describe how it feels – its smoothness, coolness, the edges, and whether they curl or have straight lines – and then get them to imagine what they could do with it. Once this has been done, try with different objects. Just make sure each piece is age appropriate, or you could be visiting A&E!

PIANO TONE

HOMEWORK:
Again with closed eyes, settle the kids and then tell them to listen to this piano key, and to put their hands up when they can no longer hear it. You can strike a bell or use another instrument if you haven't got a piano, and after their hands go up, ask for a moment's silence to see what other noises they can hear.

SMELLY

HOMEWORK:
Choose a thought-provoking smell. With eyes closed, encourage any emotions or associated memories with the smell as they describe its scent. Just avoid any nasty smells like old nappies!

BREATHING BUDDY

I got this idea from a study carried out in schools in The Bronx in New York. The boys get soft toys and place them on their chest, and when they get distracting thoughts, they imagine them disappearing like bubbles. They need to be attentive to the rise and fall of their favourite toy for a minute. Bedtime is easiest, however it was also used to settle kids prior to class, and worked well.

HOMEWORK:
Place a favourite toy on your kid's chest and get them to focus on how their breath moves their toy up and down.

RELAX AND SQUEEZE

This is just a tense and relax exercise that can be used in so many different ways.

HOMEWORK:
Start in a relaxed position with nice, deep, slow breaths. Then get the little ones to think about travelling around their body, relaxing and tightening as they go: their toes, ankles, knees etc.

HEART SENSE

HOMEWORK:
After getting them to jump about, again with eyes closed, ask them to sit or lie down with their hands on their chest and let them feel how their heart's pounding falls away. Then, gently encourage them to talk about their feelings and emotions, and if they feel things in their heart, tummy, or knees etc. This brings in body awareness.

HIDE AND SEEK

I enjoy playing this game with my nephews, aged two and four, and whilst I'm writing this, I am giggling about the way they play it. It teaches them to be aware of their surroundings, their vision, their hearing, and their sixth sense.

One evening, Raf and Rue had a big thing about hiding in a colourful blanket in the middle of the room; they were hidden, so how come Auntie could find them? Well, for one thing Reuben filled his nappy, which meant we could smell him! Another time when they were searching for me they found me straight away, and Rafael explained that they'd both peeked a little, just enough to see where I went.

Then we had counting at speed, or missing numbers out to give the person hiding less time to hide. Eventually they caught on to the need to be quiet themselves when doing both seeking and finding, and to tune into any sensation of the hidden person's energy field. Instant verbal encouragement gave fast Pavlovian conditioning, and it started worrying me as they could hide a little too well!

HOMEWORK:
Go play and good luck!

SKYLA, SHAPING BABIES' MINDS

At the time of writing this sentence, my niece is 11 days old, and looking at her reminds me of how we start as a ball of cells and then grow and grow incredibly quickly. In the first month of her life she will form trillions of brain connections – about one thousand new connections form every second. By the time she is three, her little head will be three times heavier.

She has a basic genetic blueprint from my brother, Jez and his wife, Sara, and my brother says that 25% of it will be the same as mine, generously sharing the responsibility at the moment of a very smelly nappy… yuk! However, a combination of this and her own experiences sculpture her brain. Strongly stimulated connections grow in complexity and unused ones get pruned away. Neuroplasticity is all about use it or lose it – the same goes for your thingy too!

What Skyla eats and hears and touches and feels will form the neural networks for health, intelligence, social skills, and language. God help her… just kidding, guys! I have never met such loving parents as my two brothers and wives. Baby Skyla will hear all sorts of languages as she develops, then she will select the most often heard, communicating in this way and pruning away all unused languages.

This is when my younger brother will curl up his toes, so Jez, go and make a brew. I used to play magic lifts with him, when he was a tiny brother with fluffy blond curls and wearing big nappies, and we would go to different lands and see imaginary places and people. Imagination is so strong when you are young and healthy; I wonder if he will do the same with his daughter. With my older patient and wise brother, Rich, when we were little kids I think I must have tested the patience of a saint; I always wanted to swim all the time, but as he would take me roller skating and trolley racing instead, I would wear my swim wear, goggles, and carry my float to all the boys' activities. I also sat in puddles and filled up sinks full of water to sit in them. Yes, he loved taking me out to play with the boys' gang, NOT! My imagination at under five years old enabled me to enjoy activities in my own strange way and feel happy. I guess I haven't changed much – I go swimming when I can, but I no longer sit in sinks.

John Medina in his book *Brain Rules for Baby* wrote, 'the greatest paediatric brain boosting technology in the world is probably a cardboard box, a fresh box of crayons and a couple of hours' (Medina, 2010). I enjoy that still, and I would add paint to that too… paint everywhere…

HOMEWORK:
Pay attention to baby. Speak a lot directly to baby with colourful, fresh, inspiring vocabulary. Communicate with touch, facial expressions, and body language, as language is not there to start with and baby associates more with body language. Your heartfelt body language responses to baby's needs and calls sculpture intellectual and emotional stability in the child. Get in the right state of mind as best you can around baby, as they are acutely sensitive to your mood/energy. Practice my mind techniques, especially with your breath and heart, before handling the little one, as it can be exhausting and frustrating at times, and you will transmit this strongly. If you practice energy healing or massage, baby will love that. Reiki is great too; kids and humans in general love healing energies. My cats love their daily reiki – their response is similar to the kids', there's just a lot more fur everywhere.

ADULT EMOTIONAL STATES, MOOD AND STYLES, WHAT ARE YOURS?

This new way for scientists to look at how we live our lives has led to the development of adult self-help tools. Now steady on, keep it clean; I mean meditation and neurolinguistic programming courses, F.E.T (meridian tapping) and HeartMath. Emotions are really just fleeting responses to the real or internal world, and if the emotion persists over hours, it becomes a mood. Emotional style is a consistent way of responding to things in life, and you can have these brain pathways identified and mapped out by lab equipment. Understanding how we colour our lives with emotion is the key to a happier life.

Dr Davidson, whom does a lot of work with the mind/life institute in California, writes and presents about different personality styles, of which he says there are six (Davidson, 2012). These are:

Resilience: the speed of recovery from adversity. Do you quickly recover and throw yourself into the fight of life, or collapse in a puddle of despair?

Outlook: do you have a sunny outlook on life, or are you pessimistic? How much time can you sustain being positive?

Social intuition: how adept are you at picking up social signals? Can you pick up body language cues as to people's emotional state and needs? Or are you blind to this?

Self-awareness: how well do you understand that bodily feelings reflect emotions? Are you in tune with your thoughts and needs? Or is your inner voice unheard, introspection not done, and you feel threatened, jealous, and anxious?

Sensitivity to context: how well do you control emotions? Bearing in mind the context you find yourself in.

Attention: how sharp is your focus? Can you be appropriate and sensitive to role-playing and the situations you find yourself in?

HOMEWORK:
Can you score you and your friends? Either using 0 to 10 or a point on a line, ask yourself questions on the previous six personality styles. How much of each do you have? For example, a teaspoon of self-awareness and a bucket of resilience?

According to Dr Richardson's work, there are five main personality traits, using the descriptions of styles:

1. ***Self aware:*** focused, strong social intuition, high in openness.
2. ***Conscientious:*** focused, strong social intuition, acute sensitivity to context.
3. ***Extrovert:*** resilient, and rapidly maintains positive outlook.
4. ***Highly agreeable:*** highly attuned to context, high resilience, maintains positive outlook.
5. ***Highly neurotic:*** outlook insensitive to context, unfocused.

HOMEWORK:

Where do you fit in? Here's a few more… I'm not sure if I wholeheartedly agree with these, but let's have a look at what psychologists say about these emotional styles.

Unhappy: negative outlook, low resilience.
Anxious: negative outlook, low resilience, very self-aware, unfocused.
Shy: low resilience, low sensitivity to context.
Impulsive: low self-awareness, unfocused.
Optimistic: good resilience, positive outlook.
Patient: high self-awareness, high sensitivity to context.

I HAVE TO GET INTO MY DEPRESSED POSTURE OTHERWISE I JUST CAN'T FEEL IT

These are all feelings, and while some people believe they can change these at will, others do not. We often have to assume a body posture to get into a feeling, and you can go into a sequence of postural adjustments to fuel an emotion. For example, our depressed patients do not stride in, head up and smiling. Factual words, facial expressions, and body posture reveal how you create depression. I can remember Tony Robbins asking members of the audience to change into different emotional states and their matching body language was remarkable. There is a program to run to get into an emotional state: they see something, feel something in their body, possibly smell or hear something and then change their posture. It is easy to change a baby's state by a sudden, distracting action, but it is not so easy with adults and their learnt responses. What program do you run when you feel a certain emotion?

A quick aside about emotions here: there is recent evidence to suggest that beyond the brain, emotions are stored in the fascia, which is a tight sweater over our muscles. An 'electrical grid' is said to connect our emotions through meridians and chakras, hence touch makes us emotional. There will be more about this in the next two volumes, especially when I am explaining the acupuncture I use.

THE HEART-BRAIN LINK, HEARTMATH TECHNOLOGY EXPLAINED IN DEPTH

I have HeartMath technology I use to demonstrate to audiences how emotion affects our health, and emWave is advanced technology that will help you reduce the negative effects of emotional stress, bringing awareness to your state and giving you more clarity, better emotions, and energy. The 'em' in the title is to empower you to shift your emotional status.

The Institute of HeartMath is a world leader in the dynamics of emotional physiology and heart-brain interactions. Doc Childre's research started in the institution back in 1991, when I had just finished my physiotherapy degree. Back then, I was so frustrated that the impact of the mind was seen to have such an insignificant role to play in recovery from illness and trauma. My background in psychology led to some very strong difference of opinions. I wasn't the best of students; my attention span was always short when I was bored with lecture material. I had earpieces and tapes running with different material in lectures and I wrote with coloured pens in my left hand to help me stay focused. Stupidly, I shared this with a local radio station during a live interview about what it meant to be a student. My poor tutor at the time was Julie Walters' brother, and I am sure he thought I was very weird, but I was just being honest and I got in trouble again! Anyway, back to HeartMath and relaxation. Wearing the HeartMath earpiece is acceptable at work, as no sound is coming through, so you can concentrate on your breathing without anyone knowing.

Working towards a higher state of coherence means being in a highly efficient physiological state in which the nervous, cardiovascular, hormonal, and immune systems are all working together efficiently and harmoniously. More coherence means fewer detrimental emotional stressors; in simple terms, this makes us happier. So how does this technology work that I carry around in my handbag and have in my office? By the way, yes it has batteries but fortunately it is a square shape, so it doesn't look like a sex toy, unlike the shockwave head. This little black box analyses the subtle beat to beat changes in the time intervals between heartbeats. This is called HRV (heart rate variance), an important indicator of physiological resilience and emotional flexibility. With the latter, that's me f**ked.

When I get angry, frustrated, irritable, and anxious, I am often not in a position where it is appropriate to share these feelings, however my heart rate rhythm pattern becomes irregular and incoherent. This is aging me, fattening me, stealing my happiness, and disrupting my digestion, brain function, and cell division to list just a few physiological changes. My voice, manner, and behaviour need to hide these emotions whilst in lengthy clinics or meetings, however if I was connected to HeartMath, my heart would betray these emotions to you. So often we are acting in 'an appropriate way', and we lose sight of who we really are and how we truly feel about things, just to make sure others feel secure and happy. Internalising emotions is not always healthy, hence debriefs or a cuppa and a hug go a long way.

This long-term emotional guarding and stress is unhealthy. Exploring and releasing emotions is very healthy, and then, by using meditative activities, you can rewire yourself back into how you actually feel. Then, and only then, can you encourage more positive, life-affirming, joyous, peaceful emotions. Furthermore, spend at least some time with people who emanate these feelings to recharge your batteries, but be wary of those 'well meaning people' who profess to counsel you. The safest way to journey through life is to understand and love yourself, warts and all.

HEARTMATH TECHNIQUE

Here are three steps to stress relief that don't include sex:

Step One: Heart Focus

Focus your attention on your chest in the area of your heart. Think about your heart and what your heart means to you.

Step Two: Heart Breathing

Imagine your breaths flowing in and out of this area. If you have an emWave use this, otherwise do what man has being doing for thousands of years in meditation, yoga, chi kung, and tai chi: take slower, deeper breaths and be very aware of your breath.

Step Three: Heart Feeling

Think of your breath bringing in light, positive, healing energy, and like an exhaust pipe, breathe out any negativity. Think about an emotionally inspiring time for you, and as other thoughts flow through, acknowledge them; greet them only briefly but then let them go, like the Queen greeting lines of people and giving a brief handshake. Then return to your happy place. Create an emotion of caring, joy, and most importantly, gratitude. This exercise is very useful with heart surgery patients.

They have now shown the equivalent of brain cells in the heart. In 1991, Dr Andrew Armour introduced the term 'heart brain'; he showed the heart's complex nervous system and qualified it as a little brain. Researchers at the signature Institute of HeartMath (IHM) discovered that the intelligent heart is intentionally experiencing emotions and sending information to the brain. In just one study alone, hundreds of participants were asked to work on positive emotions, and the effect was more coherence, and a more rhythmical heart rate. This empowering psychophysiological state is known to improve mental, physical, and sporting performances.

STRESS, AND HOW I ATTEMPT TO COPE WITH IT

They say we need a certain amount of stress to feel alive, but too much isn't fun. Now, our nervous system can be related to two systems: the accelerator and the brake. We have our foot on either one at any time, and this decides our actions and the chemistry that is unleashed, which then starts pumping through the body. Basically, the engine is revved up or slowed down, and these systems are called the sympathetic nervous system (SNS), the accelerator, and the parasympathetic nervous system (ANS), the brake. With too much stress, brain cells die (Gambarana et al. 1999). We get more negative, fear-inducing brain juices that are squirted out from the alarm system, and the amygdala gets stronger. The decision-making office then packs up under chronic stress in the frontal cortex – it goes bust. However, let's not get too carried away with joss sticks and sandles and candles; we do need some stress in life to thrive.

We all need to experience life full on with drive, determination, apprehension, and passion, however we need to learn how to cleverly feather the brakes. Learning how to brake effectively and timely, like in a driving test, will give you a more balanced approach and therefore a longer, happier, healthier life. In my driving lesson this was called 'feathering', and no, it's got nothing to do with *Fifty Shades*. Furthermore, relaxation alters gene expression and reduces cell damage due to stress (Dusek et al., 2008; Benson et al., 2000).

PEDAL ON, PEDAL OFF

So, here's the dilemma: too much stress is bad for you, and too little boring. An experiment with a monkey pressing a lever in a safe environment looked at getting a predictable reward, an unpredictable reward, and no reward (Fiorillo et al., 2003). The dopamine pleasure-giving brain juices reached the highest levels when it was an unpredictable reward. Interesting, eh? Well it makes sense to me. Life is a balance between comforting predictability and unexpected, adrenaline-driven surprises. Why else do we wrap presents up? It's in the feeling and guessing that we often experience more pleasure from rather than knowing what you're getting. You could apply that to a lot of things, eh ladies? Nudge, nudge, wink, wink…

If I'm feeling overwhelmed at work, I find a breather between lists of stressed patients: simple things like washing my hands or going up to the clinic kitchen and washing up – feeling warm, soapy water is soothing. Or if driving home, I love having the roof off to feel the breeze on my face. If writing, I will check posture and any locked up muscles, and light a candle for its visual softness. If bored, I do something outrageous or risky or creative to get the brain juices livened up. What do you do?

HOMEWORK:
What do you do when you're overwhelmed? How about when calming down? How do you change gear to relax?

HOMEWORK:
Take a few deep breaths, as this helps to change your brain state, and it costs nothing but a few seconds of your time. Place your hand over your tummy and feel your hand rise on the in breath and move away on the out breath.

HOMEWORK:
If you have time, try progressive relaxation exercises, bringing awareness first to your breath, then to various parts of the body. Keep it steady, feel it, and let go. You can add in breathing exercises and imagine your breath travelling into different areas of your body to relax and heal. With reiki techniques, we imagine light doing this.

Now let's tickle the brake: take a big breath in and out, no not breast… *breath.* Touch the brake again and find a simple, pleasurable sensation. For example, touch your lips (or ask a good-looking friend to!). Simply getting inside your body and building physical sensations calms the mind. I was taught some 30 years ago, by my meditation and psychic friend Ken Douglas, to develop a visualisation in my head and to literally smell the flowers. I was and am so easily distracted, and Ken has been known to put his hand over my mouth to shut me up, when everyone else was happily drifting into meditation.

POOR HRV CAN LEAD TO A HEART ATTACK

To be frankly honest with you, I am trained in healing and meditation and yet my heart rate variability is poor, as I am a passionate, stubborn, driven character, forever racing around, helping others and doing stuff. I can confirm that I am too throttled out with my software program, with my headaches and nose bleeds. I drove my heart so hard in my twenties: working in the National Health Service, running a department, setting up clinical teaching sessions, studying, running private clinics in the evenings to part fund all the studying, designing new treatment programs, frustrated to hell with long waiting lists and with no interest in my ideas on preventative medicine, I collapsed with chest pain like there was no tomorrow. I do know what to do to prevent this happening again and again, hence please read this book and don't beat yourself up when you go off track at times – we all do it.

Being a patient on a coronary unit was interesting: some young male nurse suggested he flannel my bits, and I had injections in my stomach, hourly blood pressure readings, lots of visitors, vases of daffodils, and interesting monitors showing me that yes, the old ticker was beating, even if slightly erratically. That visit was purely my body saying brake please; you have worn the accelerator out. I was fortunate in that my love of swimming and running meant I was physically fit, and I discharged myself when a stroke patient was admitted and needed a bed – I sneaked into the toilet and changed, told them I was feeling great, and that their need was greater than mine.

Did I learn my lesson? No… but I did change jobs, you bet; you can only hit your head against a brick wall for so long. After that embarrassing incident, I stepped up my interest in alternative medicine and the effects of stress. I remember my first meeting with June, my dearest friend and reiki guru, and she reached out and told me that she saw a dark patch in my heart, which was rather disconcerting. There's no chance of secrets when your closest friends are healers and psychics!

Controlling stress so that your heart rate variability is low is a good idea if you want to avoid a heart attack. Now, there exists research to suggest this is a good indicator of healthy cardiovascular, immune, and emotional system, if you'd like to read further (Luskin et al., 2002; McCraty, Atkinson and Thomasino, 2003).

STRESS MAKES US RATTY

Back in the 80's, when I was at university studying the psychology of stress, we had reports on rats' physiological reactions to stress, poor things. Not exactly what I'd believed my psychology modules would be about, however the conclusions stuck with me. In an experiment carried out some ten years previously, several poor rats received small shocks, just enough to stress them (Weiss, 1972), and they were put in different situations to see if feeling less stressed about the shocks changed their physiology.

The first group had no way to distract themselves, and they developed stomach ulcers. I believe a Nobel Prize was awarded when it was shown that ulcers were a combination of bacteria and stress. Another rat had company, and every time he got shocked, he went and bit the other rat – very human-like. Mind you, my patients haven't bitten me very often. That rat did not get an ulcer, and this is echoed in humanity: times of economic stress shows increases in child and spouse abuse. A third rat chewed on wood after and had no ulcer, whereas another had a light before the shock, telling him how bad and long the shock would be. Through this knowledge, he too escaped having an ulcer. Another could 'cuddle' another rat, getting no ulcer, and yet another rat had a lever to hit to control the shocks – ditto, no ulcer.

The moral of the story is that if you invite rats into your living quarters and they have activities to take their mind off a stressful day – such as scurrying about in your trash – their ratty medical bills will be less. The building blocks of stress include: not being able to express your frustrations, feeling out of control or having no control, having no prediction of events, feeling that things are getting worse, and finally, having no shoulder to cry on.

When we perceive we are threatened, our body steps into survival mode; the muscles need energy straight away, and our blood pressure climbs as the heart pumps faster. All non-urgent activities stop, such as cell division, healing, digestion, and immunity. Mammals who are chronically stressed and unable to undergo an adaptive stress response can actually die.

As I've mentioned, short-term stress is great: you have more dopamine, more focus, better memory recall, and more oxygen and glucose. Long-term excessive stress causes hippocampus neurons to die, and new brain cells and neural connections are less frequent and will also die (Davidson,

2001). I find it interesting that people believe meditation is just switching off and relaxing, when indeed it is not. The correct measure of stress leads to a laser focus of attention, and this art strengthens the ability of the frontal cortex to regulate emotion, which is echoed by electrographic responses. We have stress centres in the brain to focus our attention on biological needs, emitting exhaust fumes and gaining fuel. In the brain there is a Barrington's nucleus, which receives messages from our viscera. It interrupts our thoughts whilst driving, sending signals to the locus coeruleus and then on to the brain's stress centre, the hypothalamus.

SOME STRESS IS NECESSARY

Some stress is like a vaccine to the immune system; in limited doses it sparks brain growth, like a stress inoculation. Stress is a gift of evolution. It engraves a memory created by a stressful environment to enable us to survive and remember how to deal with it better next time.

STRESS IS OUR FATTY MIDRIFF

Exercising when we are feeling stressful is a good idea, however do you notice some marathon runners still have a fatty midriff while the rest of them are skinny? That's our mind; a stress juice called Mr Cortisol converts muscle into a sugar store in the form of glycogen that stacks up as fat. It's like a bunker of energy storage for a never-coming nuclear explosion.

STRESS ANALOGY IN THE OFFICES OF THE BRAIN

Stress creates focus, a need to refuel for action, and the ability to memorise the events connected with the perceived stress. Let's briefly remember the HPA axis: the alarm bell Mr Amygdala gets Mr Adrenal gland to pump out adrenaline, which gets glucose fuel moving. He gets Mr Hypothalamus aroused into heavy breathing, pumping the heart and shouting in the ear of Mr Pituitary to squeeze some cortisol currency out of Mr Adrenal. Cortisol keeps the brain cells stacked up with glucose so they can think through the problem. Meanwhile, Mr Amygdala tells the librarian who works for

Mr Hippocampus to record the happenings and get some tapes and books done. All the non-fiction books and biographies get erased and Mr Hippocampus can only focus on fear and terror and murder stories. Glutamate gets boosted to help with the photocopies being efficiently produced, and the story is recorded correctly.

I came across a comment by Bruce McEwen that sums it up well: in his book *The End of Stress As We Know it*] he says, 'The mind is so powerful that we can think ourselves into a frenzy' (McEwen and Lasley, 2002).

STOCKPILE FAT

We all need some stress to move and get started. However, the modern mismatch between physical activity and mental concentration to achieve getting food is making us fat. We also know that stress can stockpile it around your middle.

However, Paleolithic man walked 5 to 10 miles a day and thought about how and what he could eat. Our genes these days are encoded with a certain energy expenditure; we need to move more, as exercise helps metabolism. Glucose comes into a brain cell to be converted to a fuel called ATP in the powerhouse, the mitochondria. This fuel powers all the metabolic reactions, and 'exhaust fumes' are given off, called oxidative stress. Special 'green' enzymes keep cell pollution to a minimum.

If you diet too strictly, then oxidative stress happens – this occurs if the brain cells don't get enough glucose, and ATP cannot convert it to fuel. Therefore, your fuel pump at the gas station shuts. Also, at stressy times too much excitatory glutamate drives ATP too fast and the cell runs out of fuel faster, throttling out, and with a gurgle, you stop. Balancing exercise and fuel reserves is so critical to the brain as it uses 20% of the total amount of glucose in the body, and chronic stress can upset this. Look out for your friends with a big midriff, and ask if they have a stressful life… politely, of course.

DO ANIMALS FEEL STRESS?

I believe the answer to this question is well summed up by a quote from a 19th century naturalist: 'The ox cannot endure even a momentary severance from its herd. If he is separated from it by stratagem or force, he exhibits every sign of mental agony; he strives with all his might to get back again and when he succeeds, he plunges into its middle, to bathe his whole body with the comfort of close companionship' (Galton, 1883). Get my point?

CAN WE THINK UP STRESS?

Yes, it's like sitting down to a movie. The movie in the brain has processes that encode and synaptically link emotional, cognitive, autonomic, and somatosensory components, running the movie as if you were acting in it again, just like it is for real. Then, the stress brain juices flow.

EMOTION, BELIEFS AND KINESIOLOGY

This is an interesting tool that I've watched my sports therapists use when they suspect an underlying psychological block – something emotional – from preventing a physical skill being achieved, which the client is consciously not aware of. It is a mind body tool used in body talk and psychology to tap into underlying subconscious emotions and beliefs. Anything deemed as stressful, negative, or untrue leads to a poorer muscle test response.

With a partner – or someone else's partner, just kidding – get them to stretch out their arm. Tell them to hold their arm there, then press down briefly just above the wrist. Ask a question like, 'Do you live here?' and repeat. Yes or no? Retest, and get a baseline. You can ask, 'Is your name Jo, yes or no?', a bit like dowsing. You will soon get a feel of positive confirmation or a negative reaction, and this is the subconscious responding through the body. If alone, play alone… try the sway test: choose yes or no for forward or back, and again ask the questions.

Now, if a belief or emotion is not healthy, you need to reprogram and work on a new belief. This technique suggests the following posture, whilst repeating out loud the new belief. If this doesn't work for you, neurolinguistic programming can help and I'll talk more about this in a later chapter.

HOMEWORK:
Reprograming postures. If you're right-handed, cross your right ankle over your left, with the right wrist over the left in front of you. Grip your fingers, then uncross your legs. With your hands in the chapel position, look through your hands and say out loud your new belief. Step high on the spot, touching the opposite knee, and then twist your spine, repeating out loud your new belief.
You can also draw a shape slowly and again say it out loud, or you can invent your own and make it interesting! Then retest to see if you have reprogrammed yourself.

THE POWER OF LAUGHTER ON THE MIND

In 1964, Norman Cousins – the author of *Anatomy of an Illness* (1981) – developed a fever that confirmed ankylosing spondylitis, a spinal inflammatory condition which is part of the rheumatology family. He found out that his back pain and stressful lifestyle of reporting – and the heavy dosages of painkillers he was taking – were stressing out his adrenal glands and his immune system, fuelling his degenerate disease. As Tony Robbins will often say, he got to the point where it was too uncomfortable not to change.

He watched lots of funny films, ate foods of high nutrition and with anti-oxidant qualities, did gentle exercises, and decided he would laugh and will himself back to health. He did just that. Since his day, research has shown that laughter boosts natural killer cells in our immune system. You can measure raised IgA (immunoglobulin) in saliva, and laughter also lowers our cortisol levels, lessening our stress response. Laughter tears carry more toxins out of the body when compared to tears from crying. Hence, I prescribe you daily laughter.

I was known as the 'Patch Adams' of hospitals wards, and being on call always brought out my wicked sense of humour; I deeply believe that laughter – used in the correct context – is a great healer. There was a real Patch Adams, and in the great film of the same name he was played by Robin Williams, an incredible artist who sadly battled with depression until his recent death. Anyway, back to Patch: he was an American doctor, clown, and social activist, and he went on to fund free medical healthcare to help thousands of patients in Virginia. He is still gathering funds for a free hospital and believes that happiness boosts healing above all else.

CONTENTMENT AND NATURE

This mindstate is all around us, and you just need to learn to tune into nature, like when an animal stills between the kill or escape, and is just simply being. Nature can teach us about being mindful human beings, and connectiveness drew me to biology, though its peacefulness is not echoed in modern medical practice.

I am asked to talk at gardening guilds a lot, partly because of my love of nature, but also due to my understanding of appreciating healthy, home-grown food, pretty wild fauna and flora, and the need to keep our bodies flexible enough to garden; connecting with the planet in this way grounds us. Although I'm not an expert in gardening, when I have my hands plunged into the soft soil in my green house – or 'plant hospital' as it doubles up as – I feel peaceful; I love creating new plants and listening to nature, to the birds talking and feeding. Don't you?

When I was small I was forever bringing in ill birds, mice, and fish, lovingly placed in shoeboxes and bowls. Yes, my animal hospital was often a sanctuary for animals – usually dying, smelly, and dead! I have always had a tenacious, never give up nature, although in that case it wasn't very endearing with the smelly dead birds. As soon as I learnt to crawl, I also had mixtures of concocted 'medicines' hidden everywhere in the house, for a 'just in case' moment of smelly foul mixtures!

When nature needs to heal animals and humans from a toxic or emotional trauma, the body sometimes has to shut down on a very deep level; they can be comatose for days, and even appear dead. Hence the bell that was attached to the toes of buried humans for the gravedigger's watch. That's my excuse anyway for attaching them to inactive friends!

Ecopsychology is the posh word for the contentment and connectivity gained through nature. David Abram, Gill Edwards, Theodore Roszak, James Hillman, and Chellis Glendinning to name just a few have written about this concept (Abram, 1997; Roszak, 1995; McLuhan, 1996; Goldman and Mahler, 2000; Norfolk, 2002).

THE HUMAN ENERGY FIELD AND SHAMANIC HEALING

Katha Upanishad said, 'Beyond the senses there are the objects, beyond the objects there is the mind, beyond the mind there is the intellect. The great self is beyond the intellect' (Deussen, 2010).

The shamans I have met over the years talk about our soul essence giving a blueprint of how our life force, energy, mind, emotions, and body should be. It is a script for the universe to direct experiences and to manifest relationships. They heal with soul retrieval, as they believe parts are given or taken in relationships or with trauma. Unlike western doctors, shamans give meaning to an illness, not a description of what the illness is and what will happen – they help make sense of why the illness occurred. Shamans are gifted and experienced psychologists, seen as essential to a community's cohesiveness and emotional wellbeing, and the guardians of moral code. When someone succumbs to illness, not only the victim but also the villagers have to publically declare any grudges and resolve any conflicts. The shaman is exhausted at the end of a day's work and always receives healing for himself as well.

I will be exploring this more in my next volumes, looking in depth at energetic healing, meridians, and Chinese acupuncture. Energy exercises such as yoga, tai chi and chi kung all bring with them an understanding of chi and chakras, which I touched on with my *4 Keys To Health* book.

The biosphere is said to connect the invisible realms of consciousness with the physical body, and former NASA scientist and healer, Barbara Brennan, described it as the missing link between medicine, biology and psychology (Brennan, 1988). My mother brought me her book, *Hands Of Light*.

It is suggested that negative beliefs and emotions, which form in our complex, exquisite energy field, later become physical and mental issues. Valerie Hunt suggested that emotions are crucial to organising the energy field, energy being incoherent in disease (Edwards, 2010). The aura is likened to a mirror of our human consciousness, a known wisdom of our ancient cultural heritage. Just as our body has canals and rivers of blood, so too do we have 'electrical circuits' zapping through our fascia to all our organs and to our 'valves', the chakras. Like the tapestries on my clinic walls, these emotions are interwoven into energy patterns, and vibrate at a high frequency.

Modern day energy medicine uses acupuncture points (found on meridian lines), which are tapped over with specific commands. These points may either be depleted or too full of energy. Shiatsu training taught me a lot of patience with this concept.

Now, I want to very briefly mention the body's energy system in its relationship with emotion, and to techniques such as meridian tapping (EFT). A chap called Roger Callahan got a certain recipe widely accepted with the help of an engineer, Gary Craig, where you tap acupuncture points in a set sequence. These points are demonstrated in Gary Craig's free download at www.emofree.com, and are also discussed in my first book, *The 4 Keys To Health*. Now, let's play…

EFT (OR FET), TAPPING EMOTIONS BACK INTO PLACE

Here is a whistle-stop approach, enough for you to start playing with this on your own. For this recipe, you need to work on about 10 acupuncture points in sequence, roughly tapping 5 to 7 times with two to three fingers.

While you're doing this, think carefully about a situation that causes you concern that you wish to resolve. As you start, choose a level 1 to 10 for the subjective units of distress (this is your SUD score).0 means no emotional reaction to thinking about it, whereas 10 is extreme anxiety.

The script to follow is this: "Even though I have, or felt, or… (fill in the blank) I want to totally love and accept myself." Repeat this three times on each point. Tap the edge of your hand, the top of your head, your inner eyebrow, the side of your eye, under your eye, under your nose, on your chin point, your inner clavicle, beneath your arm, on your nipple, and on your inner wrist. Tap three to five times a day for several days and then check your score. If it's working for you, you should feel less anxious – i.e. I was 8 out of 10, and after three cycles, I am now 5.

Then you can implant/hardwire a new belief on these same acupuncture points. I now choose "to be at peace, or be healthy", for example, or you can be more specific about your changed belief. This is an anchoring technique that uses invisible, intelligent energetic key points on our energy matrix – the sensory system of the ghost in the machine, not the nuts and bolts of a robot. This technique is known as emotional acupuncture, the kind without needles.

Now, you're probably thinking, are there any studies about this? In 2003, in the *Journal of Clinical Psychology*, Steve Wells tested the act of tapping against deep breathing techniques, when concerned with a phobia (Wells, 2003). A single 30 minute tapping session resulted in 4 out of 5 physical tests being improved, and an improvement was still present after nine months. A team of scientists headed up by Dr Harvey Baker in New York compared tapping to an interview technique. Tapping won and still had an impact up to a year later (Baker, Siegel, Wills, Polglase, Andrews, Carrington and Baker, 2003).

HEALER'S TOUCH

As therapists, what are we doing to the brain when we touch? Our brain juices are neurochemicals that sculpture it, and our brain is hardwired to protect our life. Touch is translated into electrochemical signals that fire neurons in certain patterns, and this nerve firing can be read by EEG. If chemicals are injected that mimic natural brain juices, such as GABA or acetylcholine, the change in brainwaves can be read, as well as the shift in specific areas of electrical activity. Touch is known to change the brain juice, and it is also known to open glutamate receptors that have laid down neural networks housing traumatic memories. Touch can make these memories pliable, like plasticine, then remodelled.

So what we say whilst we touch, or inject, or use acupuncture, or do reiki is key and yet NOT covered in any detail in training for medics, physios and nurses. With every touch, subliminal messages flood the subconscious, and touch generates 1 to 2 Hz. Combining gentle touch with tapping and eye movement, you can explore traumatic memories made pliable, and that can be healed in trained hands. This is an exciting window of observation to healing arts such as reiki, seen through a lot of medics' and physios' eyes as witchcraft. Now beyond spiritual implications, there are stronger scientific implications for treating pain and trauma, and the associated depression and anxiety (Rasolkhani-Kalhorn and Harper, 2006; Harper and Drozd, 2000).

FREUD FUELS FEAR OF TOUCHING PATIENTS

Freud helped to stop touch being part of psychoanalysis for fear of erotic misinterpretation. I personally have not found this to be a problem as the words and energy surrounding healing are very asexual. Touch eases pain, loneliness, lack of belonging, acceptance, and trust, and touching the face, head, and arms are said to give the most sensation of safety to do with the mother-child interaction (Field, Diego and Hernandez-Reif, 2005). Not only do I like to ask how stressed people feel after treatment, but if time allows, I also like to check with HeartMath to give biofeedback regarding the change.

NEEDLING AROUSES EMOTIONAL MEMORIES

If I step into my biologist's shoes, I know that emotions were programmed in to help with our survival, and I like to think of emotions as the colouring pad of our soul. 30 or more states wash up on our beach of emotion every day and melt away to be replaced again and again. I ride the peaks and troughs of my patient's emotions; you have to be ready for strong emotional releases if you treat pain. If you combine a light trance with a memory of a life-changing event and with a physical therapy technique, magic can happen. It makes a mockery of prescriptive numbers of sessions and outcomes.

Emotion is from the Latin word *emovere*, which means to move out. I like this quote by Silvan Tomkins: 'Without its amplification nothing matters, and with its amplification anything can matter. It combines urgency and generosity. It lends power to memory, to perception, to thought, and to action' (Tomkins, 1982). I find time and again that when I ask my patients about previous accidents, there is no memory. Then I place a needle in a tight muscle and the memory of the previous injury comes flooding back. The traumatically-encoded pain associated with that event is centrally encoded so will NOT respond to narcotics, as it is not an opioid-dependent pathway. Men more than women feel embarrassed about the emotional component, but I have known some patients to cry all night. They tell me the next day that the pain has melted to a more tolerable level, or better still, gone, and that they feel an overwhelming feeling of release and relief. That is after they wanted to punch my lights out for initially making the ache worse!

It goes without saying really, but fear needs to be gently exposed and the treatment carried out in a caring, clean, and safe environment, one that matches the patient's expectations and beliefs. When my patients get angry or upset, I moderate any physical intervention and maintain a firm though gentle dialogue to avoid panic and lessen the intensity of the reaction to treatment, refocusing on going back to the reason for being there – to heal the trauma – and not just to replay emotions and get stuck in the loop.

So what is happening when you touch someone and you get an unexpected emotional response? Essentially, the memory is being fired up. If your friend or client is talking about a time or place, it is an encoded, non-emotional, conscious, factual memory, housed in our good old friend Mr Hippocampus – the memory library. However, if emotion is bubbling up, chances are it's the earliest memory system at play. This starts before age four, well before Mr H the library was built. These memories are hidden away in different, partially unknown places. They are unconscious sensations and feelings, postural and learnt habits. When we get nervous, our brain juices (norepinephrine and cortisol) enhance these memories being made and relived. If we are slow at calming down the treatment or touch that is bringing up the emotional memories, the cortisol level climbs and flashbacks can occur. This can happen all too fast if you lack experience.

THE RIGHT CONDITIONS FOR TRAUMA TO EMBED

So why does a traumatic memory exist on one occasion and not the next? Well, four conditions need to come together: the event must produce emotion, it must have meaning, the brain juices must be at the correct level, and it must be perceived as an inescapable injury or event. This is probably why injections and needles as a kid (and adult) create a traumatic emotional response.

Today I was treating a very gentle soul who was a fireman – they see such terrible sights on all our behalves. Anyway, whilst treating a back injury, he recounted a sad story about witnessing a meaningless death of two young children, because someone thought they could talk on a cell phone and accelerate and overtake in a truck at the same time. He was not moving through the happening at the time his trauma memory recorded, and the four things were all there to encode the memory as traumatic: emotion, meaning, inability to escape it, and the brain juices were correct.

RESEARCH BACKS THE SUCCESS OF HEALING ON TRAUMA AND PAIN

The past is always present, as noted in the great book by Dr Ruden (Ruden, 2011). A month ago I was giving a talk on the 4 keys when a co-presenter told me to look his research up again, so I did. It was good to see that he understood how using eastern healing maps, spiritual energy chakras, and acupuncture points could help the mind, and that it was not unscientific at all. These thousand-year-old systems use unmeasurable thought fields and healing energy transmission, and recent research suggests that healing/acupuncture points have stem cells and also switch physiological responses off and on.

I have always combined ancient healing techniques with modern medical/physiotherapy treatment, and Dr Ruben's research agrees that a combination is good for the mind and can reverse traumatic memories. He selects tapping, light touch, and mental distraction techniques, and he calls his recipe 'havening'.

HAVENING TECHNIQUES

Dr Callahan used his own special tapping approach (more info on www.tftrx.com): to get the patient to recall the trauma, he would give an intensity score of distress from 1 to 10, then tap a chosen series of points 5 to 10 times. Dr Roger added in a point just under your ring finger called the GAMUT point, and he called his approach havening.

This is an example of one of his distraction techniques: close your eyes, open your eyes, point your eyes down to the left then the right, circle your eyes one way then another, hum a tune, count to 5 aloud, then hum another tune/nursery rhyme. These combined treatments were seen as the Devil's work back in the 90's when I was a physiotherapy manager in hospitals, during which time I was fighting to preserve one-on-one, hands-on treatments, and group discussions.

IF YOU WANT TO CHANGE A BEHAVIOUR, USE A VERB RATHER THAN A NOUN

A verb rather than a noun? I remember an island off Vancouver where the islanders used a language only having verbs. They say it is easier to change a behaviour with labelling verbs, not nouns. Saying and believing "I am disturbed" is harder to change that saying "my current behaviour is disturbing".

COMBINING THERAPEUTIC MODALITIES TO SWITCH ON HEALING IN THE BRAIN

In my work I use reiki, IMS dry needling, acupuncture, NLP, and light touch and mobilisations. I may add in laser, shockwave, ultrasound, and light trance too (which I'll explain further in my next book). Occasionally I'll give my patients some homework of acupressure or FET, but always with light, trance-like music to encourage alpha wavelength, which initiates relaxation and healing. I find that by using IMS deep needling in a place of chronic pain and memory of suchlike, I can trigger an emotional explosion.

Only a week ago I placed a needle into a point of emotional intensity, into a teenage rugby player and in front of the patient's mother. The child cried all night before finding a release and escape from the pain. The treatment of an area of previous trauma needs to marry up eastern and western techniques; touch (somatic) and talking together is needed to create a long-term healing response. As I've mentioned, a couple of clever dudes called Dr Roger Callahan and Gary Craig did a lot of work on tapping techniques whilst saying mantras out loud – you can find all the points listed on the internet.

When patients (who have already seen everyone else) come to see me with normal scans and x-rays, and when all my known tests – including IMS muscle grab tests – are negative, the warning bells sound in my head. The emotional traumatic memory is at play, so it's a case of sending in the fire engine to quell the flames, then of starting the slower rebuild of neural pathways in the memory. The memory is usually blocked as to what initiated the trauma, but physical treatment can unblock it. The unconscious has played a clever hand at switching emotional pain unconsciously into physical pain, and it does not appreciate Snazzy Sherlock Holmes snooping about.

Cecil Helman (who wrote *Suburban Shaman*) stated: 'In fact the art of medicine is a literary art. It requires the practitioner to have the ability to listen in a particular way, to empathise and also to imagine, to try to feel what it must be like to be the other person, lying in the sickbed, or sitting across the desk from you, to understand the story teller as well as the story' (Helman, 2006).

Here's an interesting meeting that led to more seriousness about 'new age' techniques. One of my key lecturers in NLP was Richard Bandler, and he taught Paul McKenna (NLP), whom talked with Dr Ruden (research fellow and doctor) whom then contacted Dr Callahan (guru in tapping), and the blend of all these ideas added great value to the argument for both verbal and hands-on treatment for reprogramming the mind.

Exciting discoveries in emotion, thought, and motivation are driving forward the wiring of consciousness into robotic brains, and at the same time building an awareness of what makes us human. It questions how modern medicine can justify a simplistic biochemical model of drugs when clearly we react profoundly to human touch, healing, and empathy. It is summarised in this wonderful quote by Norman Doidge (neurologist): 'The discovery that the human brain can change its own structure and function with thought and experience, turning on its own genes to change its circuitry, reorganize itself and change its operation, is the most important alteration in our understanding of the brain in 400 years' (Doidge, 2015).

It has been known for some time that the meaning someone puts to something – like a healing touch – is key to the outcome. Plus, the quality of the relationship with the therapist also influences the outcome. I remember Dr Cyriax's assistant (Dr Cyriax is a late orthopaedic doctor who instigated a teaching programme in orthopaedic medicine – more of this in my next book) telling me that whilst teaching, he would click a clicker device in his pocket as he manipulated someone to demonstrate the psychological response to the reassuring sound. Curing suffering can be like trying to find a needle in a haystack, unless you have a magnet. My patients proudly tip their drugs out over my desk: antidepressants, antipsychotics, antispasmodics, painkillers/opioids, anti-inflammatories, specific nerve painkillers, and so on. Then, I touch them – as light as a feather – and they scream. I say, "these pills sure work then"... get my point?

WASHING AWAY TRAUMATIC MEMORIES WITH YOUR WINDSCREEN WIPERS

So, why is it that if we gently tease out threads of a traumatic memory, and then, by using distracting techniques and gentle specific touch, we can reprogram it? Well, if it is appropriate I will get my patient to talk about the emotional core of a problem and paint over the disturbing memory with a new picture. I will come to brush strokes of gentle touch and distracting mental activities shortly.

This is how it's believed to help: the brain juice glutamate painted the traumatic picture and it is activated on the recall of working memory, finding all associated memories just like a librarian. The juice glutamate glues together the emotional memory within Mr Amygdala. This is vulnerable to delinking; like a spark plug, if not fired up, the engine won't start. Healing can be like pouring water on your spark plugs. Happy juices such as serotonin and GABA soar, glutamate gurgles and dampens down further, emotions play out more kindly, the brain purrs into delta range – a low frequency engine purr – and then the open spark plugs get soggy.

YOU HAVE TO CRACK A FEW EGGS TO MAKE AN OMLETTE

Next time Mr Brer Rabbit jumps out in front of our headlights, we feel less panic and can logically work through a calmer response, metaphorically speaking saving another paint job. I have always felt strongly that in order to make an omelette you have to crack some eggs, and it's true that treatment can be painful in order to cure a problem. However, it is our responsibility as healers to minimise pain and not deepen emotional pain at the same time as the physical pain heals. It is the knowledge and experience – the why and when and how we treat trauma – that in my humble opinion makes a great practitioner. There are many different approaches, and I have seen many variations around the world. Many are as good as each other and work in different ways, in specific circumstances with the uniqueness of the person involved. Treatment is interacting with the belief systems implanted by other therapists (deformation professionelle) as well as the lifestyle and parenting experienced by the patient.

SHIATSU SMACKED MY WRIST

I remember being taught a big lesson when I was a shiatsu student (this is a form of Japanese physical therapy, where you hold acupressure points whilst moving joints. You feel the energy in these points and then tune them with your own energy). I was at that time trained in reiki, however I was feeling tendons and muscles and struggling with grasping the emotional meaning with these physiological switches at these key points. My lesson was that a very emotional night followed, after the teacher specifically created a reaction from her treatment to teach me a lesson: "Involve me and I will understand." I concentrated on the importance of healthy energy flow through meridians much more after that, as I got that by pressing on acupuncture points, the brain experienced emotional reactions.

BIG STUDY TO SUPPORT TOUCH

In the 90's, Dr Andrade looked into the effect of methods of healing, involving meridians, energy flow, acupoints and sensory input such as tapping. These methods led to the association for comprehensive energy psychology (ACEP), which, as you can imagine, is a highly controversial subject. In fact, my last book of the human trilogy (Soul) will raise a few eyebrows.

Anyway, back to Dr Andrade's study in Uruguay, a big study featuring 29,000 patients over 14 years (Andrade and Feinstein, 2003). You could certainly blow a raspberry to non-believers after collating this research. This study was about comparing the effectiveness of talking therapy, CBT, and drugs with alternative healing techniques. The combined healing approach fared better: there was a 76% cure compared to 51% from cognitive behaviour therapy and drugs. The latter needed 15 sessions compared to 3 of the former, that is five times as many. The research was said to be watertight and close to a double blind controlled standard.

If I have a good trusting relationship with a patient, I will explore what was happening in their life before and during the time of the trauma and how it affects them now. I like to relax their breathing and mind with music and voice control. The dry needling techniques for muscle contractures carry an emotional trigger, which is often totally unexpected, and if necessary, some gentle trance techniques can help.

Relaxing instructions of climbing stairs and steps connects with the visual spatial working memory in the mind – the bit that creates images in space – and gentle humming can trigger the phonological part of the working memory. Reiki, light massage, shiatsu, or yoga can create a safe haven, and all this can melt the glutamate receptors in the library of traumatic memories associated with the pain I am working on. Just a word of caution: I am not suggesting for a minute that we dabble with patients who have severe depression, bipolar, dementia, or chronic fatigue unless we are very experienced, although I have seen improvements. These techniques, however, are best suited to curing patients who have pain associated with emotional trauma.

HEALING WITH A FRIEND

HOMEWORK:

Do you want to play therapist and patient? Phone a friend, put on some quiet music, and get the atmosphere energetically conducive for peaceful healing and connection. Choose a mildly stressful memory and SUD score it 1 to 10 in terms of anxiety. Don't play with deeply painful emotion. Start a tapping technique chosen from a book or internet under FET, and repeat 5 to 10 times with a mantra that the patient says out loud, then get your friend to do some eye stuff: close, open, look down and left, look down and right, circling their eyes one way and then the other.

Then, with their eyes closed, do some imaginary walking up or down stairs as if going into meditation (this is called visual spatial). After this, do some light pressure point massage or reiki, then some phonetics, counting and humming a nursery rhyme. Continue with touch therapies, and repeat the eye movements. Do some slow, deep breathing and then hum a nursery rhyme or tune (or simply go "ommm"). Continue with the hands-on therapies – tapping, acupressure, massage, reiki, or whatever your skill is – and then ask for their SUD score again.

Then swap or repeat, choosing and evolving your own methods. The goal is to gain trust and relaxation, and to change your brainwave pattern and mindstate to accommodate the rewiring of the painful memory whilst feeling both in control and safe.

BUILDING HAPPY MEMORY BANKS

We drive through life at speed, and if you're anything like me, you probably don't stop to savour those special moments as you jump to the next problem or negative energy. I replay special moments when I run, and this helps to keep me sane. It's about transforming fleeting, nice experiences into lasting moments of memory networks and biochemical releases. We are wired from our ancestors for focusing on negative stuff – it sticks – while positive stuff slips off like Teflon. We all have emotional, positive needs: safety, satisfaction, love or connection, and these are the pillars of contentment.

When I have a good experience, I do my best to enrich the colours, sounds, taste, and words to etch it into my mind and link in positive stuff that is happening at the same time. So much of my time over the years has been spent with souls in pain, who have a dark, upset, fearful, untrusting anger that wraps a cloak around pain and keeps it embedded in the body. These energy imprints stick like Velcro, and despite all my psychology training, leave me drained, so when I do gain a wonderful experience, I play the memory over and over again.

HOMEWORK:
Can you practice this for me? When you recall something, imagine that just like a video camera, you are scanning around the room and picking up all the good points. It takes time to get good at this. If you lose your memories of hope and happiness, you can lose your way. When you experience caring, love, and joy, weave it into the tapestry of your brain whilst putting a hand to your heart, taking a deep breath, and spending 10 seconds to firmly embed the experience in your mind. Remember, 10 seconds is needed to embed contented memories.

Your attitude is chiselled out by memories of experiences with challenges, the vulnerabilities you hold to them, and the strengths you have to hit your challenge head on. Every day I take pictures of people and places on my phone that leave a footprint on my heart, then, when I'm feeling lost and sad, I look through the latest pictures and see how many good experiences I keep adding. This reminds my memory banks of happy times.

When I am hurt by a troubled relationship or painful news, I feel as much of it as *I am able to cope with,* that it feels safe to, and then, little by little, I let some of the details go, focusing instead on something good that came out of the experience.

For an example of how you could find a situation difficult to cope with, my father recently cut a piece out of the paper about saunas being good for the heart, and I placed it on my desk. I paid little attention at the time, but when I arrived at Hoar Cross spa the next morning, Father had lost consciousness after spending time in a sauna, and it was a long time until his blood pressure came up. To avoid having a traumatic memory, I overlaid the image of his pale face with the crowd of caring, thoughtful, and compassionate souls gathered around him, then with the amazing attention he was getting at the hospital, making sure my brain was wired in a positive way. Father was fine, and a little more wary of newspaper ideas. During that experience, I did not align the four things (emotion, meaning, inability to avoid/escape, and stressed brain juices) needed for a traumatic memory, and was able to think about it in a positive way. We cannot always be responsible for or change what's happened, but we can change how we feel about it.

Then, on that same day some four months ago, I dashed over to my friend June's bedside to see her shortly before her death. Her distorted, bony face started haunting me again, so I paid attention instead to the friendliness of her relatives and the caring nature of the nurses, imbedding these memories on top of her face. These techniques did not stop all the pain, but the experiences left a softer imprint on my heart.

HOMEWORK:
Go and practice this.

USE IT OR LOSE IT

Our brain is sculptured by our predominant thoughts, and as the least dominant ones die off, it could be called neural Darwinism. Survival of the fittest: the most used. This changes in minutes with accompanying blood supply, glucose need, and gene manipulation, and its posh name is experience-dependent neuroplasticity. Actions speak louder than words, and repeated actions cause sustained change, for example regular meditation helps to suppress stress genes.

Start thinking about what you are choosing to remember. The psychologists talk of two types of memory: explicit, which are your personal stories and an encyclopaedia of 'what it is' data, and implicit, which involves how to do things, your values and beliefs, your expectations and assumptions, your inner strengths and weaknesses, and pain. Unfortunately, the latter is negatively wired, so any disappointments, fears, and dislikes get a priority seat booking, all buckled up before the good stuff gets on board. You have to cling to a positive thought for a few seconds otherwise it jettisons off your memory plane, seeing a last flicker of its parachute as it sets off to pastures new, and you are left with a memory plane full of grumpy passengers.

HOMEWORK:
Please count to ten while thinking about a good experience, and breathe it in. Write down the good points next to the problems, and work hard at it as our Stone Age brain is about survival and misery. Tell yourself and others – at every opportunity – real, true, heartfelt, genuine compliments. Genuine compassion is life-saving, and gratitude is inspirational in how we all could see life.

I write this from my perspective, where I battle with sadness and disappointments many times over. I am brave enough to put myself in situations which I know will constantly challenge my happiness and beliefs, and that's why I know these methods are a life buoy, and I am throwing it to you. I have actually been a lifeguard in my youth… but that's another story.

JELLYFISH MAN

Now let's look at our accelerator and brake pedals, our sympathetic and parasympathetic systems. Remember the snake, mammal, human model?

Well, alongside this our nervous system grew out from the brain, feeling and tasting the world and growing feedback loops to our organs. I think of this as the brain being a jellyfish, with its tentacles spreading throughout the body.

The autonomic nervous system has both a brake (parasympathetic) and accelerator (sympathetic). The vagus nerve is also part of the autonomic system; it is calming, and as well as causing freezing, and it sends signals into the larynx, heart, and facial muscles to give social signals. It has the opposite role to revving up the autonomic system of fight or flight, and it drives it towards rewards. I like to think of it like yin and yang, and just remembering things can cause the pedals to be pressed as if it is really happening.

HOMEWORK:

Can you sense how easily you keep pressing the accelerator pedal, and are you aware what words trigger this?

Add in the human need for connectiveness in the cortex and we have a simplified model of all the drivers to action. Feeling connected to others is key to contentment – do you feel more content when you're with people you have good relationships with? When we have a green mindset, we feel safe, satisfied, and connected; we cope better with challenges.

HOMEWORK:

Look to my book on the 4 keys of health and score your mindset. Have a giggle and let happy juices flood into the brain such as oxytocin and opioids (in the subgenual cingulate cortex). The biochemistry of pleasure counters aging, and nitric oxide is a great balancer of all brain juices. Herbert Benson said its release in peak experiences climaxes meaningful, spiritual, and creative experiences and slows aging. I wonder what the nuns were up to in that earlier piece of research I mentioned!

HAPPINESS CAN GROW WITH MEDITATING

Research demonstrates that meditation is an effective intervention for cardiovascular disease (Lopez and Snyder, 2011).

The new science of brain imaging lets us watch networks glow and hum, and we can actually explore what happiness is. For a long time we believed we were born with a measure of happiness, and that was our lot. I can remember reading in a Deepak Chopra book that 50% was set in stone unless melted with deep meditation. Here's a brief collection of research to show the importance on mindfulness training and happiness.

A clever chap, Dr Davidson (from the Mind and Life Institute) did some fascinating electroencephalogram [EEG] recordings on the prefrontal cortex to show how our moods switch between happiness and unhappiness (Davidson et al., 2003), using sensors on the scalp to measure electrical activity, or by fMRI scanning. When emotionally upset or angry, the right prefrontal cortex lights up more than the left, with the left lighting up when happy and enthusiastic, hence Davidson created a mood index based on the ratio of electrical activity between the left and right prefrontal cortices. It was a predictor of daily moods (Davidson et al., 2004).

A series of simple daily meditation exercises can break habits of thinking and behaving that stop you from living life to the full. Many judgmental, self-critical thoughts are habitual, and breaking them in order to think more positively and be more mindfully aware brings joy, allowing us to experience the world calmly, non-judgmentally, and compassionately. We used to believe that happiness was pre-set genetically, carved in stone. However, Dr Davidson showed that meditation allowed people to pull free of their emotional set point. Davidson and Kabat Zinn got a group of workers to try his 8 week mindfulness meditation program, and the results of the EEGs showed a change in the way the brain dealt with sad or disturbing memories or happenings. Their mood index shifted towards happiness and it actually improved their immune system. They then looked at antibody reactions to flu jabs after meditation sessions, and bingo! An improvement (Davidson et al., 2003).

A similar program can be found at www.mindfulnesscds.com and the accompanying book for the 8 week course is *The Mindful Way Through Depression: Freeing Yourself From Chronic Unhappiness* by Mark Williams, John Teasdale, Zindel Segal, and Jon Kabat Z (Guildford Press, 2007).

Dr Sarah Lazar showed that years of meditating structurally changes our mood thermometer in the insula (Lazar et al., 2005). This insula has enjoyed a lot of attention thanks to functional magnetic resonance imaging (fMRI), and this area is linked to our viscera and our overall connectedness. This is key to compassion, empathy, and loving kindness for another being as well as yourself. What a different world it would be if we all worked on this area of our brain! It positively glows with loving thoughts, and through meditation it enhances happiness throughout our lives.

Here is another observation: Kirk Brown and Richard Ryan looked at the benefits of a mindful approach in people, and they found that meditators spend more time doing things they valued as opposed to what other people asked of them. I find that true; they are a group of people less needy for others' approval.

Barbara Fredrickson showed that just 9 weeks of meditating brought a sustained, positive zest to life and an increased sense of purpose, and that weaknesses such as headaches, congestion, and chest pain were reduced (Fredrickson et al., 2008). The techniques taught in Norwegian medical schools showed that encouraging conscious observations, becoming more aware of routine daily activities, and observing and attending to ordinary everyday tasks consciously, rather than using automatic responses, enhanced happiness (Shroevers et al., 1995). I had a go at this idea, thinking about what I was doing rather than thinking about anything but the activity I was carrying out, and I felt spaced out. I did try to explain to Alan my newfound research on attentive housework, but he just said, "Yes, you are weird."

Why not prescribe meditation instead of drugs? A study in 2005 by US National Institutes of Health showed the following: a 19 year study discovered that a form of meditation practiced since the 1960's in the west – transcendental – leads to a massive reduction in mortality. There was a 49% reduction in death due to cancer, and 30% reduction due to cardiovascular reasons, with an overall reduction in mortality of 23% (Schneider et al., 2005) – that's no small number, now where's my meditation CD? Ah… John Parker (my chum), I think I will listen to your CD and extend my life (Schneider et al., 2005).

Here's yet more proof for you: in 2010, Zindel Segal and Willem Kuyken carried out a study to prevent relapsing depression. They showed that an eight-week course of meditation for people previously on antidepressants resulted in them doing as well or better as when they'd been taking their meds. I think you will agree there is a lot of scientific proof that meditating makes you happier (Kuyken et al., 2008).

Meditation activates the parasympathetic nervous system through multiple pathways to tilt your body, brain, and mind towards peace, wellbeing, and health. You can do this through big exhalations, touching the lips, body mindfulness, HeartMath, and of course, meditation. This increases your compassion and empathy to all situations, healing and nourishing the immune system, and you also feel more secure, less threatened, more connected, and securely attached to places and people of refuge. It increases grey matter in the insula, hippocampus, and prefrontal cortex (Holzel et al., 2008), and it also reduces cortical thinning due to age (Lazar et al., 2005). On top of this, meditation improves gamma wave reach within the brain (Lutz et al., 2004).

MINDFULNESS MEDITATION

I have sat and carried out mindfulness meditation over 30 years with my learned friends, Ken, June, and Lesley. We would sit down or lie down, relaxed, with our eyes closed. We had to choose an approximate length of time to meditate for, as Ken could just go on and on, whereas for June, sleep usually called!

Start with an awareness of your breathing, feeling the chest going up and down, and gently allowing your wandering mind to return to the breath. Increase the number of breaths you can stay present with – this skill gets better with practice, as initially your mind will keep racing away. Just allow thoughts to wash through; greet them but don't get into them. Be aware of what it feels like to let them go, and what it feels like to be aware of spacious awareness itself. We often took it in turns to lead a meditation, taking us on a journey through the universe, or in forests or on a beach.

HOMEWORK:
Have a go.

Transcendental meditation is another form of meditation based on ancient Hindu writings, by which one seeks to deeply relax, repeating mantras whilst meditating. It is said to have been founded by Maharishi Mahesh Yogi (1911-2008).

SEARCHING FOR HAPPINESS: IS IT UNDER THAT ROCK?

Staying happy all the time is not natural or possible, but staying unhappy all the time is just dumb. As Stephen Hawkins said, "Life would be tragic if it weren't funny." Did you know that the international society for humour studies exists and holds conferences on humour and health? They research the effect of humour on biological sciences and the anatomy.

I find that playing with my niece and nephews reminds me how to laugh and feel happy in the moment. Too many years in front of patients have made me forget how to be spontaneous and how to be a child – as the kid's cartoon character Homer Simpson said, "The little boy reminds me of me, before the weight of the world crushed my shoulders."

As Richard Rohr (*Quest for the Grail*) said, 'We begin naïve, now that's the true fool, we don't know anything, but the end of the journey is what I like to call second naïveté, returning back to another kind of innocence, maybe we weren't wrong when we spoke of second childhood, a kind of no need to impress people, be important, a freedom to say silly things, because there's no competition anymore – that's a great freedom" (Taken from www.cac.org/richard-rohr).

My clinical days are very long and full of lost souls looking for HAPPINESS in a marriage, kids, money, a car, looking under this rock and that. That's the problem with labelling things: happiness is a verb not a noun. We live a journey, a process, rather than an encyclopaedia of facts. Happiness is hard work, it's seeking out people and activities that give you a purpose, that make you feel joyful and amuse you. You have to learn to avoid problems, as well as stressful, negative situations and people, and drive towards the ones that make you happy. Happiness is not luck or chance; it is an achievable state if you want it. Getting into a good attitude of mind is your responsibility and yours alone. You have to stop waiting for someone or something to make you happy, as you will experience transitory happiness only.

Staying happy all the time is not possible. Our nervous system knows night from day and black from white because it needs both to build in recognition of opposites. Experiencing unpleasant feelings like pain, hunger, thirst, sadness, anger, and disappointment is to drive you on to achieve more and sort the problem out. Take the prompt, deal with it, and move again towards happiness. This is brain science: think positive and you are positive.

HOMEWORK:
Write a summary of your day, of how you felt emotionally at different points in your day. Why did you feel that way? Do you know your triggers? What did you do to tackle any unhelpful emotional states? What did you achieve by looking at this? Share with a friend.

Remember when I discussed the anatomy and physiology of the brain? This incredible structure sees, tastes, smells, and touches the world through your nerves and your bodily senses. Then this information is processed and made sense of within the constraints of our understanding, beliefs, and past experiences. We then form a model, an interpretation, an architectural plan, a map if you will of your unique reality. This map is either fit for purpose or not, and once we understand ourselves more, our map changes and our life follows.

LET'S SHOUT ABOUT OUR ACHIEVEMENTS

I get my patients to verbalise or draw out in big colourful headings their physical possessions and the abilities they have achieved, as well as any qualifications and skills they are proud of. It's an empowering thing to do – go on, try it! In England we are trained to be modest, as success is often met with envy and not love; achievement can often make another feel less significant so they hit out to cover this up. As adults, in order to feel more love and to fit in, we hide our successes and excitement to the point where we feel unfulfilled because we hide them so well we can't find them. We trade happiness for connection. When success makes us stand out, or allows us to potentially move away or be needed by more people, those closest to us kick out in fear of losing us; they don't want to be different so they need to pull you down to their level to feel more certain of themselves. It's called cutting the tallest poppy.

HOMEWORK:
Write down things you've achieved, such as: I built my own greenhouse, I ran a mile without feeling any pain, I lost half a stone of fat. See it, and colour it in: how does the achievement make you feel? Then add any emotional strengths and tasks that you're proud of and have honed, such as: I am a good listener, or I run to time. Feel it in your heart and believe it. Then list your quality, reliable relationships. See the name, and in your mind's eye see their face and hear that person's voice.

HOMEWORK:
Then, prioritise those skills and people that have the most meaning and which call out to you the most. For at least 10 seconds per statement, think about why those qualities impress you and resonate with it. Breathe it in and feel it in your body. Where is it? How does it move? Loop it and enlarge the experience, then anchor it by pressing on a location on your body. I will pick an experience whilst out jogging and run it around my head. I see how it makes my legs feel, and how the speed of my feet changes, as well as the pace of my breath.

MIND OVER MATTER, IS DISEASE HELD IN THE BODY OR THE MIND?

Is consciousness in charge of disease? In 2002, a study in the *New Zealand Journal of Medicine* illustrated the power of the mind. 180 osteoarthritic knee patients believed they were having operations, a washout or a cartilage debridement, but not all of them did. The control group had sham surgery – just incisions – and two years on, the results were no different to those who had the real surgery (Moseley et al., 2008). In 2009 in Canada, fake surgery again concluded no difference in outcome (Kirkley et al., 2008). Is it possible that the healing came from the belief in the whole ceremony of the procedure rather than the procedure itself? fMRIs teach us about brain control in specific regions, and can help with emotions such as fear and happiness (Schwartz, 2005). Researching with this tool could shed some light on this mysterious brain.

PERSONALITY IMPACTS DISEASE

Personality impacts disease. For example, a person with a type A personality (remember that phrase?) often has more heart attacks. Meyer Friedman was a key guy to discover this, and he was a driven man who really cared for humanity; he saw his last patient at age 91, just a week before he died. He lived through his own heart attack at 50 and listened to what he discovered about hostile personality traits causing disease.

I have always believed that the magic in healing lay in our mind, and in our belief in the caring ritual that the shaman/doctor performs. This opinion blows a lot of clinical trials out of the water, and naïve scientists do not value this outcome. Wake up and drive your own mind and health.

We know that optimistic patients are more likely to survive and suffer less than miserable ones (Giltay et al., 2004; Allison et al., 2003). Sadly, clinical trails more often than not only value drugs and surgery, and a lot of preventative treatments aimed at a healthy lifestyle are seen as new age nonsense. It is just a 'placebo'... but I argue, who cares what it's called if it heals without harm?

My book, *The 4 Keys To Health*, was about making people accountable for their own health and happiness, and in my opinion this is a critical step for lasting health, otherwise the responsibility is mistakenly handed over to the practitioner, partner, child, boss, and so on.

Remember the HeartMath technique? Again, think of an emotionally-charged, joyful experience. Play it over and over again, smell it, colour it, listen to it and smile through it. Place your hand over your heart if it feels right, or if not, move your body in a way that feels right. You are wiring your brain for pleasure, and not only is it priceless, but it costs nothing. This blends in reiki with neurolinguistic programming NLP techniques. I touched on this in my last book, and we will also explore it further in this volume.

I remember being taught how to improve my imagination, a gift we lose as we become adults, and one that I am reminded of in meditation, trance, and distant healing techniques.

NLP IMAGERY TO IMPLANT A HAPPY SWITCH

Think of a sensual, spiritual, or exciting experience that was mind-blowingly pleasurable. See it vividly: enlarge the picture, the sounds, the colour, and the smell. Step into it and pay attention to your senses. Loop the experience – don't allow an ending – and run it at different speeds, with different sounds or tunes. Feel it in every part of you; push the feelings of pleasure to the extreme and anchor it by pressing onto part of your body. Steady on – I didn't mean there! This gives a key spot on your physical body to return to, like a switch, which is in effect what you are doing inside your brain. There is a gene (5-HTTLPR), which is a happy gene and which affects the happy juice, serotonin. However, your own life choices will affect this gene (I wonder if there's a grumpy gene or a sleepy gene?).

I can remember seeing and experiencing this first-hand on courses with Tony Robbins, Richard Bandler, and Joseph McClendon – the latter whilst co-presenting Z factor – when they were rewiring pleasure buttons. It was certainly an interesting mix with our kundalini yoga expert, Goedele, there! I also remember June and Ken, my dear spiritual tutors, working on a deep meditation years ago and exploring the spiritual essence of kundalini. June told us how she had a memorable climatic experience involving a tree, where she visualised tree roots growing through her body, much to Ken's shock and my amusement!

VALUES: DO YOUR MATCH UP WITH FAMILY AND FRIENDS?

At my work, we go over our values and prioritise them from our top 10 down to our top 3, then we sit down as a team and see if we line up. Conflicts in key values will always cause disharmony, but do be as truthful as you can: we found that people wrote down what they wanted their values to be, but which, in essence, were not what they really thought. For example, 2 out of 10 colleagues put money down as a value, but when asked if they would treat patients for less money, no one put their hand up. We wrote everyone's values onto a large flip chart and discussed where they conflicted. One chap wrote family and business growth, whereas one would have to take time away from the other, and he was tired and in some conflict. When working in clinics on preventative health, health was a key word I thought was a given – silly me!

We have roles to play at work, at home, and with friends, and I thought about my curing of suffering in terms of a pilot: in a clinic I need to be experienced, responsible, and able to prioritise landing the plane over any attributes of being amusing, pleasant, friendly, generous, creative, spiritual, and so on – get my point? However, these attributes around family and friends would not lead to connectiveness and happiness.

HOMEWORK:
Lists of values are readily available on the internet. Write yours down and see what you've put: is there conflict? Do they line up with friends or family? When we now consider emotional intelligence, values, and beliefs in employing people to successfully complete tasks, this leads to more happiness.

Aligning life's purpose ultimately creates a path towards fulfilment and happiness… or does it? Be ready for disappointment; success and wealth can make others feel less significant and you can end up feeling less liked and loved. If you place love and success together, you have conflict; I have met lonely, unhappy celebrities who no longer fit in with those friends they love. Accept the responsibility of what life will throw at you in order to achieve your goals.

Remember to check if your life goals align with others, and if they don't, then understand that and proceed with knowledge. Remember the rat stress tests? Knowledge prevented ulcers. Travelling towards your goal can make you happier than achieving it, again like in the rat experiment.

HOMEWORK:
See your goal clearly: its colour, place, smell, sound, and walk through attaining it, how it feels to achieve it, and then having achieved it. Act as if it's a given. Play that one out.

People who win the lottery often get through the money and end up depressed – the responsibility to find happiness is too much for them. This is talked about more in *The Paradox of Choice* by Barry Schwartz.

Professor Layard, Britain's happiness Tsar, said that happiness and wealth were only married together until $15,000 (Layard, 2003), and the Easterlin Paradox showed that poor nations were not necessarily less happy, it was more about how they felt (Easterlin, 1974). Buddhist monks – and HeartMath – certainly believe in mindstate and the importance of love, peace, and gratitude. The 2008 study by Stevenson and Wolfers proved the opposite: a strong increase in happiness married to better socioeconomic standards, with no tapering off. Richer equalled happier (Stevenson and Wolfers, 2008).

The SES socioeconomic scale showed that your position brought you a longer, healthier, happier life. In fact, 70% of happiness could be due to strong, quality social bonds, more years of education, a high status job, and more friends and neighbours – they all directly impact on psychosocial and overall wellbeing.

HAPPINESS GENE

Is there one? Yep. 5HTTLPR controls the transport of mood and serotonin, and people with this gene favour bright and positive over the negative. However, don't despair; the thoughts you have will influence genetic expression (Lipton, 2008).

CHANGING YOUR STATE

I remember doing the following on NLP training courses, and it's like creating a watcher within. Think of an emotional state that gets triggered in certain circumstances, and work out how you get into it. Is there a thought, a noise, a smell, a body posture?

HOMEWORK:
Write down answers with sensory-based words, and then write down how you would prefer to be. Describe the setting, your tone, and your feeling, as well as any colours or noises, and have a positive, affirming statement to match this movie. Choose an easy to manage emotion before going for a difficult one. Feel your physiology reacting in both situations, and make a note of the difference. Sportsmen imagine themselves successfully competing, then go beyond this to think how it would feel to win, with every cell in their body.

HOMEWORK:
What is one of your states that you go into every time something happens? If you could rewind, what would you change and why? I remember doing this in pairs in class, closely observing our body language. Relaying these subconscious traits back and making them conscious brought awareness, as well as a tool to change that state.

Tony Robbins and Joseph McClendon shared their secrets of how they changed their state before they had to get up in front of thousands of people. They would do certain movements and mantras that they'd pre-programmed for success, and as a result, their mood switched. My stage fright used to be huge before learning from these masters; getting up on stage with Joseph to entertain the audience changed from nerve-racking to enthralling. I learnt how to break my pattern of reasoning, and with it, my emotional state.

PAIN: IS IT REALLY ALWAYS MY ENEMY?

I've spent far too many years puzzling over why one patient feels intense pain while another feels nothing for the same problem. We can all rattle off the name of painkillers, however, if you ask about the causes of pain it's a whole different ball game.

Did you realise that pain can be triggered off by upset, anger, frustration, lack of love, sleep, lack of attention, boredom, worry, overeating, poor diet, poor exercise, and poor posture? As you can see, it is completely embedded in our modern lifestyle. Just because pain doesn't have a physical explanation doesn't mean it is any less important, and the so-called conversion hysteria has its roots in emotion. I have always believed that education about optimum health is the best way to minimise health issues, which is why I wrote *The 4 Keys to Health.*

Psychogenic pain is real and is caused by hostile, upsetting, grieving, frustrating, and stressful modern living. Painkilling drugs deaden the mechanisms that alert the brain there is a problem, and the body may – and can – pay with its life whilst drugs stop the brain from doing something about the cause of the pain.

In the future, I intend to look into ways to interweave preventative lifestyles into children's schools. Why should it only be elite athletes who understand about health as toddlers? Wouldn't it be great if you had lessons on optimum health and the true role of pain? As children are taught to fear pain and cover it up, they have no idea how to befriend it and naturally extinguish it.

Some of my elite athlete patients compete with pain that would send you and I insane. Their mental state is exceptional at honing coping mechanisms, although this is not wise for anything other than short-term measures, as long-term damage is harder to repair. The mind is trained to override discomfort due to injury, and driving through it with confidence, the athlete can still win. I like to treat these guys with solutions for longevity, and there is more about cartilage repair technology and cell health in my next book.

I FEEL NO PAIN AND I LOSE MY LIMBS

I remember one wintery day a few years ago, a pleasant Canadian lady came into my office clutching a book about a leper colony and a world without pain. She said, "Hey, if you're the painkiller, you should read this and consider a name change." I gave the book back a month later, enthralled by the story of a doctor working in a leprosy colony. Then I forgot the name of the doctor and the book. Even so, this book struck a chord with me, as in my sleepy Norfolk village, a delightful camp man – who worked behind the bar with me in Hermanus for a summer holiday job – told me an enthralling story. This was one of his guided walks about the ruins of a church, which went back to the 13th century. He explained that it was once a leper colony and that the 'unwashed' had to be invisible to the villagers, and so moved through tunnels running beneath. These tunnels were later used by soldiers in the First and Second World War. The church is still there if you visit; hidden by the trees.

Recently, I was listening to Tony Robbins talk about meeting Norman Cousins. Norman was a guru of laughter, and of using laughter to heal patients. Anyway, I looked up one of Norman's old books and lo and behold, there was a mention of the book and Dr Paul Brand – the author of the book the lady had lent me! So I am now able to share this with you. In the 1950's, this orthopaedic surgeon, Mr Paul Brand, initially worked on reconnecting damaged nerves in the forearm of lepers. Then he re-educated the brain to redirect and transmit messages to the lower forearm instead of the hand. After his initial absorption with corrective surgery, he started looking at the bigger picture.

Leprosy is a disease of painlessness; bacillus leprae killed nerve endings. I can remember resonating with this research, as here the lack of pain was actually destroying humans. Dr Bland looked at the tremendous strength possible with lepers' hands and realised that in normal individuals, the pain from pressure receptors prevented tissue damage and restricted strength. Interesting, isn't it? Healthy people can have exceptional strength if they override the resistant pressure firing off pain – like mothers lifting cars off their kids to save them. In cases of leprosy, limbs were lost, especially in kids as the lack of pain meant that physical damage arising in play resulted in severe trauma.

HOMEWORK:
Think of all the things you do in your daily life that require stressful physical activities.

Here's one you probably didn't think of: we blink many times because a subconscious message tells us to blink, to wash the eye as an irritant is present. Lepers went blind as there was no stimulus to blink, until the Doc rewired the muscles from the jaw to the eye and gave his patients supplements, especially Vitamin A.

Leprosy is not a highly contagious disease; it is caused by not being in optimum health, by poverty, malnutrition, and filth. Paul Brand believed, far beyond surgery, that a more vital part of treatment was psychological rehab; Lepers who were once beggars were helped to mentally adjust to earning a living and gaining respect in their community, and to work with other men in a humane, productive, and socially enjoyable way. Here, the loss of pain was the loss of a gift. The protection, defence, and integrity of a fragile, physical body is in the hands of Mr Pain (Brand et al., 1961).

MR ANGRY GAVE BIRTH TO MR PAIN

I like Dr Sarno's work and books on repressed emotion, where he talks about giving muscular trigger points of pain – little puddles of unreleased anger – and he and his students have written a lot about how shoulder and back pain can be physical manifestations of unresolved, internal, mental conflict.

Pain can easily somatise, that is, transfer from emotional pain to physical pain, and I personally see mind and body interweave a lot when it comes to pain. This is especially true of my child abuse patients, where there is a need for connection and trust, and where there are physical traumas embedded in the tissue as well as the mind. These poor, tortured souls have a bubbling anger and overwhelming feelings whilst bringing care for everyone, controlling everything, doing everything for everybody, and at the same time pre-empting any chance of rejection. I find that giving reiki and deep needling to specific areas can and does unleash these emotions.

TMS (tension myositis syndrome) is an avoidance mechanism, a distraction, a deception by the brain to avoid facing unacceptable thoughts. As I've mentioned, the brain communicates to the body through a hardwired system called the ANS and SNS – the autonomic and sympathetic nervous systems, the on and off brakes and the accelerator. The ANS regulates and brakes breathing, heart rate, viscera, and other things, and when anger and deeply hidden emotions start to emerge, the brain triggers the ANS to create physical symptoms including pain. This initiates in areas of muscle tissue of reduced blood flow and oxygen, and fires off pain receptors; in a fraction of a second, painful emotions vanish behind a smokescreen of physical pain. The stage is set, and the mammalian emotional brain plays out the act. The brain then slips behind the curtain and takes a bow, while Mr Pain distracts the mind's eye from unwanted memories. Emotional shadows become just that, and the mild oxygen deprivation fires up Mr Pain to scream out. In many ways I see similarities with my fibromyalgic patients – who also have a mitochondrial defect – and there is more of this in my next book.

So, there we have it: emotions are buried alive whilst the mind sets about hurting the body. This tension-induced hypoxia could in part be responsible for many aches and pains, and without exploring the mind, therapists may have a long journey ahead of them. I find that by bringing awareness to the possibility of stress, or a post trauma being rerouted to a physical manifestation, a patient can begin their cure.

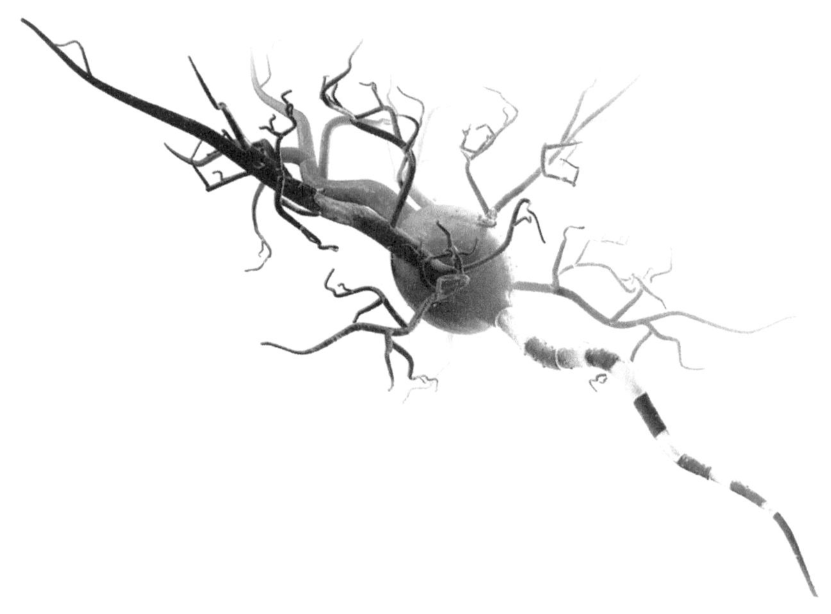

Brain neuron

Chapter Three

"God gave us the gift of life; it is up to us to give ourselves the gift of living well."

Voltaire

MULTIPLE PERSONALITIES

Who are we really? And what do I mean when I say 'myself'?

The idea of more than one self in the body sounds crazy, eh? Well, it's more common than you think, and I have actually met it on more than one occasion. Just a simple change in verbal tone and posture, and a patient slips into another personality, with its own memory and its own associated pain and illness.

We all develop several personalities as kids, and while those that are fed grow more connections, those that are discouraged shrink away; some individuals have several similar key personalities as adults, whereas others will just have one. Each personality is expressed just one at a time, each with its own memory, immune system, illnesses, and so on. I've found that patients have a very different level of pain in different personality states, as well as different levels in their ability to heal.

Abused children are known to use multiple personalities to hide away from the self that was hurt. For example, one young boy transformed himself into a cat to escape memories of abuse, purring and meowing and jumping up on tables on all fours; it was very sad. Traumatised victims invent new personalities – though often only temporarily – and I have seen this many a time.

Joe's Personality Was Left Behind In The Car Wreckage

One spring morning, my patient Joe struggled to get into my office, shuffling badly on his crutches, his scruffy jeans on, a cigarette in his mouth, and a bad scowl on his face. After shouting some angry expletives, he struggled to get onto my couch. He then explained in a slow monotone that he had been messed about: the doctors knew nothing, nobody had helped him, and he hurt so much – he couldn't breathe, walk, or function. He said he'd come in by taxi and really thought that I was going to be a waste of time. It puzzled me that he had car keys, and yet he had come in a taxi, and also that he was smoking – his records said that he didn't smoke.

I wondered whom I was really talking to, as trauma can create temporary personalities: either an earlier, existing personality is brought to the fore again, or a new one is made out of the trauma. Some people put on their personality with their uniforms, or it can depend on the friends they're around or the locations they're in. How often do you hear the phrase, "I don't know what got into me!"

Plato saw the psyche as involving the rational self, the spirit, and the appetite, whereas Freud looked at the id, the ego, and the superego. Many of Shakespeare's characters had multiple personalities – 'Wherefore art thou, Romeo? Hamlet? etc…' – so the concept is not new.

Eric Berne said that every communication would be as if speaking as a child, adult, or parent to either of the three. Hence a child-to-child conversation would be very different to an adult-child exchange, regardless of age and actual relationship (and more to do with the intent and meaning of the communication). I remember Berne also talking of one to three stroke exchanges of greetings, according to the depth of the relationship, leading to appropriate cues and responses. For example, when I run past a stranger, either of us might say 'morning' or 'evening', and if I knew the person well, they would be offended by a brief retort. A stranger, on the other hand, would be confused if I asked them what they were doing and what plans they had for the day.

Anyway, back to the story. There followed for me several painful weeks of an angry, non-thankful young man in my office. His fractures were slow to heal, and his back muscles were in spasm and hitting the thalamus, ramping up his pain like there was no tomorrow. I used a lot of techniques that will be described in volume 2; I linked MRT (magnetic resonance treatment) for bone healing with exercises, and IMS dry needling with electroacupuncture and NLP (neurolinguistic programming). His pain lessened but he still struggled with life; he received food packages, and believed that he couldn't walk or work. He explained what had happened to him: he'd chosen to drive into a wall to avoid a family in a car that was clearly out of control. It seemed to me that his body was clearly furious at this incredibly brave and self-sacrificial gesture, which did not fit the current psyche of this quite frankly testing individual.

One morning towards the end of his treatment he became slightly calmer, and I thought I should work intuitively; I used shamanic reiki and NLP. In surprise, he explained that he saw a grid of light connecting the dots, and that's when I got it: I was working with a subpersonality. I sent him home to get all of his old photo albums out, and when he came back the next week, he was wearing a suit, he had a job, and he was using one stick only, as he'd found his old self and was healing nicely.

Professor Robert Ornstein, at Stanford, stated: 'The mind contains a changeable conglomeration of small minds, fixed reactions, talents, flexible thinking… these different entities are wheeled into consciousness and then usually discarded, returned to their place after use' (Ornstein, 1986). Functional magnetic resonance imaging allows us to watch this kaleidoscopic brain activity: as one personality turns off, so do the neurons associated with that personality, and the next one switches on. Which 'you' is reading my book? And did one aspect of your 'self' forget the last bit because another you was reading it?

Back in the 18th century, a physician called Franz Mesmer found he could manipulate mindstates by a form of early hypnotism ('hypnos', by the way, is a Greek word meaning sleep). His work came to an end when he cured pianist Marie Theresa of blindness; as her sight came back, she lost her pianist and composing skills, and therefore her wage. A French physician, Pierre Janet, could hypnotise patients so that they wouldn't see objects and furniture. Also, he could get a subconscious reply (verbal or written) whilst another part of the brain was unaware and fully engaged in another activity. He called this 'disaggregation' to explain the separation of existences. The second self receives the subliminal message and the subconscious replies.

They say marketing companies make use of this.

THERE WAS MORE THAN ONE HEAD TEACHER IN HER HEAD

I remember one quietly spoken head teacher who once told me she was in pain following an assault at school by a pupil. She had a slow, rhythmical voice and flowing hand gestures. She said she had an excellent tolerance to any physical therapy or injection techniques, and she loved massage. While I was assessing her back, we discussed her love of music and poetry, and while she said that she could never grasp languages, she adored English. Her joints moved freely and there was some mild, mechanical lower back pain when pressing her spinal joints into extension.

I left the room to get a glass of water, and when I returned I was humming a tune we'd been discussing. "What a noise!" she snapped, in a shrill voice with a French accent. She was tapping her foot in a clumsy, agitated way. "That was my attempt to hum your favourite tune," I said sheepishly, and when she replied, she said, "I have never heard such a poor attempt, and hurry up! I hate therapy and I hate being touched; I hurt too much. Are you going to assess me and explain what you're doing?" After that, sure enough – she screamed at anything other than a light touch.

I spoke to her in my clumsy French, and well I never, she replied. She then sat up, and as she did so, she slipped back into the person I'd met earlier – the personality I did the assessment on in the first place. She then said, "Oh, and I've been diagnosed with a multiple personality disorder triggered by stress." "Really?" I asked. "You don't say, how interesting!"

THE HIDDEN OBSERVER

I have always been fascinated by what Ernest Hilgard (a Stanford professor in the 1970's) called the 'hidden observer'. I saw it first-hand being a student of trance and hypnotic suggestion, when at a Bandler course a couple of years ago. Whilst your subject was relaxed, you could suggest to them that they could not – for example – feel pain, and ask them to lift a finger if another part of their awareness *could* feel pain. The finger would rise without any conscious awareness.

I myself have had four operations, and each time I was happily unconscious. The anaesthetists, often colleagues of mine, would joke that I was about to have 10 bottles of gin to switch off my conscious brain. However, if I were to slip into trance by a colleague, my 'hidden observer' – the watcher within – would have something to say about the pain during the surgery. An unsettling feeling, don't you think?

Overall, I've gathered many opinions that multiple personalities are real and common, and have also been shown different sets of neurons firing in the brain (Ciorciari, 2002), a phenomenon not seen with actors.

OLIVER SACKS

Oliver Sacks is a professor of neurology and psychology, and he wrote the book that the film *Awakenings* was based on. He quoted in his book, *The Mind's Eye*, 'It is often said after a stroke or brain injury, no further recovery is possible after 12 to 18 months' (Sacks, 2010). He goes on to say that neuroscience has confirmed that the brain has more powers of repair and regeneration than once believed, and he also discusses how the brain is not hardwired and relays true stories to back up his belief. Sacks mentioned an Australian psychologist who was blind at 21, and who replaced roof guttering on his own. He did this by developing internal imagery, constructing a virtual visual world. He could manipulate a totally pliable and responsive mental space.

In *My Path Leads To Tibet*, Sabriye Tenberkens tells her inspiring story: as a blind lady, she travelled alone across Tibet, establishing schools for the blind and creating a Tibetan braille alphabet. She used verbal descriptions, visual memories, and a strong pictorial and synesthetic sensibility to construct pictures of landscapes and rooms with her vivid imagination (Tenberkens, 2003).

In *The Man Who Mistook His Wife For A Hat*, Oliver Sacks states, 'I am compelled to ask with Nietzsche, as for sickness; are we not almost tempted to ask whether we could get along without it?' and, 'Constantly my patients drive me to question, and my questions constantly drive me to patients' (Sacks, 2007). Sacks told stories about folks who lost senses and abilities such as speech, facial recognition, reading, sight, and 3D sense. He explored crazily clever adaptations of the brain, like 'tongue vision' (what blind people navigate by), and by studying a prolific novelist who couldn't read, and a concert pianist who couldn't read music or recognise objects.

I remember visiting a pile of rubble on a hot Greek island called Kos, and being told that Hippocrates came from this place – I remembered his name from the Hippocratic oath. Hippocrates introduced the case history, a description of the disease that tells us nothing about the suffering, personality, or lifestyle of the person. There is a need for a story to deepen the connection of the human subject – mind, body, and soul – turning a patient's number into a being of substance, and his approach to medicine did nothing to marry physiological processes to biography. Oliver Sacks called it, 'Neurology of identity, for it deals with the neural foundations of the self, the age old problem of mind and brain' (Sacks, 1986).

Back in the days of looking after head injuries and strokes, I found so many research papers about the left side of the brain but very few on the right. Strange, isn't it? Neurologists described the left side as a computer attached to a primate brain, designed for schematics and logic. The right side was more of a mystery, more to do with self-awareness and spatial orientations. Back in the 1960's, the stronger knowledge was thought to be in the left hemisphere, due to much more research gained from 'the man with a shattered world' (a soldier with a severe brain injury) whom had left brain problems. In Russia during the Second World War, A.R. Luria and his team created 'neuropsychology'; Zazetsky (the soldier and the subject of the study) had a big lesion in the left side of his brain, hence the focus of the study. The right side was believed to be less evolutionarily developed as it was less specifically defined, mostly due to the ignorance of the researchers (Luria, 1972). At this time I only found one comment about the right side of the brain and of it recognising reality in order to aid survival. Good job we covered this in chapter one.

POST TRAUMATIC STRESS DISORDER AND WHAT HELPS AT THE TIME TO AVOID IT?

This is a difficult question, as every trauma is uniquely stressful to humans. If we think of the rat experiments and how knowledge about the shock or trauma, a distraction at the time, or having company all changed their response to stress, we find that this is equally applicable in humans; we're just less furry and don't have a tail.

Early childhood education would help to teach and warn us about how traumatic events affect us. It would be rewarding if knowledge could help to pre-empt a reduction in the anxiety response, so that when the trauma is experienced, an inner strength will be instilled, a knowledge that something can be done and that they are not just helpless victims and observers.

TRUE STORY ABOUT A CLASS OF KIDS BEING KIDNAPPED

On a hot summer's day in 1976, a school bus carrying 26 kids from a Californian school (all aged between 5 to 15 years) was part of a kidnapping. Two vans took the kids to a disused quarry and locked them up in a trailer that was buried there. They were entombed in the dark and terrified, facing a slow death. They were literally frozen with fear.

Luckily for them, after 36 hours of hell, one boy leaned on a support and it gave way, causing soil to starting pouring in and the roof to collapse. The lad, called Bob, dug at speed, shouting out commands to dig up and crawl through the small hole. Thankfully, all of the children escaped burial.

The kids all got medical checks, and the parents were told that one kid may need a psychological evaluation at some point, but that they generally believed children were resilient to that sort of thing. On a follow up study six months later, only Bob was fine. The rest showed violent tendencies, as well as having nightmares and experiencing social problems. Their overwhelming fear and the inability to move through the problem at the time continued to haunt them. That's why, with clever counselling and hypnotic techniques, getting people to change their memories and move through traumatic events can help change them emotionally.

My training in psychology and hypnosis is only basic compared to the many incredible experts out there, however I have recognised traumatic imprints on patients' behaviours and have helped them by physically moving their body and implanting the suggestions of moving through the events that haunted them. Near drowning patients respond well to believing that they kept kicking to the end before they were rescued, but if they were fatigued right at the end, it really troubles them. I had a few cases where their back pain was the reason they came to me, but their hardwired thoughts told me their pain was strongly connected to their mental trauma at the time.

I remember Peter Levine, author of *Waking The Tiger*, saying in a study of a thousand Americans that 40% had a trauma within 3 years. 30% of pregnant woman were beaten by spouses, 15% had panic attacks and 75% had psychosomatic problems. 75 to 100 million Americans were sexually abused as kids! This is a very impressive record to present to an alien debating on whether to invest in human consciousness or instead go for a robot engineer. These poor souls are our doctors, teachers, parents, and friends, and when they knock on our door with back pain or a migraine, should we reach for a painkiller or a cup of tea and a hug? Get my point?

HUMANS DON'T COPE WITH FLYING INTO WINDOWS

Birds fly into a window, freeze, then go through a trembling reorienting process without interruption, to remobilise and fly off. This process, if interrupted, will result in shock and death. When caught by a wild cat they can go into a freeze response, appearing dead so the confused cat thinks this bird may be old meat. It comforts old Snazzy to know that it feels no pain in this state. If the cat loses interest, the bird reorients and simply flies off.

As a kid, my room was full of shoeboxes of very stiff birds I'd rescued, and I had to be very gently told that they weren't coming back to life. I remember one instance when I rescued a dead fish because it was floating, which led to me getting my own tank of fish. As my fish grew, I worried about them having enough space, so I kept getting bigger tanks and therefore fatter, longer fish as they continued to fill the space!

JEFF'S ANXIETY STORY

Jeff came to see me with a bad back and anxiety issues. He had an impending feeling of dread – a belly full of fear – that became worse following an accident in his lorry. He felt like he was in a plane crashing to the ground, and this feeling would seemingly come from nowhere. He had tried every pill you could imagine, all carrying their own side effects but many easing his terror. Jeff's HPA (hypothalamic pituitary-adrenal axis) in his brain was slammed into a high gear, whilst he was sitting still, if you like, at traffic lights. The engine was revving and he was going nowhere.

I worked on his damaged back – and you can read more on physical treatments like this in my body book – but I really needed to help his tortured mind. I knew that exercise would be great for his anxiety once I could get him through the threshold of the fear of doing it, as well as his belief that it would make his back worse. So, I told him about how getting my heart to pump hard with exercise eased my own fears, and then told him to visualise himself running. His heart rate and breathlessness would start as the anxiety of exercising percolated away. I stayed in the room with him and he worked through it without going into a panic attack. Then I got him to walk, starting with a short walk a day with his wife and dog, and then by putting trainers on, and singing and jogging a little with some company.

Slowly he started to gain confidence, and he realised that when his heart raced and his breathing deepened, this physiology was associated with a good reason, not pure fear. I did not interfere with his meds as they can be a very useful bridge to enable exercise, and as the effects of exercise on anxiety can take weeks to mature.

HOW MUCH EXERCISE DO WE HAVE TO DO TO REDUCE OUR ANXIETY?

This depends on how extreme our problem is, as well as our general health, but we can look at a few studies to see the effects of exercise on anxiety.

In 2005 in a Chilean high school, 198 fifteen-year-old kids were divided into two groups over nine months. This experiment looked at a once a week 90 minute gym session compared to three freestyle 90 minute exercise sessions. The first group showed little change: 3% improvement in anxiety and 1.8% in fitness, hardly significant. However, doing more resulted in a 14% reduction in anxiety and 8.5 % improvement in fitness, which says to me: do more (Health Promot Int, 2005).

In 2004, a researcher named Joshua Broman-Fulks at a university in Mississippi looked at a small group of 54 college students to see if exercise reduced anxiety. They were divided into two groups: one exercising at 60 to 90% heart rate and the other at 50%. Only the group exercising at a higher heart rate had less fear associated with the physical symptoms of anxiety (Broman-Fulks et al., 2004).

Between 1960 and 1989 – before I was born and then up until I graduated as a biologist – there were no fewer than 104 exercise/anxiety studies archived away, and these showed that exercise eased anxiety. Sadly, the lack of double blind, placebo-controlled trials allowed drugs companies to largely ignore the data.

In 1999 at Duke University, James Blumenthal looked at 156 people over 16 weeks, studying depressed subjects and the impact of exercise versus Zoloft medication. They were split into three groups: the first one took Zoloft, the second group were exercised at 70 to 85% max heart rate, jogging and – to prevent injury – a 10 minute warm up and 5 minute cool down, while the third group had both. After 16 weeks, guess what? That's your homework.

Well, OK: all three groups had a reduction in depression and half of them had no symptoms. At six months, however, out of group one – the druggie group – 52% remained depressed. In group two – the exercise only group – 30 % remained depressed, and in group 3 – the greedy ones having both – 55% remained depressed. Not very promising results, however in the long-term, exercise won (Blumenthal et al., 1999).

In 1997, German psychiatrist Andreas Broochs carried out a random controlled double blind trial, looking at exercise versus drugs for anxiety. There were three groups: the first had regular exercise, the second took the drug Imipramine, and the third had a daily placebo pill. For the first two weeks, all improved, with the second group improving most significantly. Interestingly, however, the improvement didn't last, and the placebo group got all the symptoms back before the end of the 10 week trial. After week 6, the exercise group matched, but they weren't better than the drug group in terms of improvements. However, the drug group were experiencing side effects. After 6 months the first group of fit patients showed the lowest anxiety and the second group were also doing well, except for the side effects (Broochs et al., 1997).

In 2006, a Dutch study of 19,288 twins showed that exercise reduced anxiety, depression, and neurosis, and also improved social interactions (De Moor et al., 2006). In Finland in 1999, 3,403 people took part in a study of exercising three times a week, and they all showed a reduction in depression, anger, stress, and distrust (Vaccarino et al., 1999).

So Jeff asked me, "Why do I feel less anxious after running?" and I answered with my train analogy –
this is what I told Jeff about the impact of his exercise: your muscles are constantly working and breaking down fatty molecules into fuel. Meanwhile, fatty acids are bouncing about in the blood stream, competing for seats with one of eight essential amino acids called Mr Tryptophan. The body knows what it needs. If you can imagine that your brain is a train at a station, the guard sees Mr Tryptophan waiting to get on the train and pushes him across the platform and onto the train before the crowd.

Once on board the train, he can see that the passengers are a little dull, and asks the guard to get his friends on board: Mr Serotonin, laughter juice, and Mr BDNF, a nice, calming character. He also calls for Mr GABA so he can apply the train brakes if the driver gets carried away, and he brings his mate Mr ANP (atrial natriuretic peptide), a special super breaker, to calm down the train's speed to ensure a nice, safe journey.

Jeff looks at me, puzzled; I guess the train analogy wasn't my best.

I NEED TO KNOW WHERE MY CONTROL BUTTON IS IN MY HEAD TO SWITCH OFF THIS DAMNED ANXIETY

So I tried again…

I said to Jeff, imagine a really loud radio blaring out. The volume centre – in the prefrontal cortex in the front of your head – is set on high, though it should normally reduce the noise. In some humans this control area is very small, and jammed on full volume. When the mammalian alarm centre (Mr Amygdala) is not quietened down, it sees danger in everything and lays down anxious memories about innocent things. His chum Mr Hippocampus (the library of memories) can't be heard, so he fails to calm down Mr Amygdala. You have a raised alarm system, Jeff, and by exercising we are literally putting a silencer around the alarm bell. Do you get my point?

All of us are somewhere between these extremes, from 0 to extreme anxiety, 10.

HOMEWORK:

Where are you? Where would you place your friends and family on a scale of 0 to 10 in terms of anxiety? Laid back? Or f**ked up and neurotically anxious?

This reminds me of a medical acronym: FINE. It stands for F**ked, irrational, neurotic, and emotional.

HOW ABOUT MY DRUGS, SAYS JEFF, DO I NEED THEM FOR EVER?

You are on a tricyclic antidepressant, Jeff, and it is commonplace to use it initially in a firefighting capacity, especially after experiencing a trauma. It works like Mr. Serotonin, a happy brain juice, and interacts with adrenaline like serotonin does. In the base of our reptilian brain, a trigger point – Mr Locus Coeruleus – senses our blood pH and sends messages up to Mr Alarm Bell, adjusting our breathing, our heart rate, and our blood pressure. Running slows your Mr Snake's trigger finger to send a signal to Mr Alarm, keeping you calmer.

YOU ARE ALSO ON B BLOCKERS

That's why you feel under power, especially at the start. They are your brakes on your life's activities, calming your SNS (sympathetic nervous system). This drug blocks adrenaline-docking ports in the brain and Mr Alarm does not ring so hastily; he lets you sleep in. Good exercise and diet may lead your doctor to safely reduce these drugs, as you are ready to do so.

YOU HAVE ALSO TRIED PROZAC

This drug works by blocking the recycling of serotonin, so the happy juice is in more abundance. Jeff, your exercise is like Prozac, and it also boosts dopamine receptors in the reward centre of the brain, without any side effects. So keep moving, Jeff, and remember the E in emotion.

THE HEART IS THE CENTRE OF OUR EMOTIONS, TRUE OF FALSE?

Hippocrates would say that emotions come from the heart. With heartfelt sense, we give heart-shaped romantic gifts, but why? I think ancient man knew a lot more about our bodies than we do.

When I got Jeff running, his heart juice (ANP) slipped through his blood brain barrier to add to more ANP made by Mr Snake, the trigger finger, and

Mr Monkey, the brain alarm. Mr ANP works on the body's thermostat/regulator and Mr Hypothalamus tries to calm Jeff down, slamming the brakes on his anxiety.

In summary: running distracted Jeff's mind from his worries, relaxed his over taut muscle spindles, brought more oxygen to his body, and built up more happy brain juice, cementing happy memories associated with raised heart rate and breathing. Other brain juices (GABA and BNF) further helped the prefrontal human cortex – the front of the head – to calm Mr Alarm. The mind learns to accept this step, and a change in physiology can be a good thing.

DEPRESSION, CAN IT SHRINK MY BRAIN?

The answer to this question is YES, but you can exercise your biology and grow it back. From the year I left biology behind in 1991 and went on to study physiotherapy, functional magnetic imaging and positron emission tomography were gaining a stronger foothold. A long time ago, my late uncle and aunt did a lot of charity work to raise funds for one of the early scanners at the Q.E. Birmingham, and they were laughed at with the same suspicion as a Dr Who Tardis by some old-fashioned doctors, who are now eating their hats. I am currently up against this claptrap, old-fashioned nonsense myself, bringing new technology to the UK that stimulates cartilage growth to delay and help avoid replacement joints. There will be more about my time machines – called 'fancy pants machines' by a recent patient – in the next book.

Anyway, back to the diagnostic skills of MRIs. The MRI's hyper intensity patches of brightness and contrasting darkness show brain shrinkage in the human cortex of clinically depressed people. This is also shown in Mr Alarm (the amygdala) and Mr Library (the hippocampus), suggesting a changed response to stress. It is not an isolated brain effect; it shows how interconnected areas are affected, explaining the emotions of emptiness, despair, and the inability to learn, focus, or sleep. Furthermore, sleep, eating, and sex all suffer too.

Drugs companies will soon be researching and mapping out genes affected by depression. However, last time, the genome project fell flat due to the huge number of unique proteins and the very apparent ability for lifestyle to control the switching off and on of genes. The research to date, although a little haphazard, strongly points to exercise being able to help a lot of depressives due to the increase in the following brain juices: BDNF, VEGF (vascular endothelial growth factors), FGF2 (fibroblast growth factor), and IGF-1 (insulin-like growth factor), responsible for nerve cells to grow and connect. It's so exciting to think that exercising increases all these juices, but our crazy modern lifestyle is stripping out our brain by giving us convenient technology and taking away the biology of exercise. Bad news for drugs companies, eh?

It's crazy, isn't it, that simply walking, running, cleaning, and gardening can heal the brain and reduce stress and depression. This ensures that we are less likely to succumb to Alzheimer's and other brain rot diseases. It costs us nothing but time reallocation.

I'm currently committed to projects that keep me anchored to my office and clinic for far more hours than is healthy, so I don a head torch at whatever time and go for a run rather than not exercise. I know I should be doing at least an hour a day, and I do, making sure that some of it makes my heart pump. No, not *Fifty Shades of Snazzy*, but running, swimming, and cycling.

PROBING UNDER MY BONNET

This little experiment reminded me of my car mechanic probing my sports car's engine recently. I don't know many details as the information is second hand via Dr John Ratey, however, it goes something like this: a neurologist called H. Mayberg placed a probe in six very depressed patients' brains to give deep brain stimulation. And yes, they were depressed prior to being prodded – I'm not sure they would feel too happy afterwards otherwise! She placed it at a key connection point called the anterior cingulate, where information goes between the human cortex and the mammalian brain. She was literally rebooting the brain. This resulted in reprioritising and integrating cognitive and emotional signals in a more healthy way. Four out of her six subjects felt better, and two died… just kidding. The moral of the story is: if you don't exercise and start to feel down, some lady may stick a probe in your brain to cheer you up.

So how much do I need to wriggle and giggle to get happy? This was another experiment relayed to me by Dr Ratey. Trivedi and Dunn worked with 80 depressed patients. One group (the placebo group) stretched with a chum, while another four groups worked out with different intensities. The high intensity was a workout burning 1,400 calories over 3 to 5 times a week, and the low intensity was a workout burning 560 calories, and ditto the times per week. In the intense groups the depression halved, and in the easier sessions a third were better, compared to the placebo stretching where nothing much happened.

In answer to the question above: roughly eight times your body weight in calories.

I'd like to include just a quick mention here regarding bipolar disorder. I haven't come across any papers on this and exercise, but any comments I've come across from my own patients have been positive.

GET DISTRACTED EASILY? HAVE YOU GOT ADHD?

HOMEWORK:

Are you – or do you know anyone who is – late and disorganised? Do you struggle to focus, go off subject easily, and have relationships that also go off focus?

fMRI is able to look at the reward centre (Mr Nucleus Accumbens) and measure activity, and he is needed for the human brain to invest in activity. ADHD sufferers appear to need instant gratification and don't relate to delayed rewards and actions. They also have a patchy attention brain system; signals coming from the arousal of the snake brain, Mr Locus Coeruleus (sleep/wake/focus), go to Mr Chocolate/reward (nucleus accumbens) then to monkey brain (emotion), the human cortex, and Mr Cerebellum (our ballerina). Mr Alarm feeds emotion, and if left unchecked, fuels unpleasant feelings and ADHD tantrums.

The brain juice dopamine talks to the reward centre (nucleus accumbens), where all other stimulants gather, and when he is stimulated, he shouts to the human brain for action. Usually with severe ADHD, it is about instant need and gratification. The human cortex working memory is needed to sequence and plan out actions; it's the higher level executive function. I think I show some aspects of this, when just as I know I should leave for work, I start texting or playing with the cat!

It's interesting that Mr Cerebellum also regulates and smooths information to the prefrontal cortex and motor cortexes, then onto think and move centres, and finally along to the basal ganglia. Dopamine brain juice acts like transmission fluid in an automatic transmission of information. However, in ADHD, the gear change jams when it comes to attention, either slamming into 5th gear at the traffic lights or not being able to get out of first gear at all.

Disciplined, timetabled exercise consisting of complex movements during heavy exertion – such as martial arts – is perfect for ADHD sufferers; it activates balance, sequence, timing, good fine motor control and the need to focus. 30% of ADHD sufferers also have dyslexia, but physical coordination exercises twice daily for 10 minutes can help this a lot. Practising this system is called DDAT treatment, and kids have shown an improvement in reading and writing, and coordination and cognition thanks to this treatment.

I experimented with these ideas by playing with my cats before playing with my nephews, running around the garden with toys and getting them to leap up. This should boost the brain juices dopamine and norepinephrine, and stretching out to grasp toys stimulates the brain fertiliser, BDNF. Mr Amygdala's (the alarm bell) screams quieten, toys appear less scary, and the brain juice dopamine further reduces brain noise to get signals through more clearly. Anxiety lessens as physical skills improve. Then I applied what I learnt, playing hide and seek with the boys. They went hyper… so back to the drawing board it is.

PARKINSON'S ROCKS MY BOAT

Parkinson's research has highlighted problems with the brain juice dopamine in the basal ganglia in the monkey brain. Activities of daily living and DIY tasks all get slammed as coordination is affected. Tremors give clumsy hand movements, poor handwriting, poor spinal posture with the head forward, a mask-like face, and a shuffling gait.

At the time of writing this book, I have a delightful Parkinson's patient whom is battling to prevent the disease progressing. It is very hard to motivate him to exercise, as his motivation point is also affected and his lack of coordination rocks his confidence. It's a case of encouraging gently where able, and I can help with suggesting rhythmical tapping, drumming to movements, and getting adequate rest. He also needs to understand that stress causes a big irritation in the symptoms due to the role of dopamine.

ADDICTION

There is a difference between liking and needing; addiction is an unpleasant, demanding need that shouts over all other stimuli. It stems from habit, due to repeated stimuli, as neurons wire together. The library (the hippocampus) is programmed by the human brain to memorise the pleasant scenario of gaining the desired object, at all costs. Dopamine amplifies it, and a new hardwired connection is made in Mr Reward, again further amplifying the problem. They say sex increases dopamine in Mr Reward from 50 to 100% depending on how skilful your partner is, and cocaine from 300 to 800%, and both together… who knows? Wham bam thank you ma'am?

Clever fMRI scanning found the hidden site of Mr Reward in the brain, so they could actually map the activity. Experiments with poor rodents in McGill University in Montreal, carried out by Milner and Olds, showed that jolting this area was ecstatic to rats; they kept self-zapping by pulling a lever at exclusion of all other activities. You could literally call it a masturbation zone of pleasure.

Gene variation D2R2 allele is known to rob Mr Reward of his dopamine happy juice receptors. These party poopers are found in 25% of the general population, 70% in alcoholics, and 80% in drug addicts. There is a tentative genetic interplay with addiction, and there is still lots of research to do on this subject.

WHY DOES MY MIND MAKE MY BODY SUFFER, AND IS IT REALLY MY SHADOW SELF?

René Dubos (1901-82), a deceased microbiologist, stated: 'What happens in the mind of man is always reflected in the disease of his body' (Dubos, 1969). How much suffering you and I feel is a complex interplay of our biological makeup and the environment – that is, in a nutshell: our life experiences and beliefs. We taste and hear and see, and we gather memories and beliefs about our reality. We all love and hate parts of our mind and body.

Carl Jung called the hidden part of our personality the 'shadow self', and this means that the unconscious can hide aspects of self-loathing in physical ailments within the body. Both eminent psychologists Jung and Freud understood that psychic (Greek for spirit) events are subconscious. When the mind chooses to distract itself away from an unlikeable event or behaviour, burying it into the body with anger and transmuting it into physical pain, there is no conscious knowing of this happening.

Freud described three aspects to the personality. The first is the id, the baby/child-like part, needy and desiring instant selfish gratification with unconscious awareness. Its aggressive instincts need the 4 F's (well, not the fourth if a child), and it exhibits anger easily. The second is the ego, the face we show the world. It is the growing child or grownup, doing what is necessary to survive, its awareness mostly conscious with an understanding of reality and weighing up the best options. The third is the superego, which is like a parent to the other two. It is mostly consciously aware of actions, it is self-sacrificial, and it does what others want, often against the ego and certainly the id's wishes. Inner conflict often bubbles up amongst the threesome. Jung called a personality aspect a 'persona', which is similar to Freud's ego. It manages the opposite views of id and superego to come up with a face, the ego to show the world.

HOMEWORK:
Can you think of a situation today where there was conflict in your head, and then you felt your neck and back ache or your stomach tighten? Now can you now make the link? For example, at work we may have a boss whom in our opinion makes a bad decision in a meeting. You think about the mortgage and your relationship with your work peers, and instead of saying anything, you smile and nod in agreement. Then you stand up to leave and your back locks. See my point? The id is raging at the superego, saying, "He's wrong, kill him, idiot!" The superego, meanwhile, is saying, "Be kind to him, don't show him up, and think about your security in the company."

Another psychologist, Carl Rogers, used a more client-centred therapy, where the patient talked and looked within to find resolving solutions, a sort of talking catharsis. Carl Rogers is known for saying: 'It is the client who knows what hurts, what direction to go, what problems are crucial, what experiences are deeply buried' (Rogers, 1951).

MY MOTHER NEVER LOVED ME

I have a friend who carries that 'victims' chant' around as if to excuse his poor relationship skills and general behaviour. He had and still has no attunement, no connection with his mother, and so he stumbles through life looking for that connection to lift him out of the abyss of darkness that comes out of nowhere and swallows him up. He is constantly searching for who he really is, struggling with different aspects of his mind that rage at each other, and going from one counsellor to the next to tell him what to think. He may say he has a headache or muscle ache from exercise, but will rarely say that his mind is troubling him – it's a shame for such a gifted, brilliant mind with a hidden, caring heart.

If we move on from Freud's picture and think of the brain physiology, the hypothalamus (the control box) is the heart of the autonomic system. The control box sends signals through the ANS (autonomic nervous system) to transduce thoughts and transform emotions into switches. These in turn modulate bodily functions and visceral functioning to come up with perceived pain in the body.
Early baby trauma or separation from the mother will overregulate the ANS, housing the ying parasympathetic (brake) and the yan sympathetic (accelerator). The involuntary, subconscious messages can cause unnecessary pain, and the hypothalamus is considered to be a very important mind-body-pain link (Colbert, 2003).

Over many years of experience, I now know through spending time talking to patients that by bringing awareness to the mind-body link, new perceptions and beliefs can chip away at the problem, creating new biochemistry and neuron networks. However, it is a very difficult journey; I have seen so many people with unrelenting backache reflect on deep, unresolved emotional traumas from childhood, disrupting the ANS time and again. Tendencies towards feeling more pain are definitely both biological and developmental through experiences.

I have so many stories I could share with you, but here are just a couple. I have heavily disguised them to avoid anyone being recognised.

AUSTRALIAN HOSPITAL CARRIED IN MY BACK

Years ago in my old office, my dearest June brought a friend, rather like a parcel being delivered on my doorstop. "She needs her backache to go before she flies home," she told me. On assessment, her neurology was sound, however there was some very deep tenderness in her lower back muscles.

I decided to put her in a light trance, before placing a laser then a needle into the muscle contracture. By doing so I triggered a sudden flashback; the memories embedded in the matrix of her muscle cells communicated with her brain to locate long lost memories in her hippocampus. "The disinfectant smells too strong; this hospital trolley is not very comfortable, and why am I waiting so long?" she asked me.

I released the muscle as I gently as I could, then brought her around. It seemed that the back pain was associated with surgery at a hospital , which she'd blanked the memory of. It seemed deeply personal and I saw no need to delve deeper, and to her surprise, as I brought awareness to where she'd hidden a pocket of emotional pain, the ache melted away.

MOTHER HIT ME THERE

On another occasion, I was puzzling over clear scans and x-rays, as well as years of injections and therapies, for a middle-aged man who was suffering with pain between his shoulder blades. I could not locate any structural issues apart from muscle contractures.

I put some music on to get me to a level of relaxation, so I could feel more sensitivity in his muscle tension; it has been shown that therapists are more sensitive if relaxed, and in alpha rather than beta wavelengths. I needed him to go into either delta or theta, so I used some specialist music and lowered his breathing rate with mine. I then employed a shamanic reiki technique to check out his energy in that area. It was at this point that he sobbed, "Mother, stop hitting me!"

ABUSE LIVES IN MY JOINTS AND ROTS THEM

Another dear patient, who was abused as a child and consequently terrified of being near other people, constantly went from one surgeon to the next to try and convince them they had to operate on her joints – her mind projected her inexplicable memories into painful joints. She was the kindest, most thoughtful, brilliant soul I have ever treated and yet she believed she should die and had attempted this many times. Surgeons stared at her joints and not at her heart, and she went under the knife time and again.

SHE PAINTED PAIN INTO HER SHOULDERS

A delightful artist came to see me with arthritic pain and stiffness in her neck, with tense, trapped muscles, which were especially sore after her mother died. We discussed how grief can hide away in the body, and together we eased the flare-up in the joints due to the immune system ebbing, and with reiki I eased the pain transference while with acupuncture the local tension ebbed away.

THE PAIN OF HER HUSBAND'S DEATH MOVED INTO HER NECK

Grief likes sitting on shoulders. Another lovely lady came to see me, not able to move her neck after her husband's passing. His spirit would sit in the chair next to her treatment couch and pass messages to me. There will be more of this in my spiritual book.

HOMEWORK:
Who do you know who has been traumatised emotionally and was consequently in physical pain?

CHRONIC FATIGUE SYNDROME (CFS) AND WHAT CAUSES IT

Today I got an email from an artist who mentioned in passing that she'd had a diagnosis of CFS, so it is an apt time to mention it in my book. She explained how she could not cope with the run up to her exhibitions, how she felt the fear freezing her actions; her need to help other up-and-coming artists and please her public made her feel in despair. She understood that a lot of her headaches were down to her newly diagnosed CFS, but she had no clue what it was and what it meant. This is what I wrote back.

A lot of research about the body's ability to cope with stress has been applied to CFS sufferers, and in particular to the freeze response survival mechanism of CFS. I have covered the freeze response in more detail in this book whilst writing about trauma and stress, and I have written about how the brain redirects emotional into physical pain in tension myositis (TMS) patients.

In relation to CFS, a specialist in hormones (endocrincologist) Mr Selye wrote about applying the three stages of stress to a CFS response, the first being the old mammalian alarm ringing the bell, tooting the horn and saying, "Be alarmed now!", whereby a 'perceived' threat stimulates the brain and initiates a cascade of stress hormones. He called the second stage 'resistance', where the body adapts to chronic stress with autonomic changes in the mind and body, fighting to maintain homeostasis with stomach, heart/chest, and head pains. Moods at this stage bear a lot more resentment, anger, and depression.

The third stage is exhaustion or chronic fatigue, a self-imposed pressure to continue to do well beyond endurance. It is the human superego pushing all the ego's and id's buttons to go beyond the call of duty and its safe comfort zone. The hypothalamus can trip – yes, it can literally go haywire trying to sustain optimum health. Emotional repression messes up all our systems, including sleep, and the hypothalamus can no longer control the lack of delta sleep essential to survival. It's a freeze response stage, and if repeated without learning how to move through it quickly, it will be detrimental to longevity.

In the animal kingdom, animals move through it, their muscles transforming their biochemistry and their brains not ruminating on what was considered to be stressful and which has now passed. They don't lie awake wondering if their predator will be back and what mood he will be in, or how they could have run a bit better or swerved a little quicker. Well, maybe they do and we just haven't researched this yet.

An extreme illustration of this freeze response was in Oliver Sack's *Awakenings* book, which was made into a film with our loveable clown, the late Robin Williams. In the film, the L-Dopa drug slowed the mind to match body rhythms, pulling patients out of their sleep. I digress as this was not a health film about CFS, but one of my favourite films, along with his *Patch Adams*, a true story about a doctor and the power of laughter.

In summary, CFS sufferers are believed to subconsciously overreact to stress, leading to symptoms of tiredness or pain, and see-sawing in different amounts. Once again, the mind-body connection can be seen to be going awry.

I told my artist patient that the havening techniques covered in this book could help her, as well as exercising, having a good, nutritious diet, and doing some meditative practice. See my *4 Keys To Health* book for tips.

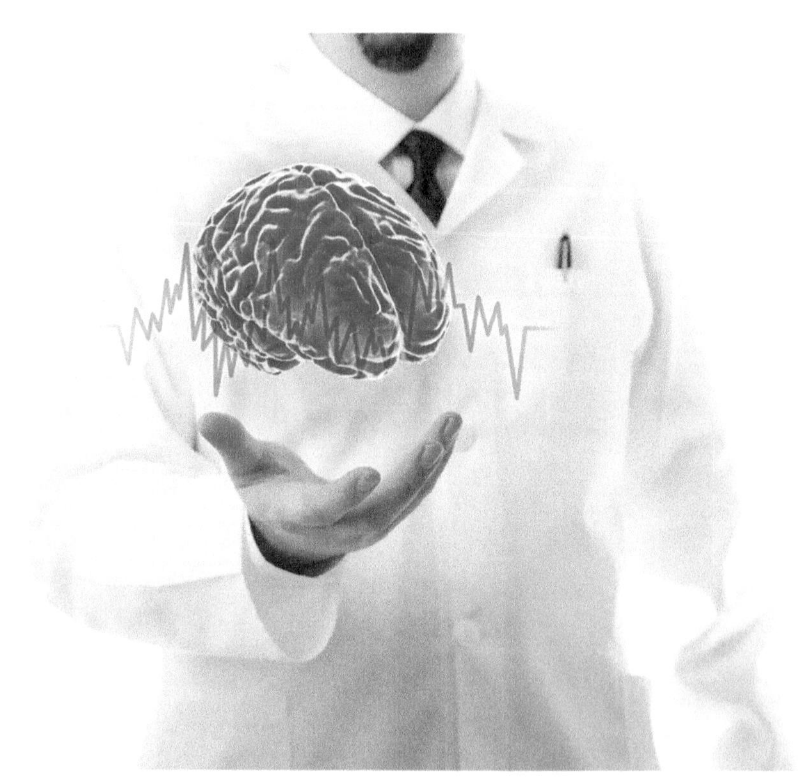

Heart mind connection

Chapter Four

"Finish each day before you begin the next,
and interpose a solid wall of sleep between the two."

Ralph Waldo Emerson

HOW EXERCISE WILL IMPROVE THE PERFORMANCE OF YOUR BRAIN

Why can physiotherapy help brain damage? Interestingly, Buddhist monks have always believed that the human brain can transform through training – one of my dearest professors in pain was a Buddhist and he explained this all to me.

Back in the '80s, I was led to believe – whilst researching in the biological sciences department in Birmingham – that the brain matured in the infant child and had little power to grow new neural networks, heal brain trauma, or change a person's IQ or temperament once they were past the infant age. I was told that these brain functions were somehow carved in stone after a set time. This partly entrenched belief led me to carefully put my keys, phone, and glasses in a known place this morning, as in middle age, brain rot may get me!

My biological lab in the 80's was close to a little train station that ran between my library at the Q.E Hospital and various lecture halls. I remember seeing stroke patients getting on and off that train, and I used to talk to one in particular who was a biologist, and who was at that time studying the psychology of the brain and the mind. I remember feeling so sad that those poor patients were now permanently brain damaged, as we were taught that the brain was hardwired and unable to heal very much from brain injuries. I would walk along beside them, noticing that with careful repetition, their footsteps became steadier.

These chance encounters in life are rarely chance, as within a year of those talks I had commenced studying at a different university, illustrating how physiotherapy helped stroke victims function.

HARDWIRED BRAIN – I DON'T THINK SO?

The scientific belief that the brain had little chance of repairing led me to many controversial questions when I was in my twenties and working with head injury and stroke victims. This old belief did not explain why my stroke patients relearnt motor skills with repetition, or how they relearnt how to speak again up to eighty years old. I believed that the brain was resculpturing itself, and I wrote so in my notes.

What really excites me now, in the later stages of my clinical career, is that new research really is showing that mind training is changing the brain. This evidence is being achieved with the proof of functional MRI brain imaging on humans, building on earlier experiments with animals that I will briefly cover in this chapter. Related to this evidence is the notion that the brain adapts and expands in areas relating to repeated activity. When your mind changes, your brain changes. For example, male London taxi drivers have great visual spatial memories for streets, hence they have a large hippocampus (Maguire et al., 2000). Also, when you are less grumpy and happy, your left prefrontal cortex grows (Davidson, 2004).

So you see, this research backs up my experience of unfocused thinking leading to a disappointing lifestyle. This really does make me sit up and think about how my habits shape my future, and how your habits determine your future. Not especially good news for my butterfly-like mind!

Now scientists have additional new evidence showing that the brain can adapt and take on different roles in response to trauma and malfunction. For instance, the visual cortex can help blind readers interpret brail, and the ever-emerging field of epigenetics backs up these findings. I was amazed to learn that even embryos' minds were sculptured by the mothers' emotional reaction to the environment; whilst pregnant and during childhood, the mother learns repeated responses to her environment and her habitual fears trigger specific proteins to switch her child's genes off and on. This is now known to shape brain function, as well as the size of specific emotional centres in the mind. The good news is that neuroplasticity exists in adults, which means that the brain can remodel and that new brain cells can grow, under the right circumstances. This gives fresh hope to therapy that enables abused children to feel compassion (for example), long after these centres in the brain have been mostly switched off in childhood.

For many years in research institutes in the USA, Buddhist monks and scientists compared notes on the influence of our thoughts on brain sculpturing. The power of the mind and its ability to cause neuroplasticity is a fascinating mystery, where science meets what was previously thought of as mysterious spiritual knowledge. The brain can change as a result of our thoughts and can change the amounts of cortex assigned to new functions. Neuronal connections can be altered well into adulthood. Mental training – especially in the form of meditation – is about growing new qualities until they become integral parts of our brain.

Let's go back in time now and see how brain mapping and early experiments got us where we are today. According to my psychology textbooks, early brain mapping started way back in 1886, in order to prove that specific parts of the brain carried out specific unchangeable tasks. In 1861, Pierre Paul Broca (a French anatomist) discovered lesions at the back of the frontal lobe in patients with damaged speech, and he named the speech area after himself (Broca's area). Then it became a bit of a fashion – everyone wanted to have part of the brain named after themselves.

In 1886, Carl Wernicke named a part of the brain after himself (Wernicke's area) that focused on understanding in speech. A German neurologist who studied dead bodies, Mr K. Brodmann, named 52 distinct areas in the cortex after himself, calling them Brodmann's Areas or BA – the same initials as British Airways – which were based on appearance only. Now, ladies: BA 10 is our multitasking spot, and it has grown over the years – not unsurprising. In those days they believed it was like a geographic map, that the boundaries and function were set in stone.

In the 50s, a man named Penfield stimulated the somatosensory cortex area to map all of our sensory zones. A touch over the face area, for example, felt like he stroked the face itself. A bigger area dedicated to an area of the body meant more precise and greater sensitivity, like the tongue and genitals compared to the back of your hand. A Spanish neuroanatomist, Cajal, agreed with German research that the brain was predetermined and not plastic. They were all wrong.

In the early 1900s, a couple of scientists called Sherrington and Brown looked at the motor cortex (the area responsible for movement) in animals, to see whether movements related to specific zones were the same for everyone. However, the movement maps varied in every brain, like a unique fingerprint. They mapped the motor cortex out using tiny little electrodes to stimulate the cortex, causing different muscles to twitch, and repeated, habitual movements showed changes in the brain – 'Use it or lose it'. This suggested neuroplasticity, a change due to experience. If muscles were used more then the area was greater, if less, they were often smaller. This went against all previous beliefs.

FERRETS HEARD THE LIGHT

In 1976, Jon Koss studied ferrets because of a neural similarity in their eyes; the ferrets' optic nerve grows from the eye, while auditory grows from the ear, just as they do in humans. However, the wiring in humans is present from birth, whereas with ferrets the timing comes later, and this delay meant that brain surgeons could actually trigger changes. In a complex experiment with auditory and optic nerves, they showed that when light hit the eye, the ferrets' auditory nerve actually heard the light. This is proof of use-dependant cortical reorganisation, showing early neuroplasticity data. The hardware is not fixed as science had once thought (O'Regan, 2001).

SNAZZY'S BIG FINGER JOB

My fingers that I use for my precision IMS dry needling must be enormous in the part of my brain that represents my fingers. The lack of guitar playing these days means that those parts of the finger space aren't used for music anymore, and that they may have gone to help with something else, such as the fingers involved with IMS. We now know that neuroplasticity means the brain adapts to giving more space to current activities.

With better radioactive tracers and technology, scientists went on to discover the units of the brain, brain neurons, and their synapses – the connections between neurons. They then started puzzling over which activities made better connections, or possibly different ones. These scientists still argued incorrectly into the 20th century, with the only exception being that of synaptic strengthening, the notion that the brain was unchangeable and that it was hardwired. The belief they held was that early on in life, the brain has set areas, and that was that. It is never easy to shake beliefs, and it suited them to ignore random bits of research questioning this.

Having the unusual life of being a biologist before becoming a physiotherapist, I can access research in both animal and medical fields. I do not condone any animal research that captures and stresses animals, however if it has already been done it seems a greater crime to lose the findings that the studies have already gleaned. Hence, the following monkey study interested me. It was carried out the year after I'd been working intensively with stroke patients, and I write about Paul – one of my special stroke patients – later in this chapter.

MONKEY BUSINESS

In 1991, an experiment on the palpation and dexterity of monkey hands led to modern stroke patient physiotherapy and patient rehab. It was called The Silver Spring Monkeys case, and 17 monkeys at the behavioural research centre in Silver Spring, Maryland were at the centre of a renowned exposure to suspected animal cruelty.

The monkeys had their sensory nerves removed so they could not feel their fingers, hands, or arms, so like leprosy fingers they could be painlessly injured (it's already looking gruesome, I know). The lead scientist, Edward Taub, was looking for proof of stroke recovery, and he showed that a loss of sensation did not mean losing the use of the limb. In this experiment, the afferent nerves – that is, the sensory nerves – were cut when the monkeys were three or four years old, and they stopped sensing their arm for the next 10 years.

The older sick monkeys were put to sleep after brain surgery under anaesthetic, but the rest were freed and led happy lives out of the research lab. While under anaesthetic, these older monkeys showed that the brain areas had taken over feelings from other areas; massive cortical reorganisation reflected the changed input from their bodies. The area of the brain in the somatosensory cortex, that used to process information from the arm, now looked after parts of the face. The part of the brain which was no longer receiving signals had not – as believed – shut down, far from it: it had changed jobs, reflected in an increased size of facial processing. This showed that the brain can adapt and change functions, and is not hardwired as scientists once believed (Pons, Garraghty, Ommaya, Kaas, Taub and Mishkin, 1991).

I am happy to report that many of these types of animal experiments stopped in the 90's and were replaced with more humane ones. Furthermore, the monkeys' lack of freedom and the gift of their lives were not wasted, as they inspired Edward Taub to continue his research into stroke victims. He went on to write several papers with others on the subject of upper limb movement (Taub, Uswatte, King, Morris, Crago and Chatterjee, 2006).

In a series of – I think, slightly cruel – studies in the eighties, headed up by professor of neuroscience Merzenich at the University of California, experiments were done with owl monkey's hands – poor monkeys. The hand has a big representation in the somatosensory cortex (SSC) part of the brain, which means it should be easy to see any change. In one of many experiments on the sensation of touch, scientists cut median nerves in their hand, so no messages could get from the hand to the brain. The region in the somatosensory cortex that used to be spoken to from these structures then responded to signals from other areas of the hand (Stryker, Jenkins, and Merzenich, 1987). These were primitive examples of neuroplasticity in the brain.

Monkeys' hands were selected as they're close to human hands, and in a much more humane investigation called the spinning disk experiment, they looked at teaching old monkeys new tricks. Outside the cages were placed

4 inch discs with wedge shaped grooves, and the monkeys had two fingers lightly touching these harmless spinning discs. Day in and day out for hundreds of days, this activity was repeated. The result was a fourfold increase in the somatosensory cortex (SSC), the main sensory receptive area for the sense of touch. This area related to the fingers that touched the disc, and the brain used an area that was previously used by the other fingers (Merzenich, Nelson, Kaas, Stryker, Zook, Cynader and Schoppmann, 1987). This is another example of neuroplasticity.

In another experiment, a small group of squirrel monkeys were taught to sense a flutter on their fingers, making note of the tiny changes. This resulted in a 3x increase in the size of the somatosensory cortex (SCC), so the experiences changed the brain area. Furthermore, the motor cortex (the part of the brain that moves muscles) also changed by a few millilitres (Nudo, Milliken, Jenkins and Merzenich, 1996).

The monkey experiments led scientists – like Edward Taub – to devise physiotherapy treatments in the early 90's that helped countless stroke victims. Taub inferred that when a stroke damaged part of the brain, a healthy part could be trained to assume the function of the damaged part. He called it 'constraint-induced movement therapy'. So, monkey business led to stroke recovery in humans.

Decades after the monkey studies, brain imaging has revealed the success of these earlier experiments. Taub and other scientists found a large use-dependant reorganisation, where substantial new areas of the brain were recruited to take over disabled areas in order to carry out a new function, and this was exciting news for me in those years working with stroke patients. Experiments in the 21st century showed that stroke patients recruited large areas around the infarct (this is a posh word for an area damaged by a stroke) to do the job that the damaged area previously did. Whether it was the same side or the opposite side of the motor cortex (the area that controls movements) or the premotor cortex, not only did they do their own job, but also the job of the damaged area (Taub, Uswatte, King, Morris, Crago and Chatterjee, 2006).

UNLIKE A CAR ENGINE, BRAIN COMPONENTS CAN CHANGE FUNCTION

Remember the monkey experiments with the disks? Well, Taub also looked at the fingers of violinists, and not surprisingly, it was found that the brain space associated with these fingers in musicians was greater, just like the monkey research. This shows that the genetic blue print of brain mapping can be altered through training – such as learning music – or following an injury. Another bit of research showed that with blind people, the visual cortex was needed to feel braille, and to hear peripheral sounds and process language (Sterr et al., 1998). Again, this is evidence of compensatory reorganisation.

The question I then asked myself was this: is it only after a major crisis or damage that the brain changes function?

THE VISUAL CENTRE COULD FEEL AND LISTEN

Neurologist Pascual-Leone blindfolded a group of volunteers with good vision for 24 hours a day for five days. fMRI showed normal visual cortex activity pre experiment, and during the five days, they learnt braille and listened to pairs of tones in auditory tests. A repeat fMRI showed that after just five days, the visual cortex was firing up on non-visual tasks of braille and sound. This so-called hardwired visual cortex (VC) switched tasks because it received no visual stimulus. It was probably bored, and perhaps using rudimentary, unused old nerve tracts (Pascual-Leone et al., 2000).

Bowled Over

I still remember to this day my excitement at helping a so-called hopeless case of a fast bowler – let's call him Paul – who had suffered a massive stroke. It was 2009, I was on placement at a neurological unit, and the forty-year-old professional cricketer needed help. It was a harsh winter, one where you had to look carefully at where your feet were going, and it was with this in mind that I started thinking about how I was making a subconscious movement of walking to steady my feet on the ice. I didn't own a car at college (it would be another year before I was a qualified physio, when I would need a car for on call duties) and I skidded along the pavements to the old hospital department in my woolly hat and gloves. I was car less, but not careless. I arrived into its long, depressing corridors with peeling paint and the smell of disinfectant and pee – not mine, I hasten to add – ready to start work.

I had been assigned to a forty-year-old gentleman with a severe stroke, and he looked suitably disgusted to see me; I arrived with my glasses steamed up, my nose bright red from the cold, my hair in knots from the wind, and my white jacket crumpled up from carrying it too firmly, but that was just me. He was unable to speak or stand so I wheeled him into an old rehab gym and talked for the both of us. I could tell his hearing was still working due to his irritated expression, and thereafter ensued weeks of small repetitive movements and sounds, over and over again. I was literally willing his brain to start healing, and I could sense him starting to understand the caring and healing I was pouring into him in order to help his angry frustrations.

I put his good arm in a sling, sat him at a desk, and for hours made him put buttons in pots, moving dominoes and then cards – just small, repetitive actions, with a hand that once fast bowled with such precision. I also made him lift his foot up and down the same step hundreds and hundreds of times. After weeks of swearing at me – in what sounded like a foreign language – because I was making him do the same action over and over again, we walked very slowly, holding a stick and smiling, down the corridor in front of his disbelieving family, teammates, and consultant. I was so excited, and like a girly, very tearful.

HOW EXERCISE WILL STRENGTHEN YOUR BRAIN

New research shows us that exercise reverses a lot of the damage caused by our stationary, stressful lives, as we increase our happy juices, like serotonin, norepinephrine, and dopamine. Muscles produce proteins that cross the blood brain barrier and that are crucial to the highest thought processes – insulin growth factor (IGF-1) and vascular endothelial growth (VEGF) are the names of these proteins. Strong exercise sparks biological changes to get our brain neurons to bind together.

SLIM AND FIT AND CLEVER TOO IN NAPERVILLE COLLEGE

I came across a very interesting project where learning in a state of higher awareness – induced through exercise – was the mission of an American college called Naperville 203. The P.E instructors would get students to run a mile in the morning before school at their specific heart rate range, close to their maximum heart rate. The research was to assess how much impact there was on learning, when the students started class in a state of alertness following their morning exercise.

Looking at international tests in maths and science, this college ranked in the top ten academically amongst all the states. They were first in the world in trends of international science, and sixth in terms of maths. The demographics were favourable for success, but these stats far outweighed any demographic impact. Here's the bit of data that got me: 97% of freshmen had the correct body weight and fat. I'll say that again – 97% of the students had a perfect ratio of body fat!

Fitness was redirected from the usual large team games to small groups of 2 to 4 students, and they stayed in their specified heart rate range whilst constantly moving. Did you know that only 4% of Americans over twenty-four years old who play sport are actually fit? The kids were taught the importance of fitness; they worked out on equipment that set goals for blood pressure, heart rate, and body fat, and they knew how to set up their own fitness plans. At eighteen, the students at this school have a 14 page document that combined fitness scores, blood pressure, cholesterol, lifestyle, and family history, as well as predictions of disease with preventative plans. They also have lifetime designer fitness activities that they chose from 18 activities whilst at the training academy. What a wonderful idea! Hardwiring in the concept of correct exercise will keep you as well and clever as possible (Ratey and Hagerman, 2008).

MORE PROOF THAT BODY FITNESS DRIVES BRAIN FITNESS

Charles Hillman and Darla Castelli looked at 216 kids at Illinois University by using EEG (electroencephalogram), studying electrical activity in the brain, and the study showed that exercise helped executive function in the prefrontal cortex.

In 2004 in California, 13 researchers looked at 850 studies on the impact of exercise on kids. They concluded that an hour a day was needed to make changes in their behaviour and physical health such as: memory, concentration, self-concept, academic achievement, depression, happiness, and focus, as well as physical benefits in obesity, blood pressure, cardiovascular, and bone density.

In 2004 at Leeds Metropolitan University, a study asked 210 employees to spend time either doing 45 minutes of aerobic gym work with weights, or yoga. This was not a double blind, placebo controlled trial, however their analysis of questionnaires showed an overall 65% improvement in managing time, meeting deadlines, and interacting better with colleagues. Overall there were feelings of being less tired and less stressed.

CROSSING THE CHANNEL WITH A MESSAGE IN A BOTTLE

If we return to earlier discussions on who we are – a collection of thoughts, experiences, memories, and actions, both verbally and physically – the effectiveness of the way our brain cells connect is key to everything.

If I can refocus you for a moment on what I mean by this, I am going to choose an analogy of my little car going to France – I feel sick on ferries so I prefer to use the Channel Tunnel, but the ferry works much better for this analogy! Anyway, picture Sparky (my little car) carrying a very important message in a letter. I spark up the ignition, and when enough electrical activity hits the sparkplugs, the engine gets fired up and off we go along the road – not the A 1, but the AXON road (the axon is the snake-like body that connects the head and tail of a brain neuron). Sparky gets to the dock, and the ferry bolts safely into it, the dock being the receptor 'Dover'. The ferry churns up the water with its engines at the right thrust, aligning the loading platform for Sparky to drive onto.

The electrical message is now carried by a sea of chemicals called neurotransmitters. My car sits quietly while the sea – made up mostly of salt and water – carries us across. In the brain, the two main ingredients are called glutamate and GABA (aminobutyric acid). At the French coast – Calais – the ferry locks into the correct offloading site (the receptor) at the dock. Waters churn as she fits in like a key into a lock. I switch on Sparky's ignition, we get enough zap, and our little sports car is back on the road. The letter has now changed from a chemical sea carrier to electrical, depicted by dry land.

Can you see how important it is that we eat all the nutrients necessary to make the chemistry in the sea? We are what we eat, and I will go more into how you can improve on your food in chapter 5.

About 80% of communication relies on healthy glutamine to rev up our activities, and then GABA to quieten them, and psychologists tend to focus on messengers who make up about 1% of the neurons that make them. However, these brain juice guys – the serotonins, norepinephrine, and dopamine – have profound effects on our moods; like gear changes, they modify the speed that messages travel at. A key incentive for my daily jogs is my brain infusion of happy juices, and research is backing up the confirmation of the balancing effect of exercise on brain neurotransmitters/chemical messengers.

Another group of proteins called factors help rebuild and nourish the brain. One of them (BDNF) is known as the fertiliser, or the shit of the brain. In the old days out at sea, SHIT meant 'store high in transit', as manure was treasured cargo and it would protect the boat – its fumes would otherwise ignite with the lanterns and cause the old sea-going vessels to explode. The hippocampus is fragile and prone to degenerative disease. This is our library, and it is buried in shit to protect it – I mean, buried in BDNF. Exercise elevates the amount of brain fertiliser we have, and in the 1995 book, *A User's Guide To The Brain*, a small article discusses evidence of more fertiliser in the mouse hippocampus when the mice were given mouse gym classes (Ratey, 2001).

A man named Cotman conducted studies of mice running repeatedly on different daily runs, and he found that increasing the distances meant more BDNF lighting up in the hippocampus, shown with dye when scanning their brains. The hippocampus of the long distance runners lit up like giant Christmas trees. I had visions of little mice in running gear and headbands. On a personal note, I need to run further for my brain, but not for my knees (Cotman et al., 2007).

Cotman also went on to discover that exercise sped up the rate of learning. His early work paved the way for many more studies to agree with him, so get those running shoes on! Greenough looked at mice learning more complex motor skills, such as running over beams, and the cerebellum (the coordinated movement centre]) lit up like a Christmas tree as well, so it wasn't just the effects of simple running.

In 2011, Dr Reynolds at Illinois University wrote a paper based on the living quarters of mice; a team of scientists headed up by Dr Rhodes checked cognition and healthy brain tissue before and after four different lifestyles. The only key thing was the running wheel. Group one had a luxury pad of the finest toys, nibbles, and tunnels. Pad two had the same plus running wheels, and pad three had boring, plain accommodation and simple food. Pad four had the same as three plus the running wheels (Reynolds, 2011). The moral of the story is just give running wheels for Christmas presents!

Hence my first book, *The 4 Keys To Health*, emphasised the need to do exercises such as tai chi – as well as cycling or running – as it is so important in later years for balance. Circuits have to link the cerebellum, basal ganglia, and prefrontal cortex, and engaging brain cells in this way encourages learning in every sense. Repetition then thickens the nerves and myelin sheaths. Dr Northrup – a world-renowned speaker and author on women's health – loved tango as it really is a powerful brain stimulator, and I shall leave it there!

WHAT HAPPENS TO MY BRAIN WITH MY DAILY JOGS?

In 2007 in Columbia, Scott Small looked at how exercise improved neurogenesis, the process by which neurons are generated from neural stem cells and progenitor cells. By a unique way of using MRI (magnetic resonance imaging), Small found that the capillary bed increased by 30% in the library (the hippocampus) with exercising. This meant that freshly perfused oxygen beds of blood fed the memory centre to encourage healthy new brain cell growth. In the future, we may have answers as to how much exercise is good for you, but generally, exercise gives you a normal body mass index and a more robust cardiovascular system.

What do I mean by the need to exercise to grow brain cells? The anthropologist in me knows that our DNA has been honed over millions of years of chasing after prey and running away from predators. This is the modern equivalent of a mixture of low intensity walking, moderate jogging (55 to 65% max heart rate), and running (75 to 90% max heart rate). Remember: your maximum heart rate is 220 minus your age, so you can literally jog your memory – ha ha.

Furthermore, learning is enhanced for a specific skill if physical activity is included. Don't you find that if you are moving it helps the learning processes? A simple mouse water maze experiment showed that mice could learn fast with the physical application to the task of the maze, but it was a non-transferable, learnt skill (Kee et al., 2007). It did not mean they got more skilled at anything else – I guess they meant that if mice played the piano, then playing drums would not be a transferable skill. They exerted themselves physically and new cells became spry and cognitively limber.

Again, in my *4 Keys To Health* book I talk about ideal amounts of exercise. I aim for an hour a day if I'm experiencing lengthy sedentary days in the clinic, ideally in two episodes of 30 to 45 minutes each. You need to mix resistive with aerobic exercise, and you'll only be committing about seven hours a week to keeping your brain healthy. If we can't manage a tenth of our day… come on, guys…

When we push into the strenuous bit, the pituitary gland in our brain releases growth hormone HGH, the fountain of youth. This burns up tummy fat, boosts brain volume, bulks muscle, and gives a more youthful appearance. Weight lifting or strenuous exercise does this. In turn, HGH stimulates another brain juice called IGF-1, which switches on genes to grow more neurons and improve learning. A gene on chromosome2 codes for a brain juice called BDNF (brain derived neurotrophic factor), a key role in making new brain cells and protecting connections. It has been known for some time that low calorific intake, nutrients, and yes, exercise, stimulates its production – again jogging your memory.

In a recent report in the *Journal of the American Medical Association*, Professor Nicola Lautenschlager discovered a 1800% improvement in memory, language attention, and brain plasticity, just by exercising for twenty minutes a day (Lautenschlager et al., 2008).

In my spin classes at Hoar Cross Hall, just a 30 second sprint can increase my HGH for two hours afterwards at an increased level of six times. If you are fit enough, adding in interval training boosts your brain's shit – sorry, manure (BDNF). When our heart pumps fast, another body juice (ANP) reduces stress as well as our monkey chatter brain. This is probably why I feel such clarity when I am doing a nice steady jog or going for a swim.

SHORT TERM STRESS IS GOOD FOR US

Mark Mattson is the chief of the neurosciences labs at the National Institute for Aging in the States, and he understood that mild stressors – such as mild toxins and short-term stress – were essential for strengthening the resilience of brain cells. This resilience comprised of waste-disposing enzymes, neuroprotective factors, and proteins. Healthy exercise and a good diet of small helpings of food go a long way to a healthy brain.

Non-aggressive exercise also improves the energy efficiency of brain cells. With a car journey, we must have enough fuel for the drive, and comfortable levels of exercise we have trained for means fuel conversions are within demands. The fuel tanks are topped up, and the exhaust fumes are ventilated in the case of the brain by 'janitor' enzymes. Exercise increases a brain juice called IGF1, which is a glucose (energy) controller, LTP, and excitingly, a neurogenesis champion. This means that we can grow bigger, healthier brain cells and connections, and our happy and anxious brain juices are better balanced – that's your serotonin, adrenaline, and dopamine. Exercise relaxes the resting tension of muscle spindles, which breaks the feedback loop to the brain, and we so we feel even less stressed.

Sooooo get moving!

DRUGLESS INOCULATIONS OF MINUTE TRAUMAS

"What are you on about now?" I hear you cry out. Yes, you read it correctly: tiny physical stabbings into the body with needles can actually change your brain. Acupuncture is thousands of years old – the Chinese say it started between 200 and 500 BC – and it focuses on 14 meridian lines, carrying at least 361 and 2,500 additional acupuncture points. These points all have fixed locations and have quasipharmacologic functions. That means they act like medicine, changing body chemistry depending on which combination of points has needles placed in.

I have seen modern day Chinese, Japanese, Korean, and Malaysian doctors all use different acupuncture approaches, and early man (pre metal age) used sharp fragments of bone. Each point is a switch to our physiology and a gateway through to healing, with a secret code of point sequences for each imbalance in our body. The number of tender points is indicative of our general health.

My chronic pain patients have hardwired pain, with centres in the brain and the spinal cord building up pain memories, and with persistent pain also sensitising neurons in the spinal cord and brain. I have always been interested in why harpooning the body heals and helps to change brain wiring. Basically, acupuncture is a drugless inoculation of minute traumas, used to restore self-healing and cause gene transcription. Signals from needles travel to the midbrain, the thalamus, the pituitary, and the cortex.

Researchers say that you get good and bad responders to treatment: 28% excellent, 64% good to average, and at least 8% will not respond at all.

SCANNING GAVE US PROOF OF THE EFFECTS OF A TINY PRICK ON THE BRAIN

PET and fMRI gives us evidence that the brain listens for and responds to acupuncture – scans have revolutionised our understanding of the brain. In 1997, Zang Hee Cho – the inventor of positron emission tomography (PET) – carried out the first fMRI acupuncture technique. Thank you Mr. Cho. We can now image minute changes in glucose uptake and oxygen consumption in different parts of the brain, thereby observing the brain's energy metabolism and oxygenation status, with spatial and temporal resolutions to investigate the cortical responses to acupuncture. The ability to see what each point and combination of points does to the brain is a step towards understanding the ancient craft of healing.

Scans show that the human cortex has three key areas, which perceive and process pain, and they all have complicated names –the dorsal, caudal and rostral anterior cingulate cortex. Acupuncture signals are believed to travel up cables called the spinothalamic tract (STT), the spinoreticular tract (SRT) and the spinomesencephalic tract (SMT). Signals travel up through the spinal cord and into the brain stem, and here they find Mr Thalamus – also known as the dynamic pain processing centre or router. He then sends it onto the monkey and then the human sensory and higher planning areas. It's amazing what a small prick can do! When presenting pain in various countries and through translators, I found that coloured pens and metaphors helped with what can be a very dull subject to teach. If you are not careful, it becomes a boring catalogue of complicated names for bits of the brain, which is a right pain in the backside.

Pain control is the most common reason in the UK for seeking out acupuncture, but it goes well beyond this; it provokes much larger, survival-related functions. The needle poke stimulates the monkey brain limbic system as it talks to the human cortex, then it backchats to the monkey brain before talking to the hypothalamus. The acupuncture point stimulus causes hormonal, autonomic, and neurochemical changes, altering settings in Mr Hypothalamus (the central homeostatic regulator). In other words, the fear response is adjusted, as well as causing anti-inflammatory and neuro immune responses. All of this helps the brain keep the body healthy, and just from a tiny prick. This is such a huge subject to touch on in my book on the mind, so I will leave it there and return to acupuncture in my next book.

THE BRAIN CALLS THE SHOTS ON THE BODY'S SUFFERING

Injury and suffering can be very different things. Time and again I witness grade 4 osteoarthritic destroyed painless joints and healthy, normal, agonising ones, the damage bearing no relationship to the perceived pain. The difference is the brain's perception of how dangerous the situation is; whilst gathering sensory information from the tissues, the brain draws on a complex evaluation process and listens to memories of similar experiences. The conscious experience is based on the brain's unconscious and rapid evaluation of how much danger the tissues are in, and most importantly, the survival issues. Mr Pain is needed as the brain perceives a threat to tissues, and motivates us to change our behaviour to get out of danger. It is not and never has been an accurate measure of the tissue damage, it's just a 'get off your arse and do something!' signal.

NO BURGLARS AND NO FIRE

If we take a tablet and artificially block pain, the brain steps down and switches off the alarm, causing us to falsely believe we have done something to protect the damaged tissue. The subconscious stops adjusting the blood flow, the immune system, and the hormone levels in an attempt to heal, and therefore incorrectly rests.

Only this weekend we had two false alarms at the clinics; the intruders and fire only existed in the computer brain, not in reality. Head office muted the alarm on their display and correctly explained that we needed to find the fire before calling out the emergency services.

We did not do the painkiller bit but we rooted out the cause, which was a power surge that had blown various circuits. These were mended to protect them next time, and if the computer was human, it would store this memory to learn from it the next time it happened. Even though the conscious radar – the bloody loud alarm – was switched off, we investigated the unconscious systems and processes. Well, our wonderful IT team did.

I find with my patients, if they perceive that part of their body is vulnerable – and in my job it seems to most often be their back – the brain scans the environment differently. This is when I get a lecture about any slopes in my grounds, or any steps or marks on the carpet. Body posture overprotects and weakens the area further, and any situation that could worsen the injury is avoided, leading to a dull, depressing, non-sexual, non-active life. The brain even lays down extra receptors for certain chemicals or stimuli that it fears, hence unhelpfully getting us overreacting, overstressing, and generally becoming weaker. The more the brain wires pain into certain activities, the stronger the neural network gets and the more the pain grows. Understanding this and talking to our subconscious brain makes a big difference.

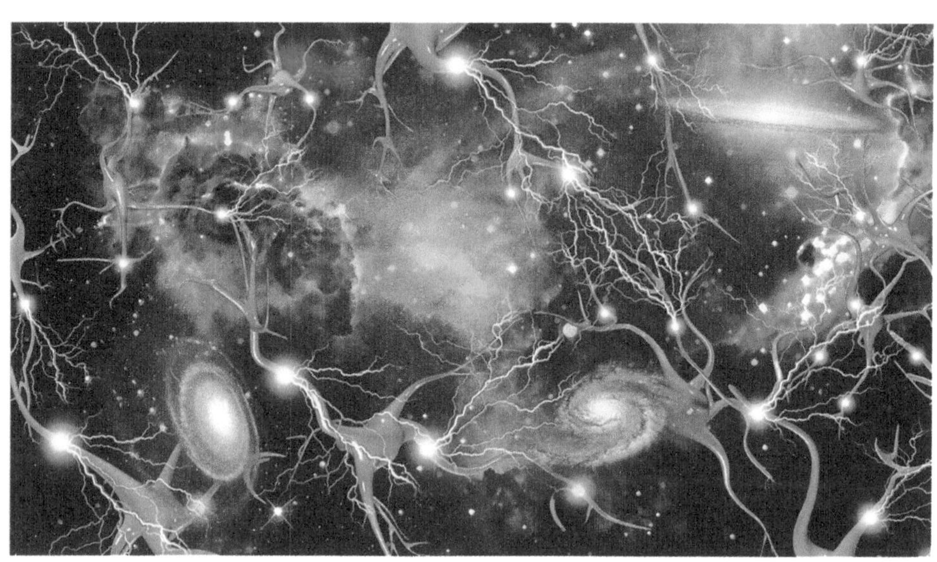

Looking into the mind is like gazing into the universe

Chapter Five

"Tell me what you eat,
and I will tell you what you are."

Jean Anthelme Brillat-Savarin

Before you read this chapter, you may find it useful to go back to my first book, *The 4 Keys To Health*, and do the mind key again in preparation.

FOOD FOR THOUGHT

How we think and feel is very powerfully affected by what we eat. Nutrients change our intelligence, our mood, and our emotional stability, as well as our mental health in the broadest sense. Our gut is also full of what you could call brain cells. I am going to share with you the food knowledge I've gleaned over the years from a handful of healthy food enthusiasts and research labs around the world.

When I'm writing my book, I often take a break to go in my greenhouse, selecting veggies to make some healthy – though not always tasty – mixtures; I am very creative when it comes to food. As I was making my creative mixture this morning, the comment I got from my father was, "That looks like shit," just as I was adding hemp and chia seeds to a Nutribullet of blackberries and veg. I said, "Father, do you eat chia seeds?" and he replied, "Yes, that sounds like a word we used in Brazil for shit." I sparkled with excitement; he groaned and pulled faces.

All this deliciously poisonous processed food has spoilt our taste buds for the healthy food that our gut cries out for. In the West, our generation is likely to live ten years longer than kids growing up today, and what seems criminal is that we are sickening because of a handful of diseases that could be easily avoided if we turned our kitchens into nature's medicine cabinet.

I enjoy giving presentations to gardening guilds as they really do get it: if you have an unhealthy plant, you look to the nutrients, oxygen, and sun level to make it flourish. I enjoy listening to farmers in the audience at my presentations who look after their animals by balancing nutrition rather than rushing to use drugs.

FOOD CHANGES BRAIN JUICES

Eating too much or too little of certain nutrients will have a huge impact on the balance of chemicals that make sure our brain works well – our brain juices – and therefore on our brain chemistry and long-term health. It's interesting to consider connections between eating fast food, feeling ill, visiting the GP, getting a prescription, and still suffering illness.

The brain is our control centre – the equivalent to the CPU (central processing unit) in our cars – and it receives messages from everywhere: externally, about temperature, movement, light, sound, and pain; and internally, about the balance of chemicals (acid/alkali) and about levels of chemicals (glucose, oxygen, and so on). The brain makes billions of decisions based on this information being constantly supplied to it. The central nervous system (CNS) has to make the correct decision to send appropriate signals out to adjust what happens in our muscles, glands, and more, to quickly make life saving adjustments for balance (homeostasis).

Here's a quick memory jogger of the neuroanatomy covered in chapter one, and how essential nutrients are. The human body has 100 billion neurons, each one connecting through wires and spark plugs (called dendrites and synapses). These messages excite or calm the mind, help or hinder digestion, aid focus and intelligent decisions, or add confusion, aid or destroy sleep, and swing emotions.
Messages are sent out from one receptor and received at another one, and these receptors are made of essential fats. As their name suggests, essential fats really are essential to keeping the brain well oiled, and we gain more of these by eating fish and seeds.

MEMORY MOLECULES

Memory molecules (phospholipids) add 'oomph' to how well the brain works; they help the brain to receive the messages about what's going on inside the body and in its environment through a complex nervous system. The snail-like outer sheaf coatings of nerves are called phospholipids, found richly in eggs, and lecithin capsules are a direct source of phospholipids.

INTELLIGENT NUTRIENTS

Intelligent nutrients are essential vitamins and minerals that fine-tune our brains. Amino acids – the building blocks to proteins – hold the keys to messages, signalling on and off at our receptors. They allow the brain to 'talk' about the signals it has 'heard'.

Intelligent nutrients turn amino acids into motivating chemicals called neurotransmitters. There are so many neurotransmitters – in essence, the signals from the brain – and here are a few key ones: laughter juice (serotonin) is for increasing happiness; adrenaline and dopamine improve levels of motivation; GABA helps us to de-stress; acetylcholine can increase our alertness, and tryptamines improve connectiveness. Melatonin, for example, is a tryptamine that affects connections to the sun's cycle of day and night.

THE WAY TO A MAN'S HEART IS THROUGH HIS STOMACH – WELL, HIS BRAIN HIDES HERE TOO

The gut – that's right, think of gut feeling – has 100 million neurons and produces as many neurotransmitters as the brain, as well as two thirds of our happy juice, serotonin. The brain-gut link is strong. The area of the brain known to transmit to the gut has been identified as the insulate, hence the brain's link with irritable bowel and ulcers.

Furthermore, new research is pointing to the need for a good, healthy bacterial flora in order to have a healthy brain. I have a product in my cabinet that claims 12 billion natural bacteria per capsule, and if I need to fire up my brain for some intensive writing, I make sure my vitamin D3 is to hand. Vitamin D3 is a hormone that is manufactured from cholesterol in the body, particularly in sunny weather, and excitingly, it regulates genes along with good brain nutrients. I also have omega 3 to hand as well as antioxidants, because I have a cupboard full of veggies that were not picked freshly today.

I understand that my supplements are helping with brain stem cell growth, which will push the onset of Alzheimer's, multiple sclerosis and Parkinson's a little further away. New research suggests that many cases of Alzheimer's are preventable with the right balance of nutrition, especially vitamin D3 (gained mostly from cholesterol) and exercise. If the cholesterol level is kept too low because of prescription drugs, Alzheimer's will accelerate.

I DON'T NEED SUGAR IN MY TEA, I'M SWEET ENOUGH

Even before people gathered vegetation, plants processed sunshine, water, soil, and oxygen to make energy in the form of glucose, and when we began to gather plants, we took advantage of this stored energy.

We rely heavily on plants to provide our healthy food, and I find it very humbling and grounding to have a garden and greenhouse to grow some of my food. The biologist in me remembers that we humans are just a small cog in the great engine of nature. We are guardians of this planet: without making sure the way we use nature is sustainable, our health will plummet and our species will not survive.

Sugar gives fuel, but too much sugar encourages brain dementia. An active brain uses up 40% of the body's fuel needs. Now, I did say *active* brains, so get thinking. Furthermore, the brain cannot function without energy, as it's essential. There is a lot written about healthy natural foods releasing sugar slowly to avoid high surges, and this is known as the glycaemic index (GI). If you're interested in this, there are many cookbooks on the subject. It is important to stay away from the long-term use of sweeteners, especially aspartame; they are known to promote the less favourable emotions as well as memory loss.

So, get adventurous in your kitchen and play creatively with healthy food. Grow and cook from scratch where possible. When you eat a food advertised as having a long shelf life, you are putting less healthy food inside you. Non-organic veg will have been grown in soil full of chemicals and been sprayed with yet more chemicals. I was interested to hear a farmer's wife at the hairdressers say that their crops are so full of chemicals that she peels any veg thickly, and if her meal is served with a jacket potato in a restaurant, she feels so strongly about the level of chemicals in it that she sends it back.

I think I need to rethink how many veggie skins I consume by reviewing my Nutribullet recipes. I have had so much fun with my juicer and I get to keep those fibrous parts that I previously resented throwing out into my compost. I will share a few of the less weird Nutribullet recipes in this chapter.

HEALTHY FATTY OILS FOR THE BRAIN

Remember back in the dissecting lab? In chapter one, I talked about the brain shockingly being an ugly ball of three pounds of sculptured fat. The brain is 70% water and 30% dry matter. Over half the weight – 50 to 60% – is fat, and a third of that fat is specifically omega 3. The point I'm making is that if we are what we eat, knowing what the brain is made up of is pretty important information to have.

There are basically three categories of mental health: emotional, intellectual, and physical, and all three need omega oils to function. The first is emotional intelligence, and this is assessed in the way we respond to situations. Mood swings and emotional imbalance will be made worse by not having the correct diet. Intellectual mental health, simply speaking, can be measured with an IQ test, being able to add and subtract, form conceptual and organised plans, as well as looking at memory and learning speed. Physical intelligence includes the mind body coordination of sport, posture, balance, handwriting, and any other physical activity.

Essential for our mental health is healthy fat in our diet, specifically omega 3 and 6 oils, and omega 3 is the best as it reduces inflammation. Our body can make some saturated fats and cholesterol itself, however it has to have extra omega oils from our diet.

So, folks, if you lost your keys this morning, dropped your phone on the floor, or lost your temper, get out your Nutribullet, and add some omega

3 and 6 brain boosts. What did I just say? Erm… I've forgotten already. I'd better rush out to get some omega 3-rich ingredients. Back soon.

BRAIN OMEGA OIL BOOSTS

Here's a quick list of foods that boost our brain with omega and other essential oils:

Chia seeds originate from the ancient Mayans of Mexico, and are rich in omega 3 and 6, as well as iron, calcium, and zinc. They help to stabilise sugar metabolism.

Flax seeds are rich in omega 3, they lower cholesterol, and help keep bones strong. They have a nice nutty, crunchy taste.

Hemp seeds are loaded with rich omega 3 and 6, and they also help regulate immunity, hormones, and the heart.

Sunflower seeds – American baseball's favourite snack – have omega 6. The combination with selenium and vitamin E helps prevent arthritis and asthma, repairs cell DNA, aids the killing of cancer cells, and helps with detoxifying.

Walnuts are rich in omega 3 and antioxidants, and are great for anti-aging and anti-inflammatory processes.

Pumpkin seeds are yummy and rich in omega oils.

You can grind all these up and put on salads or cereals, or just have them in little bowls for snacking.

The animal protein ingredients of many meals – salmon, mackerel, herring, sardines, anchovies, tuna, eggs, and dairy products – have a kind of omega 3 called DHA. Eat something from this list at least twice a week, or choose an omega oil supplement or make up a salad dressing including this type of omega 3.

INTELLIGENT MEMORY FATS ARE PHOSPHOLIPID FOOD

Free range, organic, omega 3-rich eggs are superfoods, especially when they're not fried. Egg lecithin is needed to insulate the connections for the nerves, and supplementing our diet with lecithin is said to be important in improving cognition – clear, intelligent thinking. Eggs, fish, and nuts also have choline; acetylcholine is an essential neurotransmitter and is needed to form memories. Phosphatidylserine is a smart nutrient supplement for memory because it helps brain cells communicate and is a vital part of the structure of the brain's receptor sites.

All these phospholipids keep the neuron's receptor sites in good condition, so that the brain can receive information clearly; it 'hears' the message and understands it.

PROTEIN FOOD FOR THE BRAIN

Amino acids are the building blocks – the alphabet – of neurotransmitters. Remember I said that they are, in effect, the language bites of information passed from one brain cell to the next? Amino acids can be supplemented or found in certain fresh foods. 23 amino acids – 8 of which are essential and have to be eaten – make up hundreds of neurotransmitters.

When I prepare food containing the building blocks that are amino acids, I like to daydream about what effect they will have on my brain the moment they hit. I think about it like an orchestra with the conductor signalling the violins, then the cellos, then the oboe… blending and bringing moods to a crescendo like a musical performance.

IN A RELAY RACE OF THOUGHTS, THE BATON IS THE NUTRIENTS

One way to think about how the brain works is as a relay race with coloured batons. Nutrients make up the baton, the signal. This baton is passed on, placed in a hand as the fingers wrap around it. Taking the baton is a signal for the next guy to run towards the finishing line and win.

In reality, brain neurons have lots of locks that open when the correct key – the neurotransmitter – is fitted. The neurotransmitter passes from one neuron to the next and the correct fit unlocks the signal to cause a change in the neuron it connects with. The key is broken down after it's been used, and then is recycled. It's incredible to think we change our thoughts and how we see the world with our food.

If you're throwing a supper for friends and you know one of them gets down, some good, healthy food will help raise their spirits. Get them to read up about how supplements with 5 HTP tryptophan are said to help with depression.

For your vegetarian friends, protein powder supplements are great in your smoothies, juices or Nutribullets, and they should include glutamine, tyrosine, taurine, GABA, tryptophan, and phenylalanine. Good sources of protein include chickpeas, maize, lentils, brown rice, seeds, nuts, green veggies, and beans. Fish can be used as a source of protein for vegetarian friends who eat it.

ESSENTIAL VITAMINS AND MINERALS, THE INTELLIGENT FOOD TUNERS TO THE BRAIN

These guys help turn glucose into energy, essential fats into prostaglandins, GLA, and DHA, choline and serine into phospholipids, and amino acids into proteins. The key ones for mental health are B vitamins, folic acid, vitamin C, manganese, magnesium, zinc, and D3.

Whole grains and veggies supply B1, B3, B5 and B6. B1 is needed for concentration; B2 to avoid depression and psychosis; B5 aids memory and helps stress management. B6 does the same as B5 and also helps with irritability, and bananas are a rich source of B6. If you have an irritable grump at home, boost the levels of their B vitamins.

Interestingly, the part played by whole grains in brain health is going through a controversial phase. The glycaemic index and gluten allergy are now known to affect our brains.

Green leafy veggies are an excellent source of folic acid to help with psychosis, and anxiety with depression. Any veggie crops from above ground have less carbohydrate than crops from below ground. Eggs, dairy, and fish supply B12. Egg yolk is a wonderful source of omega 3, especially those laid by hens not fed on too many grains. GPs sometimes give injections of B12 to multiple sclerosis sufferers to help generally with memory, confusion, and psychosis.

Adding fresh fruit to veggies gives a rich vitamin C supply to again help depression and psychosis. Adding nuts and seeds to veggies supplies magnesium for the usual depression and irritability, and this time, insomnia. Replacing veggies with tropical fruits, and adding nuts and seeds with tea, supplies manganese to help with dizziness and convulsions.

GUYS, SHOOTING YOUR SEED TOO OFTEN DEPLETES ZINC

Eating seeds, nuts, and fish builds your zinc levels. An interesting fact is that when guys 'shoot their seed' a lot – get my drift – it causes a zinc deficiency. This little critter causes lack of motivation, confused and blank thoughts, loss of any appetite, and loss of motivation to act on anything. In this case I am ordering a few sacks of nuts and seeds. I know a lot of people who could do with some help in this area, especially in the winter. I don't believe a likely cause is due to too much sex, sadly; however, it is an interesting question to ponder – and to be tactful about – in the absence of partners.

FOOD TO HELP STROKE RECOVERY

Whilst environment, stress, happiness, genetics, trauma, and aging all add in their penny's worth, looking at nutrition before and after the event helps overall brain health, and avoidance or speedier recovery if disaster strikes. A stroke occurs when part of the brain does not receive enough blood, resulting in a loss of brain function and needing another part of the brain to take over this function, as well as new neuron pathways to grow. Blood vessels can rupture or block in the brain, and this is a disorder of the circulatory system, so food to help this must be considered.

Diets low in artery-clogging trans fats, processed foods, and bad cholesterol help stroke recovery, and not smoking or drinking alcohol in large amounts also helps. Homocysteine tests – available through York lab – are useful predictors of strokes. Good cholesterol makes hormone D3, which is essential for brain health; we often need to supplement with D3.

After a stroke where blood flow has been impaired, you often get sleepy when you sit a lot, as well as getting absent-minded. Avoid too much alcohol and too many toxins in daily household cleaning products, and drink adequate water. Herbal teas with blessed thistle, gingko, or hawthorn will help. A massage with rosemary and peppermint is also said to help brain function. You can also drink these in teas.

Make sure if you are trying out my juices that you try out some super algae – yum yum! Omega 3 oils are essential, and food with lots of B vitamins in is a must. Psychiatrists are taking a closer look at omega 3's, calling them happy fats. This is because they are researching their use in Alzheimer's and depression and many other mental problems. We cannot make our own, so we should either plan a diet with lots of oily fish, or use supplementation. They contain eicosapentaenoic acid (EPA) and docosahexaenoic acid (DHA), both known to help brain function.

DEMENTIA

This is a gradual decline in healthy brain functioning, and tangled damaged neurons and plaques add to this problem. One form is called Alzheimer's, and hardened arteries again lead to increasingly poor brain function. Researchers are showing that nutrient-rich diets low in unhealthy fats and sugars help to prevent or lessen this illness. D3 is essential to slow the disease. If statins keep cholesterol too low, this can have a negative effect on dementia.

Loss of memory and concentration are terrible things to happen, but the right nutrition helps the brain to fight off free radical damage, improve neurotransmitter formation, and strengthen capillaries and the blood brain barrier.

Here are some herbs that are known to help this condition. Chinese club moss (Huperzia serrata) has a history for treating memory loss, dementia, and mental illness. Modern research has found a compound in it called huperzine A, which inhibits the enzyme that breaks down a neurotransmitter in the brain called acetylcholine, and this has been shown to help with Alzheimer's. I have heard that researchers in China are confident that 60% of their Alzheimer's patients show an improvement in cognition with the help of this herb alone.

Ginkgo biloba has been shown to improve brain circulation, helping dementia, mental decline, and depression. Research in Europe shows an improvement in dizziness, absent-mindedness, loss of memory, and confusion.

Age-related degenerative diseases involve inflammation and free radical brain damage. Since the brain is mostly fat, antioxidants like lycopene and alpha lipoic acid – that prevents the oxidation of lipids – are twice as effective as beta carotene. Alpha lipoic acid is both fat and water soluble and slips easily through the blood brain barrier. As an aside, in Germany it is used to treat diabetic neuropathy and damaged nerve tissues.

The soybean lecithin complex can help maintain a healthy brain; this mixture contains phosphatidylserine, phosphatidylcholine, phosphatidylethanolamine and phosphatidylinositol, which all make up the brain cell membranes. This is really important in cognitive functions – such as memory – for things like telephone number recall, short-term memory, attention, reading and memory of what has been read, and face recognition.

It is interesting that, as with Chinese club moss, phosphatidylserine is the major building block for folate and amino acids (like glycine and cysteine) to deactivate the enzyme that breaks down acetylcholine. Ethanolamine is a cell membrane phospholipid and is an antihistamine and good for sedating. Inositol is another phospholipid in the cell membrane needed for normal brain function and transmitting nerve signals.

Snow rose tea (Rhododendron caucasicum) is known to extend life span. It is high in antioxidants called phenylpropanoids to improve brain circulation, and it reduces brain damage from chemical and biological causes, as well as being a free radical hoover; just like a vacuum cleaner sucks up dirt, snow rose tea sucks up damaging substances called osteoarthritis or free radicals, an everyday product of metabolism.

PARKINSON'S AND WHICH FOODS HELP

Research being done in 2015 involves looking at gene therapy and identifying specific proteins that protect dopamine-producing nerve cells. Some of these clever experiments are being carried out on thin worms called C. elegans. Another bit of research has looked at the cell's 'shopping baskets' that deliver stuff in and out of cells and through the blood brain barrier. This research has examined putting gene therapy in these cells to reduce specific proteins, that if too great in number or the wrong shape, can kill off brain cells.

Stem cells are being taken from Parkinson's patients' fat to grow nerve cells. Another project is looking at genes in happy brain cells and those in cells that die (*Breakthroughs*, Parkinson's leaflets, UK, 2015). "We still believe lifestyle plays a role, and that the body's immune system goes overboard and attacks its own brain cells," claim Dr Geoffrey and Lucille Leader (www.cureparkinsons.org.uk). One in ten of us will suffer from this disease, which is a sobering thought; for those bean counters out there, that is six million people.

The good news is that the modern medical management of dopaminergic drugs includes nutritional management. Mood, emotional status, and personal attitude are all just as important as having the shakes, and nutrition – as explained to me by a very dear patient – makes his brain hostile to

Parkinson's. Dopamine deficiency may lead to this disease, and proteins, minerals, and vitamins all have to be present in your brain factory to make the building blocks of dopamine. You also need glucose, ideally from fruit, grains, and veggies. You have to have B vitamins, vitamin NADH, coenzyme Q10, biotin, iron, zinc, and copper. Then, with the energy from glucose, proteins are manufactured into dopamine.

By the way, the fibre in your diet helps a sluggish bowel to absorb the nuts and bolts in order for the brain to make dopamine. Healthy snacks every two hours help with sugar levels, and herbs, ginkgo biloba, hops, horsetail, passion flower, liquorice root, valerian root, and wood betony all help with this condition. Essential nutrients are apha lipoic acid, 7-Keto, coQ10, evening primrose oil, grapine, N-acetyl cysteine, super GLA, and vitamins C and E.

Remember the importance of repetitive, focused activities to drive the brain cells and neurotransmitters you are creating with good food? You need to keep exercising even when the drive to do it is missing.

Interestingly, once you have made dopamine to help physical movement and mood, Parkinson's disease also has an impact on the stress hormone adrenaline, as it is manufactured from dopamine. My Parkinson's patients are unbalanced and shaky if they've had a stressful drive over, as the brain shouts, "I am stressed! Get me some adrenaline NOW!" Then the brain replies to itself, "But the stores are low on dopamine to make stress juices. Are you sure?" If the answer is yes, movement may be more erratic. That's why my treatment needs not to be too stressful, otherwise walking afterwards is more of a stagger out of my office.

MULTIPLE SCLEROSIS

This is an autoimmune disease and is very difficult to diagnose, often presenting as pins and needles, blurred vision, fatigue, numbness, staggering gait, unexplained leg or arm pain, or incontinence. The symptoms may mildly ebb and flow for years and go under the radar, and I have seen many patients who show a mild form of this: some have symptoms that are quickly resolved, never to return, but some sadly deteriorate.

When multiple sclerosis occurs, the body's own defence system goes haywire and attacks the myelin sheaves of nerves. A brain scan showing plaques will ascertain a positive diagnosis.

Nutrients to help with this disease include evening primrose oil, flax seed oil, vitamin D3, blackcurrant oil, N-acetyl cysteine, and super GLA. Helpful herbs to add to food are ginkgo biloba and psyllium. Drinks to help with the symptoms can be made from fruits: fresh apple, apricot, grape; veggies: cabbage or lettuce; and added for taste: aniseed, basil, chamomile, fennel, mint, or a lemon and ginger infusion.

DEPRESSION

When someone has bipolar mood disorder, they can be very elated, setting unreasonable goals, having an exaggerated sense of importance, or exhibiting mania. They can talk a lot, be hyperactive, then have poor sleep. There can be many causes: serotonin or dopamine levels can be unbalanced, or unresolved emotional wounds can add to the mix.

Mood stabilisers are essential, and amino acids from protein are important. Protein supplements in a morning shake are good for this – either veggie or algae – which can be very tasty. Blood sugars need to be stable. Food with B vitamins is essential, as well as calcium, chromium, grapine, magnesium, niacin, and good old omega 3. Make use of aromatherapy in an oil burner or massage, using clary sage, lavender, and lemon to help stabilise moods. Liquorice root tea is also said to be good for mood balance, and it tastes okay too.

I find a lot of my patients suffer with elements of depression, and as well as feeling physical pain, they are wrestling with spiritual and emotional problems. Some have been abused as children or within their current relationship, for example. Pain is often stored in the body and acupuncture and massage often stores up a hornet's nest. Being an excellent listener and encouraging good nutrition helps to anchor a positive response to any physical treatment.

MIGRAINE

This is a recurrent severe headache, often with visual disturbances and vomiting. I am often asked to help with acupuncture and neck manipulations to relieve this. A migraine can be triggered by many things including stress, hormones, or food. There are basically two types: vasoconstriction and vasodilation.

The first, vasoconstriction, is a restricted blood flow, and teas of ginkgo, lobelia, or ginger can help. The second, vasodilation, means too much blood flow, and digestive bitters and feverfew are said to help. It's also suggested that cleansing the liver with appropriate herbs, like digestive bitters tonic, reduces the onset of migraine. Similarly, increase your water intake to make sure of an even blood flow.

Other treatments that can help the migraine sufferer are massage or oil burners with sweet marjoram, tei-fu, and ylang-ylang. Supplements of coenzyme Q 10, magnesium, and niacin are also said to help. Herbal teas and supplements include ginger, gingko biloba, feverfew, and lobelia.

OBSESSIVE COMPULSIVE DISORDER

This is when the sufferer fears that something bad will happen, and in order to avoid this, feels compelled to carry out driven, repetitive, irrational behaviour. Apart from excellent counselling, nutrition may ease the symptoms. Food and supplements rich in B6 and zinc are said to help.

POST-TRAUMATIC STRESS DISORDER

Any build up of stressful and traumatic events can lead to an emotional build up, resulting in post-traumatic stress disorder. This is burnout. They say pantothenic acid helps, as does the herb kava kava, as well as having a massage with lavender and frankincense.

STRESS

This is a huge subject, and a condition we will all experience from time to time. Many herbs help, a few being kava kava, chamomile, ginseng, liquorice, valerian root, and St John's Wort. I like my chamomile tea – especially the one with flower heads – which I brew up in my little red teapot I got in Bruges. I find the whole ritual of making tea soothing.

I bought some strong-tasting ginseng back from Korea, but I was a baby with the taste. Liquorice is nice, just don't drink too much or you can get the runs. Nutrients that help to relieve stress include pantothenic acid, magnesium, niacin, pregnenolone, B vitamins, and 5-HTP. Massage to reduce stress can be done with bergamot, lavender, chamomile, sandalwood, ylang ylang, and tei-fu.

PAIN, HEADACHES AND IN GENERAL

Pain did not set out to be the enemy; it's our 999, our guard and our teacher. I have the nickname 'the painkiller' as I kill unnecessary pain as best I can. Most people's idea of killing pain is a lazy pill-pushing exercise. A healthy lifestyle takes work and patience.

There are some simple steps to avoiding pain. Drinking more water is key to reducing pain made worse by dehydration, whereas breathing more deeply helps water, oxygen, and nutrients get around the blood supply to the cells. Maintaining a more alkaline system can be done by having a diet of 70% veg and fruit to 30% protein and grains. Or simply 1/3, 1/3, 1/3, favouring green veg every time. Try and add more aloe vera, anamu, hops, kava kava, lobelia, St John's Wort, valerian root, curcumin, magnesium, MSM, and omega 3.

It is easy to find natural pain-relieving gels. Just look out for: EverFlex cream, sandalwood, MSM cream, biofreeze, eucalyptus, camphor, aloe, rosemary, citrus, and peppermint oils and creams. Massage with frankincense, eucalyptus, helichrysum, lavender, or tei-fu

FIBROMYALGIA (FM)

This may cause a lot of discomfort and affect not only sleep, but also mood and the overall ability to engage in life. It is a stress-related autoimmune disease in a similar way to arthritis and chronic fatigue syndrome. I am yet to find a happy-go-lucky, smiling FM patient. This condition is both a mind and body problem.

I have still to find the right pixie dust to cure this. My friend Professor Gunn once said to me, in an annual FM meeting in Canada, that he saw fibromyalgia as a barrel of musculoskeletal dysfunctions, all separate conditions. However, as the barrel fills up it becomes a labelled syndrome called FM (fibromyalgia). Like a ball of wool, if you tear away the strands, it becomes a smaller problem. It was an interesting meeting, and that message came home with me. However, the jet lag was biting hard, the eight hour time difference between my UK clinic and Vancouver called for a catch up snooze, and Alan and I took it in turns to elbow each other to stay awake.

Out in Germany, in beautiful Baden-Baden, I was invited to the first symposium of fibromyalgia, where I looked around specialised rehabilitation centres set up by insurance companies for people with FM to stay there for intensive treatments. My German is only at schoolgirl level, so I gathered that I asked some strange questions. I really wished I could understand more, as their passion to help this condition was breathtaking.

They really did understand re-educating people about lifestyle, diet, exercise, and mindset. Have I mentioned my *4 Keys To Health* book? For the condition of FM, they gave a diet rich in high volumes of veggies, which is important, because their antioxidant properties help to reduce stiffness caused by inflammation.

There has been research to suggest that mitochondria – the powerhouses of the cell – are faulty in FM. Mitochondria, with their separate genetic code passed through the female line, are weaker and need specific nutrients to fire them up. Doctor Brownstein, author of *Iodine: Why You Need It, Why You Can't Live Without It*, believes that iodine is prevalent in FM sufferers. I do find that a few of my female patients with chronic pain have thyroid problems.

My patients often have digestive problems and irritable leaky bowel issues, and this affects nutrition absorption. Enzyme deficiency adds to this problem, then bacteria and viruses hit the gut. Fibre helps with peristalsis (gut movement) and inflammation. There are known strong links between the brain and the gut, and emotion – especially stress – is very bad for FM sufferers. Within the gut there are also a lot of 'brain cells' which play another part in how we feel. Magnesium is essential for this powerhouse to function.

Useful herbs include liquorice, lobelia, kava kava, yucca, thai-go, cats claw, and St John's Wort. Useful nutrients include magnesium, MSM, omega3, iodine (black walnut), essential fats, and antioxidants. Detoxing the liver helps, though I believe that if you are fragile, you should only do a gentle detox. Some docs believe heavy metals also hinder recovery. There is a strong link between adrenal exhaustion and FM. Highly sugary refined products should be avoided, and yoga, tai chi, and meditation encouraged.

AUTISM

With autism, a person seems to be withdrawn from reality, experiencing hallucinations and daydreaming, and there is evidence it is linked to poor immunity or food allergies, especially gluten and dairy. The diet should be rich in fresh fruit and veg, with some high quality proteins and fats. Extra nutrients essential for autism include nacetyl cysteine, co-Q10, B complex, B12, methyl folate, vitamin C, A, and D, flax seed oil, magnesium, L-glutamine, protease, omega oil, and GABA. Green tea, ginkgo biloba, and St John's Wort can also help. Massage with lavender, frankincense, and myrrh.

MENTAL FATIGUE

Mental fatigue results in a lack of mental focus and often means that the memory does not work well. Foods that can relieve mental fatigue include apricots, carrots, mint, shellfish, green veggies, and unrefined cereals. Supplementing meals with zinc, selenium, and vitamin B can also help. You can make some great drinks to help improve mental focus and poor memory by mixing apricot, cherry, and grape juices with basil and mint, or apricot, lime, and mint juice.

Here's a lovely recipe:
3 apricots
3 tablespoons of lime juice
Honey to taste
1 teaspoon of mint
Ice
Blend and add mint and ice to taste

INSOMNIA

There are many reasons why you might not be able to sleep well, and if the brain's neurotransmitters are not giving enough sleepy juice, sleep ain't happening. Insomnia is made worse by stress, anxiety, alcohol, stimulants, adrenal exhaustion, and liver congestion. If you wake suddenly then cannot sleep, it can be your adrenals reacting to low blood sugar levels. Try eating a snack of protein and fat an hour before bed. If you find it hard to get to sleep and feel groggy when getting up, it could be down to a toxic liver.

Melatonin production in the pineal gland sometimes goes awry. We need serotonin in order to make melatonin, so if you crave sweets and are grumpy and low, you may need a serotonin boost – 5 HTP helps with this. Darkness helps the conversion of serotonin to melatonin in the pineal gland.

You can improve the conditions for sleeping by doing several things. Firstly, deal with what you do in the time before sleeping. Lessen the brightness of the lighting in your room before bedtime. Remember that the TV and the computer are stimulators of wakefulness, and are not sleep-inducing. Cut down on caffeine, especially after 6 p.m.

Sleep dictates: how fat we are, how we fight off infection, how creative and insightful we are, our stress coping ability, how we learn new things and process information, and how we store memories. In a British study, sleep deprivation altered 711 genes (Moller-Levet, 2013), and these genes activate proteins to repair brain tissue. Don't get enough sleep and you can suffer from memory loss, diabetes, depression, and being a fatty.

Sleep deprivation will cause the hormone Ghrelin to soar – this increases appetite – plus another hormone, Leptin, to fall. Leptin, which is stored in fat cells, controls the urge to eat and when the levels drop, the urge to eat is ignited. Moreover, the urge is to eat naughty junk food (Taheri et al., 2004). Don't you find that when you have to get up really early you just want more food? When I'm up at the crack of dawn to go to my Harrogate clinic from my Midlands home, I have two breakfasts. Next time your fat friend reaches for more cake, ask if they slept OK – you could be saving their life!

Leptin controls all the functions of the hypothalamus – your inner dinosaur – including lots of physiological functions, from eating to sex. This survival agent coordinates metabolic, behavioural, and hormonal responses to starvation. Nora T. Gedgaudas in her nutritional book, *Primal Body Primal Mind* states: "Leptin essentially controls mammalian metabolism" (Gedgaudas, 2011).

Herbs that help with sleeping include catnip, chamomile, hops, kava kava, lobelia, St John's Wort, passion flower, and valerian root. Massage with jasmine, frankincense, lavender, chamomile, rose, or ylang ylang. You could also try an Epsom Salts bath. Supplementing with magnesium and calcium helps this condition, as well as 5HTP, GABA, and melatonin. Adjust your diet to make sure you eat more aubergine, basil, marjoram, chamomile, fennel, courgette, lime, onion, and pumpkin.

Here are a few recipes to improve sleeping:

Mango juice:
2 mangos, peeled and stoned
2 tablespoons of water
Ice cubes made from chamomile tea

Lemon balm:
1 orange, juiced
1 grapefruit, juiced
Slice of lemon
Honey to taste
Lemon balm leaf (optional)

Elder and chamomile infusion:
2 tablespoons of dried elderflowers
1 tablespoon of chamomile flowers
250mls of boiling water
Honey to taste

YOUR PHONE AND COMPUTER USE IN BED MAY BE KILLING YOU

Years ago, people didn't know anything about artificial light – we went to bed when it was dark. The sun was the source of our lighting, so people spent their evenings in darkness. We, in our modern world, on the other hand, take pride in having technology that allows us to stay up as late as we want. The amount of artificial light in the world keeps growing.

However, depression, insomnia, and the use of prescription sleeping pills, anti-depressants, and caffeine has skyrocketed. Is that a coincidence? I don't think so. According to statistics, rather than talking to each other, 95% of people use different types of electronics prior to going to bed. Stop thinking those rude thoughts; I meant TV, working on the computer, or going on your phone! These activities cause sleep disruption, which leads to insomnia, which in turn leads to much bigger health problems.

Research has proven that nighttime exposure to artificial light suppresses the production of melatonin, which is the main hormone secreted by the pineal gland – no, not penis gland – which controls sleep and wake cycles. In order to stimulate the production of melatonin by the pineal gland, we need darkness. This vital hormone maintains the circadian rhythm of our body, and our bodies function optimally when we are exposed to natural sunlight.

A recent study found that people whose circadian 24-hour rhythm is interrupted by artificial light are more likely to get cancer. Natural darkness increases melatonin and protects cells from damage, whereas melatonin suppression has been linked to cancer, impaired immune systems, being fat, diabetes, and heart disease. You need to make sure you are producing enough melatonin because it is a powerful antioxidant that has positive effects on the immune system and aging.

Staring at screens right before sleep turns out to be a lot worse than previously thought. Doctor Dan Siegel – clinical professor of psychiatry at the UCLA School of Medicine – lays out all of the negative effects bedtime screen viewing can have on the brain and body. He says that the "body needs seven to nine hours of sleep to clean up toxins from cell to cell connections. Glial cells do this in the brain whilst we sleep. We cannot think straight and get fat due to insulin disturbance, if we don't sleep enough" (Siegel, 2015).

JUICING AND SMOOTHIE RECIPES FOR OPTIMUM BRAIN HEALTH

Remember to make your juices and smoothies from fresh products, keep to small amounts, and drink them straight away. Harvest your own ingredients or buy organic produce when you are able to. Wash everything thoroughly and avoid old fruit. A juicer extracts the solid bits, and a Nutribullet or blender gives a thicker, complete drink.

VITAMIN-RICH RECIPES TO AID AGING, BRAIN SHRINKAGE AND ALZEIMER'S

Vitamins A and E are powerful antioxidants to help protect the brain from free radicals, and vitamin E helps to lessen toxic proteins, slowing down Alzheimer's deterioration (Behl, Davies et al., 1992).

Omega 3 superfoods slow down brain aging and help with blood vessels (Nutribullet Natural Healing Foods). Here are some more recipes out of my American Nutribullet book for brain food. They are based on 40% to 50% veg, 40% to 50% fruit, then a handful of milled nuts and seeds. I combine what I have available in the fridge, freezer, and garden, and I am mindful of the properties of the food. Here are some text book suggestions:

50% veggies:
Choose from:
Avocado
Spinach
Swiss chard
Collard greens
Sprouted lentils
Kale
Spinach
Sweet potatoes
Carrots

50% fruit:
2 apricots or a cup of papaya
1 banana

Nuts and seeds:
10 milled almonds
1 tablespoon of sunflower seeds, or 1/4 cup of walnuts and 2 tablespoons of flax seeds, or 1 tablespoon of sunflower seeds and 1 tablespoon of flax seeds, or 10 almonds and 2 tablespoons of chia seeds

Fountain of Youth recipe:
50% spinach
½ avocado
1 medium nectarine
½ cup of blueberries
10 walnut halves

Tea time recipe:
50% lettuce
1 banana
1 cup of blackberries
1 tablespoon of flax seeds
Top with chilled green tea

Berry buddy recipe:
50% kale
½ avocado
½ cup of blueberries
½ cup of blackberries
½ cup of raspberries
Almond milk to top up

Here are some of my own made up favourite mixtures:

Snazzy morning pre-workout special:
1 banana
1 large strawberry or a handful of berries
Almond milk, or occasionally soya or hazelnut
Milled seeds such as chia, sunflower, or pumpkin
A spoonful of Nature's Sunshine protein mix, which gives it a yummy flavour

Snazzy mid-morning juice:
1 large carrot, preferably organic
Half an apple, or a scoop of berries, cherries, or strawberries (I always have frozen blackberries and raspberries to hand, picked from the garden when in season)
Ginger or lime to add if not using berries, as it gives a nice flavour zap if required
2 sticks of celery

Snazzy mid-afternoon fruit and protein alga juice:
1 scoop of blackberries, raspberries, or blueberries
1 scoop of wheatgrass, barley grass, or green algae
1 scoop of Nature's Sunshine pea mixture – it's yummy and healthy too
1 apple

Snazzy refresher veggie juice:
Half a carrot
A small piece of broccoli or spinach
A scoop of blackberries, raspberries, or blueberries

Snazzy chocolate:
Chocolate would help the brain more than exercise if you could eat enough, but there is the slight problem of getting fat! Within the library of memories (the hippocampus), there is an area called the dentate gyrus (DG) and this is thought to show age-related memory loss. Research has been carried out to show interventions that enhance DG function. "A high-resolution variant of functional magnetic resonance imaging (fMRI) was used to map the precise site of age-related DG memory dysfunction and to develop a cognitive task whose function localized to this anatomical site. Then, in a controlled trial, we applied these tools to study healthy 50–69 year-old subjects who consumed either a high or low cocoa flavanol (chocolate) containing diet for months. A high-flavanol intervention was found to enhance DG function, as measured by fMRI and by cognitive testing." Our findings establish that DG dysfunction is a driver of age-related cognitive decline and suggest non-pharmacological means for its amelioration" (Brickman

et al., 2014). In other words, eating cocoa flavanol (chocolate) helps to slow down age-related memory problems.

ANXIETY AND DEPRESSION, HELPED BY A VITAMIN TABLET?

America – one of the leading countries in treatment advances – has over 40 million people suffering with anxiety, and I stumbled across an article that suggested a vitamin pill could stop the anxiety epidemic. The variations in the MTHFR gene mean that folic acid (vitamin B9) cannot be converted into folinic acid, which the body needs to not be anxious. I point this out to stress that we sometimes need to look outside the box, especially if it's Pandora's.

A SPOONFUL OF MEDICINE AND A HANDFUL OF NUTS... KEEPS THE DOCTOR AWAY

I make a slight adaption of the Mary Poppins song, because my love of magnesium-rich cashew nuts is a healthy one. Magnesium is a mineral used generally in many functions of your body and especially your heart, muscles, and kidneys. Your magnesium level could be too low if you have unexplained fatigue or weakness, heart arrhythmia, and even muscle spasms and eye twitches. However, its role in depression is less well known.

A handful of cashews is the therapeutic equivalent of a prescription dose of Prozac. "Several handfuls of cashews provide 1,000-2,000 milligrams of tryptophan, which will work as well as prescription antidepressants," says Doctor Andrew Saul, a therapeutic nutritionist and editor-in-chief of Orthomolecular Medicine News Service (Saul, Doctor Yourself website). The body turns tryptophan into serotonin, a major contributor to feelings of sexual desire, good mood, and healthy sleep.

Cashews are packed with protein, dietary fibres, and a rich supply of essential minerals and vitamins that contribute to overall health. These minerals are potassium, phosphorus, calcium, magnesium, iron, sodium, manganese, zinc, copper, and selenium. Cashews are also rich in folic acid and vitamin K. I never knew they were antidepressants and made you horny!

So there you go – sometimes a little bit of what you fancy can go a long way to helping you live a healthy life. Now, here we are at the end of my food chapter. I think you would agree that we are constantly bombarded by contradictory information on diets – even my clever, educated, cautious, skeptical patients go into trance over unhealthy, sugar-laden food. We trust marketing companies and so-called food experts to guide us to healthy food, but in reality, what we consume is far from healthy: sugar-laden fast food, and fruit and veggies grown in nutrient deficient soil with long shelf lives.

We should fight for the right to know who the silent brain killers are.

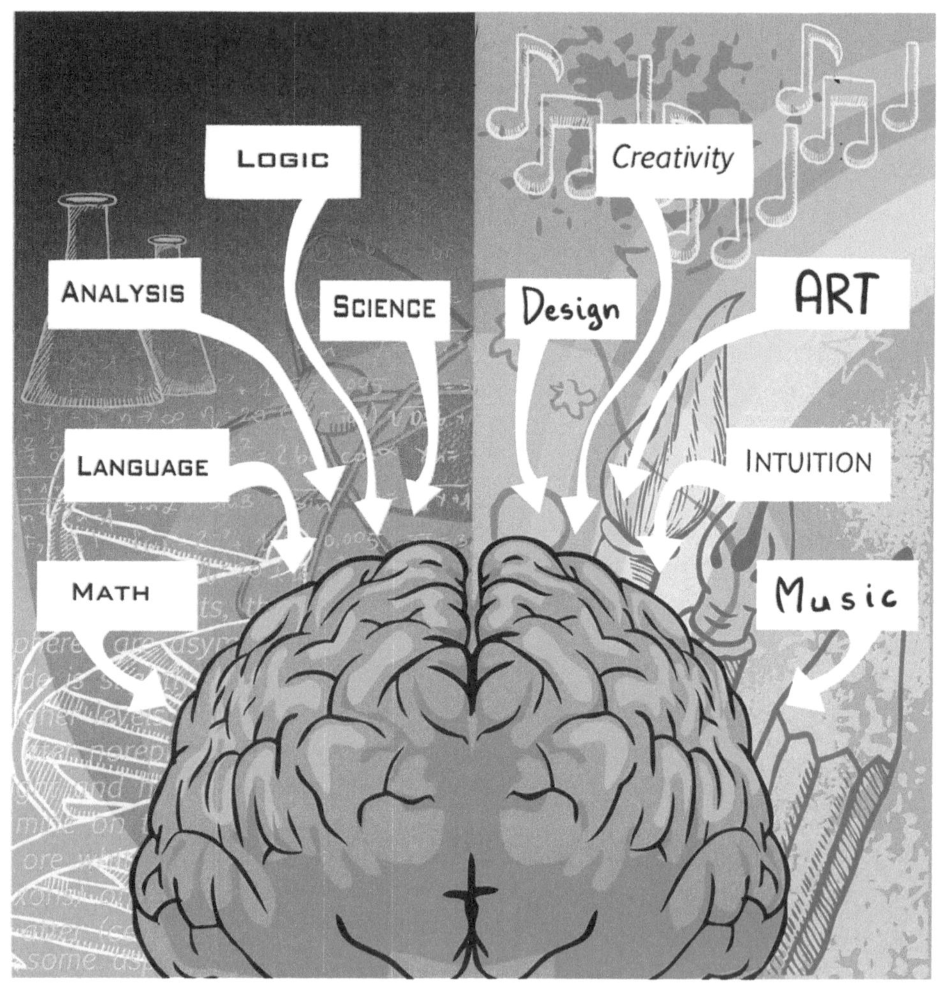

Right and left functions

CHAPTER SIX

"There are more things in heaven and earth, Horatio, than are dreamt of in your philosophy."

William Shakespeare, Hamlet

LANGUAGE

This is a chapter about words, and so you will find it woven together with a tapestry of quotes.

The cofounders of NLP (neurolinguistic programming) suggest that language imposes order on buzzing confusion. We define names for objects, values, beliefs, boundaries, species, and categories of objects with descriptive action words. In therapy, if you can make the problem a verb rather than a noun, it no longer seems like an immoveable object. For example, 'my relationship is a disaster' seems a bigger problem than 'the way we relate to each other can be disastrous'.

I have enjoyed many trips to Vancouver where the teaching centre for pain relief used to be (until it moved into the sports medical faculty at Calgary University). Anyway, whilst out there I heard about something rather special on Vancouver Island. There is a little known tribe that uses verbs where we use nouns; they felt more empowered to change everything with this fluid way of describing objects. When speaking of pain, for example, if you express it as moving, you have more of a chance of changing it, of manipulating it with descriptive changes in both speed and direction.

DO YOU HATE CHANGE?

It is not unusual for people to dislike or even fear change, and many of us engage in change avoidance behaviour so it's important to know how to identify it. Learn to be aware of how you are responding to new ideas, or activities, or people, so that you can change at will.

My mother, for example, hates change, and I think all of us love the familiar: we park our car in the same spot, we sit in the same chair, we drive down the same roads. Familiarity is comforting. New, unexpected information and activity, on the other hand, is met with a surge of brain activity to make new neurons, accompanied by unsettling changes in brain juices. Avoiding change feels safe, though it can be hellishly boring, and it doesn't challenge us. If you are pushed into something your mind reacts to as too challenging, however, it can leave a negative imprint in your brain, which in turn can lead to a wrong belief becoming associated with that action in the future.

HOMEWORK:
Think of any associations you have – any irrational responses to something – and where they came from.

ONE WORD, 25 MEANINGS

Just saying one word can release a cascade of brain juices that triggers either a fitting or an inappropriate emotional response. I find that when I use words, I am thinking of one meaning and my friend or patient is thinking of a totally different meaning. According to research done using fMRI, each noun has about 25 meanings; like fingerprints, the meaning of words is unique and linked to our own previous experiences. An acupuncture needle, for example, elicits many different meanings, and this influences the outcome of treatment. How a patient feels about their problem is more important to me than an analogue pain scale or a measure of flexibility.

'E' MOTION

I often see folks with emotionally embedded traumatic experiences inside a physical pain, and if they know when the pain started, I will check out their memory as though it were a movie. I'll look at how big the memory movie is, how bright it is, what colours are involved, who was present, the clothes they wore, the sounds and the smells featured. Did their pain start suddenly or did it ebb and flow? Did it move and if so, in which direction? Just last night, a patient limped out of my office, then stopped and said, "Why did I do that?" It was the memory of the now absent pain kicking in.

Hand movements tell me a lot too. For example, I observe whether the hand movements are soft and flowing, or if they are tight and fast moving. The way we sit, stand, and walk, plus our body language and the way we move, are all like electronic programs running in our heads. 'E' motion is emotion in movement.

If we believe we can do something, that belief is echoed throughout our body language. Look at the way you're moving today – ask yourself what the cadence of your walk is like: fast, slow, hesitant, or whatever word you choose to describe it. Ask yourself also: what personality mode are you in? Think about it – would you say your tone is gentle or sharp? How loudly you are speaking? Is the person you are today angry, laughing, determined, or defeated? At what time today did you decide that this is what you are?

Reflect on whether you feel any emotion at this time, and think about what might be causing it. Ask yourself if you can identify where this feeling is, or if it begins at one point in your body then moves to another. Once you know what you are feeling – as well as why and where – decide whether or not it is useful to hang onto the feeling. If it isn't useful, change it.

POST-TRAUMATIC STRESS IS KEPT ALIVE BY THE STORIES WE TELL OURSELVES

When any of us are exposed to severe trauma, or emotional loss or pain, or the accumulation of too many small events, it is said that we suffer from PTSD, or post-traumatic stress disorder (Peres et al., 2007). The primitive part of the brain – the part of our mammalian wiring called the limbic brain – stores the emotion without a date. This means we can overlay recent happenings that trigger an old event, and the brain plays out the rawness of the original feelings as if it just happened (Kessler et al., 1995).

I see this day in and day out with patients in so many ways: old whiplash injuries give rise to current postural change and pain, and childhood abuse is very much reinforced by well-meaning counsellors and friends. This gives rise to current emotions, behaviours, and beliefs that have no grounding in current reality. Old traumas create a circular pattern of toxic behaviour not suited to our modern day lifestyle, and relationships, careers, treatments, and fitness plans all crumble because of a subconscious program running in our brains to prove an unconscious, toxic belief.

I have some dear friends who are so damaged by life that every time an emotion or situation even faintly mirrors the past events, their mammalian brain puts up a stop sign like a lollipop lady. This is a self-destructive action, to do with the story the mind has created around the past trauma – your subconscious keeps this damaging story alive, without conscious awareness. This is why it can be like talking to a tape recording, making many therapists fail. Listening to why we have no self worth, trust, love, and belief in others or ourselves may be reinforcing neural networks and emotional habits that keep the story working against our health.

I have patients and friends who subscribe to damaging narratives. One such harmful story is: I was not loved as a child, therefore I have to be promiscuous, I cannot sustain a loving relationship, and my belief that I am unlovable is true. Another is along the lines of: I had a bad childhood, therefore now I am in physical pain and nothing can be done. I am meant to suffer. Or another common belief is: it's my genes. I will always be fat. Nothing can be done. I am meant to be this way.

"Someday, maybe, there will exist a well-informed, well considered and yet fervent public conviction that the most deadly of all possible sins is the mutilation of a child's spirit; for such mutilation undercuts the life principle of trust, without which every human act, may it feel ever so good and seem ever so right is prone to perversion by destructive forms of conscientiousness" (*Young Man Luther: A Study in Psychoanalysis and History*, 1958).

HOMEWORK:
What stories do you play out to yourself?

Neurolinguistic programming questions the psychological approach to post-traumatic stress disorders. The psychoanalyst Hillman wrote, "The failure of psychotherapy to make clear its legitimacy has resulted in psychologies which are bastard sciences and degenerate philosophies" (Hillman, 2007). A little strong, maybe, though I understand where he's coming from.

Just like how having an understanding of how a virus affects the brain does not reduce the symptoms, understanding the origin of the trauma does not change its impact on everyday relationships; you also need action in the form of guided mind exercises, healing, and good nutrition. I like this practical response: "I recommend brain nutrients, knowing these would help regions in his limbic brain heal, which would allow new, higher cortical pathways to be established through other methods I would provide" (Perlmutter, 2011). I covered this approach in my earlier chapter on brain food

PAST LIFE HYPNOTIC REGRESSION

"Although I am a typical loner in my daily life, my awareness of belonging to the invisible community of those who strive for truth, beauty, and justice has prevented me from feelings of isolation."

—Albert Einstein, from "My Credo" 1932. AEA 28–218

I have been spoilt over the years by sitting with my closest friends and being shown shamanic and reiki healings. I have been taken on spiritual journeys – under light hypnotic trance or meditation – to discover more about who I am, to learn what stories I run to explain my behaviour, and to identify whose stories they really are.

I can clearly remember Lin – a dear friend of my recently departed friend June – coming over from Australia to spend time in meditation with June, and I was kindly invited to a session. They asked me to name a fear that I had, and to say what I wanted to achieve. They invited me to tell my story.

At that time we had all studied Brandon Bays' wonderful books on her journey from the diagnosis of her tumour through to her self-treatment. With this in mind, I explained the story I told myself about not being able to set my own clinic up full-time, and why I thought I could not leave the hospital. When they'd finished with me, I realised I had just told myself a story about it all, about why I couldn't and how it could all end up being a disaster. Realising I needed to tell myself a different story, I did, then I sailed my own ship and the rest is history.

We all need a nudge from our friends, otherwise we can seem to be too safe and comfortable with our ship in harbour, telling ourselves stories about how rough the sea is out there, even though we can't see it. Ships are designed to sail. Get my drift?

WE BECOME OUR STORIES

The many shamans I've met over the years still have great faith in story telling, sharing legends and beliefs of the traditions, and in essence, the soul of the village. Remember the danger of unhelpful memes creating a culture of robotic followers? When I studied biology, I learnt about evolution and how the brain evolved; then I would reflect on my childhood with its daily visits to church and the belief of creation and order. The place where science meets religion has always been a stormy one, and that's why I'm fascinated by the Dalai Lama's deep involvement in scientific research in America.

Life can be cruel, heartbreaking, unjust, evil, destructive, and unforgiving, as well as magically enchanting, inspiring, and loving. Notice how these words resonate with a different feeling in your gut and heart: learn to feel words in your body.

HOMEWORK:
Learn to feel words in your body. See how they alter your muscle tone, facial expression, and gut.

Kinesiologists believe that you express your subconscious reaction with simple motor tasks; your physical strength will ebb and flow with your thoughts and energy, or your chi.

HOMEWORK:
When you survive your next traumatic event, stop yourself before turning it into a story in which you are a victim. Change the script, find lessons in the event to help you change, and make it into a story of epic heroism, as this reshapes who your future YOU is. We cannot always change what happens to us, but we can change how we look at it, what we do with it, and the attitude we develop from it.

I have listened to – and continue to listen to – my patients' stories about their lives, and this is my starting point for developing an understanding of where their beliefs lie. Beliefs are very strongly hardwired. If their belief is that they cannot get better, they cannot change, I then ask them why they are here. Often it is to replay the story, to compound and reinforce the belief that nothing can be done. I ask them if they wanted to come or if someone else arranged the appointment. A friend or doctor may have sent them to get help, and this can mean that they're not ready for it.

HOMEWORK:
If you're thinking about seeing a therapist or doctor, what story do you tell yourself about the outcome? How about changing the story you tell yourself about what you want the meeting to accomplish before you make an appointment?

ARE MEMORIES OF PAST TRAUMA COLOURING OUR EMOTIONS?

"If you want to live a happy life, tie it to a goal, not to people or objects."
—Albert Einstein, quoted by Ernst Straus in French, Einstein: A Centenary Volume, 32

I mentioned before that psychologists talk broadly about two types of emotion. One type is healthy, normal cognitive emotion: formed in the moment, it is original and fluid, and occurs in response to stimuli. This healthy type of emotion – whether happiness, sadness, or anger – is often fleeting, measured, and appropriate.

However, instinctual emotions bubbling up in the more ancient mammalian brain can be toxic; a past event locked into an unhelpful emotion can bubble up with inexplicable and inappropriate consequences. The loop replays again and again, and the replay causes unpleasant verbal exchanges, which are unreasonable and unnecessary in the present.

HOMEWORK:
Can you identify any smouldering, draining, trauma-linked emotions that have hijacked what should have been harmless enjoyable experiences, ruining your passion for life or a relationship? Once you bring awareness to this, you can free the experiences from the connection and shoot the hijacker.

Hypnotic regression is a clever way to be able to get people to follow a timeline backwards and see what really happened, allowing them to then move through it and escape. I remember my friend Ken and myself taking June back to a previous lifetime, where she had a memory of being buried in a mineshaft. Under hypnosis, she spoke with a different dialect, and we worked on her escaping and moving through the traumatic end to her life. She awoke with a sense of something having changed in her perception of life, and she stopped using the metaphor of being a canary trapped in a cage.

I also remember working with a young woman who had come to me with backache, who was feeling lost, was out of work, and who was unable to summon the strength to go for interviews. Every time she thought of going for a job she felt like she was drowning, which was an interesting metaphor in relation to her history – when as a child, she had fallen into the ocean and nearly drowned. She had panicked and her body froze; she was unable to move. I regressed her and superimposed on her memory her taking action rather than freezing – kicking her legs hard to escape – and rather than her listless body being dragged out by her father-in-law, I got her to help him by kicking strongly.

After the light hypnosis and back work, she recovered completely. She went back to swimming, had a daughter, and led a normal life. If light hypnosis hadn't worked, I would have added NLP (neurolinguistic programming) techniques to make the memories of drowning smaller, as well as putting it in black and white pictures, running the movie backwards, and adding funny music. I would have followed up with in-depth questions of where her emotions and pain were travelling, and in which direction, and associated them with moving.

Building on this, I would then have given her anchors, tapping places on her body – like her hand – to hardwire positive reactions. It is important that instinctual emotions (in her case, near drowning) do not linger. Toxic programs take over our neurocomputer, causing us to waste precious years in what we believe to be a loveless, abusive marriage, or a worthless, boring job. Often it is the neural networks that we fire up to engage in our current lifestyle that we need to change, and we perceive our life through these neural networks. It is important to imagine what our lives could be like if we changed.

HOMEWORK:
Imagine if, like an actor changing the lines of a script, you completely changed your response to everything your partner or boss does for a day. This would raise important issues for you: what would your day be like? Who changed your day? Who is creating your tomorrow?

Remember that I talked about our neural networks being plastic, mouldable, and dynamic, like waves on the ocean? That's how mulling over things time and again can hardwire unhelpful toxic networks in our limbic brain. This can then create false instinctual emotional beliefs about life, fixing behaviour in unhelpful patterns.

My patients replay stories of their lives to justify their behaviours and pain – the shamans again would see this as their internal map playing out their life script. Children's brains are undeveloped and see the world differently, and we all developed from this state of being a child, which is why hypnotic regression is sometimes a useful tool to probe with. Trauma is not what has happened but how it is remembered.

Often the best time – and sometimes the only time – to go deep into the psyche and reprogram through hypnosis is after loss, fasting, trauma, serious illness, or deep meditation. In moments such as these, a superhero can step into the shoes of a victim. The prefrontal cortex is the area for enlightenment, and it is here that you can come to the realisation that you are the story writer not the book, that you are the creator of the stories and outcomes. You wield the pen and become an enlightened author of your own life.

Moving from old brain myths to rewiring new wisdom in the prefrontal cortex is not easy. My shamanic and reiki masters talked to me about thinking of this as a movie, and then changing the part or role you play in it: changing from victim to hero, escaper to explorer, and quieting the older fight and flight parts of the brain. Our experiences shape our brain; changing stories changes our mind. We have the basis of our genetic code, and this becomes greatly influenced by our lifestyle and the powerful stories that shape our actions and health.

When my father recently collapsed at his health club, overdoing it in the sauna, the friend who sat with him was a talented artist. He told me how he painted his emotions out, and he explained how he painted a series of pictures throughout his sister's illness and death, and that through this, he expressed the soul's journey. This active creativity allowed him to keep from being a victim. Father recovered that same day, however, so I put aside the paintbrushes I had got ready.

HOMEWORK:

Write a child-like story with a strong theme and characters, then imagine or write it as if you are one of the characters. Look for tone and beliefs that come into this version. If you are a victim or hero, rewrite it as the different character. Rewriting stories can be an insightful process in finding out how you colour a narrative with your own beliefs. What would you write?

ACUTE HEALTHY STRESS AND CHRONIC DAMAGING STRESS

Acute stress, it can be said, gives us the juice for excitement and makes us step up to the bar to achieve great things. Chronic stress, however, is unhelpful. The HPA axis is a posh name for the old mammalian alarm system: the hypothalamus and pituitary gland in the brain and the adrenal glands in the kidneys. Together, they alert the men at the fire station, start the engine, and make sure all are ready to deal with a blaze. With an imaginary fire, it's not a useful way to spend our store of energy; we use the budget up ahead of time. For those of you working in alternative medicine, the pituitary sits at the sixth chakra, and the adrenals at the second.

Another aside: Levine (1962) looked into how positive, loving exchanges helped to reset a genetically-set thermostat level in the hippocampus that has been fixed on stress, so get hugging to avoid brain rot now! If you think about it, we only use 5% of our DNA. What if – like taking different books out of a lending library – changing our lifestyle could alter the influence that the other 95% has on our active genes?

SHAMANIC DESTRESS, QUIETING HPA

In my last book, *The 4 Keys To Health*, I talked about the chakras, the spinning energy vortices in our light body. Much of a shaman's work is done with the connections between chakras and the human body. The shaman in me knows that you can create a sacred space anywhere and at any time by focusing attention and summoning the power of the four cardinal directions, mother earth, and father sun. It is to do with connecting with primeval energies, four being an important number (the biologist in me recognises that four DNA letters form our life code). Sacred space stills the ache from the fearful primeval brain and aligns the right vibrations of creative energy for inspirational focused healing and intelligent guidance.

I was taught about healing the light body in reiki and shamanic reiki. Shamans believe the light body to be an internal map, and by changing this, they can change diseases of the inner body and the happenings of the outside world. My psychic guru Ken would always say that it is important to work on your own mind first. All the answers are there. The shamans I have been fortunate enough to meet believe that if the light body is free of illness, the gifts of seeing the future, time travel, and healing are more powerful.

In *The 4 keys To Health*, I give examples of many different sacred spaces that I can create. The one I suggest in the next paragraph is a shamanic one, and you will find a shamanic invocation in my Soul book. I always like to create a scared space where I write, treat, or carry out healing work – the shift in energy is quite tangible.

HOMEWORK:
Create a sacred space, and sit or lie down: ideally the room you choose will be quiet. Then, call to the four corners: north, west, south, and east; hummingbird, cougar, serpent, and eagle. Then begin by inhaling through your mouth for a count of four, then exhale through your mouth for four and make a noise if you wish. You could imagine negative rubbish leaving you like exhaust fumes from a car, and healing light entering. Place your left hand on the heart chakra in the centre of your chest, then feel and listen to your heart drumming away. Next place your right hand below your tummy button over the chakra above kidneys, where the fight and flight adrenal glands sit; imagine you can feel an echo of your heart beat right inside this chakra. Tune in to the softness and slow pace of your breathing. This should help with your heart rate variance and stress levels.

It is so important to have practical methods of controlling chronic stress, because when we do not, the immune system suffers. Hormones restrict the prefrontal cortex blood flow and the hippocampus shrinks, making creative learning difficult. We become like cornered animals with muddled thinking. A study of stress in rats has shown that stress produces repetitive behaviour with less creative responses and reduced problem solving ability (Dias-Ferreira et al., 2009).

Chronic stress seems to be similar in human behaviour, driving us into a rut, with our faulty transmission reducing us to repetitive cycles of futile actions, like a wheel spinning in deep mud, driving deeper and deeper into the shit. As Robert Sapolsky, a stress neuroscientist at Stanford, says, "We are lousy at recognising when our normal coping mechanisms aren't working" (Sapolsky, 1992).

However, my daily run is said to increase the protection of my hippocampus, protecting creative thinking and memory – although I can't say the same for my poor back! Eating fewer calories also helps on my healthy days, when the lid stays on my chocolate biscuit tin. As mentioned earlier in this book, the clever brain cell fertiliser – that recognises when we exercise and when we eat fewer calories – is called the brain-derived neurotrophic factor (BDNF). This the key brain-protecting hormone and rewards us with more freshly made brain cells when we behave – when we eat less and exercise more.

YOGA DREAMING

It is possible to program yourself to remember your dreams. When you settle down to sleep, take some sips of water, then take a few slow, deep breaths and say what and who you would like in your dream. Ask yourself what question you would like to be answered while you sleep. When you wake up, take another sip of water, close your eyes and bring to mind any details of the dream. Ask yourself the same question when you wake up; you will recall how your dream has answered it.

Scribble down the details and answers in a journal by your bed then get up.

MEDITATION TO GROW EMPATHY

The 14th Dalai Lama, Tenzin Gyatso, is a bridge between spirituality and the world of science. Sadly, when he was invited to the annual 2005 neuroscience society, 500 members signed a petition to say that he had no place at a scientific conference. In a book full of his scientific dialogues he said, "Spirituality and science are different but complementary investigative approaches with the same greater goal, of seeking out truth" (Zinn and Davidson, 2011).

The Dalai Lama is fascinated with the brain's neuroplasticity, and it resonates well with the Buddhist wish that all sentient beings be free from suffering; his involvement in the mind and life institute over many years is testament to this.

The 2004 mind and life meeting honed in on the results of compassionate meditative states of eight experienced meditators. Davidson projected fMRI images onto big screens so the Dalai Lama could see the explosive activity of gamma waves in specific locations in the brain, especially in the right insula (the visceral mapping control centre), relating to empathy and maternal love, and in the anterior cingulate, where cognition, empathy, and decision-making takes place. Davidson showed that meditative training heightened a brain state known to be associated with perception, consciousness, and empathetic decision-making, with the effect being imprinting long after meditating stopped (Begley, 2009).

HEARING YOUR INNER VOICE

"I admit that thoughts influence the body."

—Albert Einstein, quoted by W. Hermanns in A Talk with Einstein, October 1943. AEA 55–285

Studies like those mentioned in the previous paragraph showed that practicing mindful meditation allows more positive brain patterns, inspiring better health and fewer anxious, stressed, and depressed thoughts. Mindful meditation can have a regulatory effect on the brain, especially that part of the cerebral cortex known as the insula. The Insula maps out our internal organs, and is tucked behind the frontal lobes of the brain. It maps our body's insides via circuitry linking to our gut, heart, liver, lungs, and genitals – every organ has a specific spot; paying attention to a specific part of our body builds somatic awareness as the insula ramps up the sensitivity. For example, tuning in to our heartbeat enhances our very sense of how we are feeling (Craig, 2002).

A good perception of how to look in on our body's health makes us self aware, intuitive, and insightful, as well as making us more likely to live a fulfilling, purposeful life by listening to our body's wisdom. Effective insula activity gives good emotional awareness of self and others, and the opposite of this is called Alexithymia (Bird et al., 2010), when we're unaware of our feelings and others – know anyone like that?

Our gut feelings are messages from the insula that amplify life decisions by guiding attention to intuitively better options – called somatic messages – from our body to our brain. The ventromedial prefrontal area, a key part of the circuitry, guides emotional, complex decisions. Listening to our inner body's wisdom is a key sat navigation system to our deepest sense of purpose and meaning, and is richly connected to our gut. This internal visceral control system is strong in people who have lived a life "well lived".

Mindfulness meditation is a great way to reduce the urges of flight and fight in the mammalian brain, as you observe your thoughts indirectly, as if in the third person. For example, by responding to pain differently by thinking objectively: 'Isn't it interesting that my mind has been alerted to knee pain?' rather than, 'Help, Ouch! Knee pain!'

Meditation is most easily started by focusing on breathing. When thoughts come, greet them and let them pass through. Practice drawing awareness to different parts of the body, and really feel them. Ask questions about the area. You can carry out a body scan for five or ten minutes to practice body awareness in a non-judgemental way – see if you can sense any messages in that part of the body. Increasing self-awareness in this way can increase the size of the insula in the cerebral cortex.

Some people react calmly to internal visceral sensations communicated through the insula, whereas others catastrophise and express reactions with heightened emotions. Mindfulness meditation has a regulatory effect on the brain, especially the insula, and too little attention to internal bodily cues can increase the need to use meditation in order to focus on sensations such as heartbeats to improve self-awareness. Too great a hyperawareness and this can be modulated down to a less anxious reaction to physiological changes in the body.

When focusing on your breath and body, you realise that thoughts come and go of their own accord, and that you are not your thoughts. Like a watcher within, observe as they come and go like waves crashing on a shore. You have the choice whether or not to act on these thoughts, as well as how to act. It is important to observe without criticism but with compassion. In order to regain control, you can catch the tail of a negative thought and throw it out.

MINDFULNESS HERE AND NOW

> "Strange is our situation here on earth. Each of us comes for a short visit, not knowing why, yet sometimes seeming to divine a purpose."
>
> *—Albert Einstein, from "My Credo", 1932. AEA 28–218*

Mindfulness meditation is very much about seeing the world in the present with greater clarity. Developing timeliness of measured actions will lead to achieving reasonable goals without risking your health to achieve them (Fredrickson et al., 2004; Ivanowski et al., 2007). Regular meditation improves both mental and physical memory and stamina has been examined by many, including Baer (2006) and Jha (2007). Unlike animals, we drive our mind into the past and the future, trawling through memories associated with our mood, and predicting the future in the same way.

I have talked about the ancient brain being honed by millions of years' worth of survival tactics, and you cannot stop these negative responses altogether, but you can lessen the impact significantly by developing awareness about what you are doing. It only takes a few negative thoughts to cascade into your mood and affect your health. Chronic stress and high blood pressure can be eased by looking at accepting a situation rather than responding to it emotionally (Low, 2008). Furthermore, feeling brighter helps the immune system fight off illness, shown by Davidson (2003) in a study of alterations in brain function and immunity.

I like to change my surroundings when I feel overwhelmed, as I know my mind will dredge up similar emotionally laden experiences if I stay in the same environment. My favourite place to blow off the cobwebs is my Norfolk beach; memory is often fired off in context, so that when I am by the ocean, there is little around me to remind my brain to activate memories of any problems at my clinics. Returning to the context of the beach reminds me of freedom and experiences charged with happiness (Godden and Baddeley, 1980).

I was taught to use this imagery of my beach as a safe place to go to – imagining myself in my favourite place – in meditation also. In this mindstate, I recognise unhelpful memories as just that: unpleasant propaganda. I also remember to stop allowing my amygdala to stay in high alert all the time; this causes me to rush from one task to the next with little focus on the here and now. I slow down and talk to the seals in my mind – they're not going anywhere in a hurry.

HOMEWORK:
Surround yourself with thoughts, bodily sensations, smells, sounds, and pictures that evoke pleasant emotions, and see what memories do and don't attach to you while you are doing this. Practice mindfulness meditation with these sensations – this is good practice at managing your emotions creatively, like mixing a palette of colours.

MIND YOUR POSTURE

HOMEWORK:
The body and the mind are inextricably linked, continuously working together to share emotional information with each other; much of what the body feels is directed first by a thought. Can you feel a connection between your body's sensations and your thoughts?

In return, our posture and muscle contractions can shape our emotions, a popular subject amongst psychologists. One psychologist called Michalak looked at embodied effects of mindfulness. He studied depressed people and those without depression by attaching reflective markers to specific places on their clothing. He then asked each person to walk in front of an optical 3D motion capture system. Not surprisingly, those suffering from depression tended to slump forward and move slowly, with less arm and upper body movement (Michalak, 2010).

I watch my patients walk into my clinic so I can get an idea from their posture and facial expressions what the consultation will be like. I remember Tony Robbins working an audience I was in, teasing depressives about body language to get them to realise that they had to get their body into posture in order to feel depressed. You can test these ideas informally yourself.

HOMEWORK:
Try having a competition with a friend or partner to see how many times you can smile in ten minutes. I think I will phone a friend – as my husband Mr Grumpy may struggle with this.

Meditation helps with problems, but not all problems can be dealt with in the same way. Some problems are best dealt with emotionally, whereas others are best approached logically, and yet other problems can be viewed intuitively and creatively. Some problems need urgent attention, whereas others need to be left until the future. When I was studying reiki and shamanic healing with meditation, I was told that once I'd practised for more than three months, I would start to see results slowly. Meditative practice is a slow burner.

HOW DO YOU PROCESS PROBLEM SOLVING?

I have many patients and close friends who have a history of depression; some of the most special and thoughtful people suffer from this. At least 10% of the population are being labelled as clinically depressed; that's no small number, and depression can affect people throughout their lives, even affecting youngsters – it is not just an old person's illness. If meditation helps ease this condition, it's well worth a try and costs nothing. The World Health Organization suggests that depression will be number two in the health burden ratings by 2020. It is currently 4th, and mental health represents 30.8% of total global disabilities (World Health Organization website).

Without meditation, a fifth of the number of people affected will remain in a state of depression for two or more years. Half of the people with depression will suffer it time and again.

I have friends who always see their therapist to talk over their depression, and it seems to me that they are analysing the problem to death. I have issues with this. Rational critical thinking looks at the gap between where you are and where you want to be. When you are in the doing mode, the problem gets broken down into manageable stages. This is great for dealing with survival issues, but using this way of thinking for depression can be a disaster – it just flags up how we are failing at bridging the gap between happiness and unhappiness. If you brood on emotional problems, you can end up feeling worse.

BEING AND DOING

Here is where meditation training about having awareness of your thoughts works. The nature of the 'being' mode is that it stops self-critical, negative, repetitive monkey brain chatter to observe patterns of thought. Living in 'doing' mode shortens our lives. Living in 'doing' mode is like driving at speed to a destination, completely unaware of any surroundings en route. It is like driving on autopilot with your mind ruminating on past problems and future problems, but with little awareness of the here and now, or of achieving useful activities in the present, however small they seem to be.

Consider that if you live solely in your head and not in your heart, not tasting life for most of your time, how much life do you have? I always think that life and longevity are about the quality of how we experience the world, not the quantity of years. So you can right now – just by changing the way you think you will increase your perceived lifespan.

Switching into mindful acceptance of being in the moment changes the inner watcher into one who is not judgemental. The person who developed in this way has no need to rush at solving a problem or urgently helping to change a person or situation. Acting impulsively to stop an argument begins a negative spiral, which can be avoided if you take a breath, step outside exhaustion, disappointment, frustration, and fear, and just acknowledge the experience unemotionally. We had some of this training in hospitals, because emotional reactions to a patient's physical needs can paralyse the ability to help in a crisis. The training was brutal and forced, to make sure the empathetic emotions were numbed down. Gentle mindfulness meditation is certainly a more intelligent way forward.

Ken Douglas – my UK meditation guru – would always say: first, still all emotions to gain clarity in a gap of peace, then decide from a position of strength and push on again. He would clamp his hand over my mouth in an attempt to achieve this. Humans seem to differ from animals in that we relive past events; we 'refeel' pain and 'prelive' possible pain. Unless one day animal fMRI proves us wrong, and my cats are stressing about last week's fur cut, or yesterday's supper, or tomorrow's weather.

You have to switch out of doing mode into being mode to tell yourself you are in the now. Memories are just that, part of the past; future predictions are just that too, of the future. Neither are the reality of the moment. I am guilty of existing too much in the doing mode – packing in sixteen-hour days of rushed work activities is normal for me. This leads to me struggling to find time for pleasurable hobbies that I deem less important, not valuing the impact I have on family or friends' lives, and always looking to the next hurdle to jump to help the greater calling. Too much focus on one part of who we are is detrimental to health and spirit.

I keep physically and mentally fit, eat good food – although usually standing and rushed – and I have great supplements. Yet my immune system suffers because of too much self-driven stress. My fascination for the power of the mind has kept me sane at times, as I know what I have to do in order to avoid deep exhaustion – I just have to bloody do it more often. It's called preaching to the converted. Meaningful work is a godsend to me, so I am very fortunate to be in businesses that add real value to people's lives, but even so, too much is too much. If I let my personal spiritual mindfulness slip, I start to slide into shutdown mode and illness takes hold.

THE SELFISH MEME

MEMES, our thoughts, create our future for better or for worse. I wrote about this in my earlier book, *The 4 Keys To Health*. However, I need to briefly reiterate this here, as I feel it is important to our minds.

When I was studying biology, the popular science book that was all the rage was Richard Dawkins' *The Selfish Gene* (1976). In it he discusses how ideas become fixed into easy memory pieces – which he called memes – and how this shapes the way we see the world. Memes are passed on like story telling from one generation to the next, and beliefs, such as the world being flat, become set in stone.

Like a virus, the meme infects a host and sits in the subconscious, and false realities are often absorbed this way. Marketing has always relied on social contagion and replication through the cultural network. In today's world, this is expedited by internet-led lifestyles. Rather worryingly, memes affect our behaviour and perceived quality of life, culturally sculpting our future, just like those parasites that hardwire the brain circuitry through imitation. Similar to genes, memes survive by connecting with other humans at all costs, which is why Dawkins used the phrase 'selfish genes'.

MINDFULNESS

Why do we need to understand mindfulness? If you are fortunate enough not to be one of the one in four who are 'mentally unravelled' (a great phrase Ruby Wax uses). It is still very important to understand how your engine works.

Think of it this way: when your car gets stuck in the middle of nowhere, and you call up the AA only to be told there is a long wait, how much better is it to know how to free the car yourself? So what you need to know in emergencies is how to deal with your pliable three pounds of play dough and stop it churning over the same ground, keeping you awake, regretting, resenting, and rehashing negative emotions.

You need a toolbox to retune your play dough engine, breaking old mental habits, and creating new flexible ways of thinking and learning-focused intention concentration. The engine can only work with a cleverly organised CPU. That's your brain – you have to repeat thoughts and actions over and over again to make the engine you want. You are the mechanic, so get used to it and stop blaming the weather and the fuel and the road conditions and the navigation system. If you know where you're going, you stand a chance of arriving there. Not being able to access your memory banks of wisdom is like losing the keys of your Ferrari.

TUNING THE MIND ENGINE

There are several ways that mindfulness helps us to deal with our brains becoming stuck. Here are some approaches to be in the present through the senses, through posture, and through movement.

Touch

When I need to come up for air, I pet my cats. When I'm writing, they're usually around, sleeping next to my desk. When I need to switch into a mindfulness mode, I really tune in to their energy, breathing rate, and the feel of their fur. Then I acknowledge my thoughts like waves on the beach and let them flow away.

Smell

Find an intense, evocative smell – I like my aromatherapy vaporisers. Draw the scent in deeply, notice thoughts, greet them, and then return to the smell and what it means to you.

Sound
Be aware of sounds and of their direction: left, right, ahead, behind. Tune in to the one you most want to focus on, then change your focus. Observe and release any other thoughts.

Taste
I choose a piece of dark chocolate, but it can be anything. Explore the texture with your tongue, let it melt on your tongue, and taste it. Notice when your chattering mind snatches attention away from this pleasure. Note where you go and why you hesitate to return to it. Reflect on how much of the experience you miss by not being in the moment and not laying down a memory of it.

Posture
Focus on your position, the placement of your feet and your shoulders, and what are you touching. Then greet your thoughts again before returning your attention to your posture.

Breathing
Notice your breathing pattern, and observe it. It is a weather forecast reflecting your emotions, like clouds in the sky, and it is often used as an anchor in meditation. Focus on your breath, and observe it without needing to change it. Again, as waves flow up onto the shore then ebb away, greet the thoughts then release them.

Body Parts
Focus on individual parts of the body and breathe into them. HeartMath uses the heart with a deeply content memory. Let yourself be aware of tension, temperature, or any other sensation.

ANCHORING THE MIND

"The true value of a human being is determined primarily by the measure and the sense in which he has attained liberation from the self."

– Albert Einstein Mein Weltbild (1934). Reprinted in Ideas and Opinions, 12

Ruminating on past or future problems is not living in the now, and this being able to focus now dampens down your primitive alarm system. Notice where your mind goes when it wanders. Return the ship to safe harbour. Park the car in the garage. Do not reprimand yourself; self-flagellation is not fun. Just be aware and refocus on a breath or a sense.

Strengthening your mind is like strengthening a muscle. You can create your future by making different decisions and choices in relationships and ways of communication. Put a time limit on unhelpful thoughts, and focus on the thoughts you do want, making sure you hold onto them. I've heard it said that it takes only ten seconds for a happy thought to become a memory. Like footprints disappear into the sand, as the thought takes shape it then dissolves, letting unhelpful thoughts go.

In a nutshell, mindfulness means paying attention in the present moment in a non-judgmental way. It means not changing emotions and feeling by force, just observing them with a different lens. Regulating your thoughts is like consciously operating a car rather than driving on autopilot; just like a car can't be in two gears at once, a mind can't be in two states or brain wave patterns at once.

"A happy man is too satisfied with the present to
dwell too much on the future."

—Albert Einstein, from "My Future Plans", September 18,1896. CPAE Vol.1, Doc. 22

DOING/WANTING MODE

The other day, it was raining. Everyone felt cheated out of a day in the sun on the beach or in the garden, so they wanted some quick fix therapy – buying stuff – and they drove to my old favourite city, Norwich. I was stuck in endless queues of traffic; I felt that I was stuck in wantingness. Car parks were chock full of happiness seekers, drivers were now angry and bored at queuing. They were overtaking, jumping lanes, dashing here and there to find a parking slot, trying to imagine where there could be a gap. The sun had come back out and they hadn't noticed. This is doing mode.

When we are in doing mode, we constantly check our emails, texts, phone messages, posts on Facebook, Twitter and LinkedIn, Google, weather reports, shopping lists of things you need or want, food, clothes, and on and on and on. This may sound familiar to you, and I have to confess to taking part in this too. Needing everything to happen at the speed of light and demanding replies to often unanswerable questions is an obsessive type of behaviour. This destroys being mode and long-term health. I wonder what Einstein would think of social media!

"Man owes his strength in the struggle for existence to
the fact that he is a social animal."

—Albert Einstein, from Address, October 15, 1936. Reprinted in Ideas and Opinions, 62

In my moments of being mode, I watch my cats crawl over my writing desk, desperate for attention. I watch my three-month-old niece sleeping. I plant seeds in the garden with my nephews. Focused attention is where magic happens.

HOMEWORK:

Make a mental note of what state you are in now. You may well be in automatic pilot mode, daisy chaining together lots of 'to do' tasks so that you barely notice anything around you. Memories are not laid down; time evades you. You are in doing mode.

Huge amounts of money are spent on face creams, diets, facelifts, and mind, body and soul books to help us live longer and look younger. Here's a key that is priceless: be attentive to life around you, rather than getting through it. If we live consciously, our life expands, and time appears to stand still like it did when we were children. We all live far too much in a doing trance, in a subconscious stupor.

HOMEWORK:
Take a few minutes out of every hour to do something consciously, registering how something smells, tastes or feels. Close your eyes and check if you can recall what clothes your colleagues are wearing and what mood are they in. Begin to master the way you think. You own a trillion gigabyte powered engine: your brain. Facebook, Twitter, and other social media feed our hunger for connectedness, but those connections can be remote, unloving, and untouching.

Buying stuff to achieve status is like being a Madame Tussauds' dummy, as Ruby Wax (an appropriate name for the context!) talks about it: one day you are famous and the next just some candles on a birthday cake, when you have been melted down for the next wax figure to take your place in the hall of fame (*Sane New World*, Hodder & Stoughton, 2013). Quick happiness fixes equal long-term breakdowns. Get real, folks. Put some savings in your bank of long-term happiness. Be the observer of your thoughts.

NLP UNTANGLED PERCEPTION

"I very rarely think in words at all. A thought comes, and I may try to express in words afterwards."

—Albert Einstein, quoted in M. Wertheimer, "Productive Thinking" (1959).

I found studying this subject fascinating. I can remember being told to imagine my thoughts on a screen in front of me; to imagine them running like a movie. Begin by sitting in the audience watching your thoughts play out on the screen, then take part in the movie, noting which part you always play and why. Take note also of who is with you; what the sounds are; whether or not you can add music, speed up the pace or slow it down, add colour, or change from colour to black and white. When you have done this, are you able to sit back in the audience again, and see it just as a movie?

I was taught these techniques by my dear friend, Ken, then I learned them again when studying to be an NLP practitioner. He used to say: ask yourself what character you are playing and why. He would tell me to stay focused right now on your clothes, friends, family, job, fitness, genes, and chemistry. Culture and special relationships give us the metaphorical clothes and personality of the character we play. Consider if you play different roles in different relationships, or at home or at work – if so, this may mean that you would like to be someone else.

AWARENESS

A couple of days ago, I had a writing day on – of course – my favourite beach. I was revisiting awareness practice, and I was surrounded by papers and books with stones holding them down as I stared out to sea. Reading out loud, I practised the technique: eyes to right, boat, red; eyes to left, sailing boat, white; behind irritating large crowd of day trippers, down to left empty miles of white sands. I used observation to get the hippocampus to lay down nice memories to increase my lifespan. Great, I thought; all in hand, I've got this off to a tee.

Then, after perhaps an hour or so of writing, a little boy with his family came up and asked, "Didn't the policeman evacuate you? Everyone has gone because of the bomb being carried off the beach this morning into the café." My mammalian brain said, 'Help, legs run, bomb!' My human memory banks said, 'Hang on, you are on your safe beach, and you don't usually have bombs here, so the little boy is just playing out a story.' I decided – with the growing confusion in my head – that I should at least explore, and sure enough I had not noticed an empty beach, empty car park, or a locked up café. My awareness had simply shut down. When I found him, the policeman said in a relaxed manner, "Keep to the building line: unexploded mortar bomb by your feet."

I rang my friend, Ivan, who owns the marram grass land around the beach, and as I was telling him about the bomb, I screamed because I just missed stepping on an adder. He didn't crash his car while listening to the mad ramblings of a seemingly mad woman, but instead he calmly said, "Just another mortar bomb, and considering you didn't see the dead body last month sitting next to your car for three days, I'm not surprised your amazingly bad awareness skills were again at work." Also, please note that the adder was unhurt.

Awareness is derived from a Greek word, horan – I see, I notice you are there. Mindfulness, as I noted earlier in this chapter, is about paying attention in the present moment, in a non-judgmental way; not trying to change things, just observing what is happening. You can observe with a different focused lens.

When I look into waves and relax, I see them transforming, dispersing, and dissolving – not facts and truths, just splashes of water. Trying to regulate my thoughts has always been difficult; like a car, we cannot be in two gears at once, so I practice getting into the gear I need to achieve the outcome at that time. fMRI showed me that the memory centre, Mr Hippocampus, cannot operate successfully unless I focus and do not multitask. Focused attention grows neurons in the hippocampus; novelty, not boredom, leads to thicker neuron clusters, so focusing on the waves breaking on the beach is a good brain exercise.

Our hairy ancestors had their brains wired for survival; they could not afford to stop and smell the roses as that could mean they were sandwiches for a passing predator. I am guilty of constantly dredging up worrying memories and it only succeeds in rotting my brain. Doctor Aaron T Beck in the 1950s is said to have pioneered the branch of practical psychology called cognitive behavioural therapy (CBT), which is all about getting patients to observe their thinking patterns and question them. This approach is supposed to help unlock dysfunctional moods and relationships. However, in 1991, alongside Phil Barnard, Teasdale developed a mind theory he called 'interacting cognitive subsystems'. Teasdale says that the mind can operate in multiple modes, each responsible for processing new information on both an intellectual and cognitive level.

From this theory, mindfulness-based cognitive therapy (MCBT) grew. Developed by John Teasdale, Zindel Segal, and Mark Williams, mindfulness-based cognitive therapy is based on the mindfulness-based stress reduction program designed by Jon Kabat-Zinn. John Teasdale studied cognitive therapies for years and developed MBCT as a viable and effective form of treatment for the prevention of depression relapse. This treatment combines traditional cognitive behavioural therapy with mindfulness and other contemplative therapies. John Teasdale reported fewer relapses in depression with MBCT and has the research to back it up. In one such piece of research, the conclusion was that MBCT is an effective and efficient way to prevent relapse/recurrence in recovered depressed patients who have three or more previous episodes.

The experiment used recovered recurrently depressed patients whom were randomised to treatment as usual (TAU) or TAU plus MBCT. Replicating previous findings, MBCT reduced relapse from 78% to 36% in 55 patients with three or more previous episodes; but in 18 patients with only two (recent) episodes, corresponding figures were 20% and 50%. MBCT was most effective in preventing relapses not preceded by life events, and relapses were more often associated with significant life events in the two-episode group. This group also reported less childhood adversity and later first depression onset than the three-or-more-episode group, suggesting that these groups represented distinct populations (Teasdale et al., 2008).

DISTORTED THINKING

Ruby Wax has developed some good pointers on distorted thinking, and here are some ways of approaching distorted thinking that I have adapted from her work. Thank you, Ruby, for your honest and inspiring contribution to mental health. Get her book (*Sane New World*) or see her talk, guys.

HOMEWORK:

Look at the ten ways in which our thinking can be distorted:

1. You can only see black or white outcomes, ignoring shades of grey (no pun intended).
2. You overgeneralise, for example: every time I breathe, my back hurts. Every time?
3. Are you called a half glass empty person?
4. You quickly give reasons why a positive scenario could have problems.
5. You jump to a negative, wrong conclusion before hearing all the evidence.
6. You magnify a bad experience beyond reason because of the mood you are in.
7. You believe idiotic suggestions without questioning them.
8. You are harshly self-critical beyond reason.
9. You give yourself false and very negative names and labels.
10. You personalise every disaster as if you were there and it was your fault.

I think I can say yes to everything on the list when I am tired.

TRAFFIC LIGHTS

A bit like the approaches I use in my *Four Keys To Health* book, there has been some work done with kids on mindstate. In this way of working, teachers have a traffic light approach with cards, not keys. A red card means 'I am in a melt down, stay away'. Yellow means 'I am reversing or coming down from a melt down'. Green means all good. If the child is holding a card up in response to something the teacher has taught or said, she/he has a chance – perhaps at another time – to help the child understand what the trigger was and how to get out of red with taught tools.

If we are trying to learn and see a red light, our memory shuts down, because there is too much stress juice in the brain and less activity of new cells in Mr Library, meaning that generally there is much less oxygen getting in there. Rafael – my four-year-old Yorkshire nephew – got very upset imagining that he might struggle with getting his coat off at his new school. Buttons and ties worry him. He was at the red traffic signal, crying a lot and going red in the face. This took place in his head at home, months before he went to his new school. This then gave his clever mum – who is qualified in psychology and is a maths teacher – time to get rid of this emotional fear before he went.

HOMEWORK:

Whenever something nice happens, chew it over in your head for at least 10 seconds; your brain needs this time to lay down a positive memory. Positive memories are like Teflon, they slip through; negative memories are like treacle, they stick around. Minimise the repetition of negative memories, and replay happy ones time and again, focusing on the details of them. Rewire, redecorate, and refurnish the rooms in your head.

HOMEWORK:

You may want to try practising mindfulness with a friend using this exercise. Sit down opposite them and really focus on them, noticing the colour of their eyes, their mood, their clothes, and their posture. Then close your eyes and remember these details. Ask them if they felt more listened to when you did this – if they feel a better connection. Consider whether or not either of you were surprised by the results of the exercise.

Just like Albert Einstein (1879-1955), I did mirror writing and did not speak much when I was a kid, as I was very introverted (I still treasure my solitude even now). Today, the practical applications of Einstein's theories include the development of the television, remote control devices, automatic door openers, lasers, and DVD-players. Recognised as TIME magazine's 'Person of the Century 1999', Einstein's intellect, coupled with his strong passion for social justice and dedication to pacifism – and his wonderful quotes – left the world with infinite knowledge and pioneering moral leadership. Well, there's still time for me to catch up…

He was one for empathy, and when I think of Einstein I remember reading the following quote from him: "[A human being] experiences himself, his thoughts and feelings, as something separate from the rest… This delusion is a kind of prison for us… Our task must be to free ourselves from this prison by widening our circles of compassion to embrace all living creatures and the whole of nature in its beauty."

> "Everything is determined… by forces over which we have no control. It is determined for the insect as well as for the star. Human beings, vegetables, or cosmic dust—we all dance to a mysterious tune, intoned in the distance by an invisible piper."
>
> *—Albert Einstein, quoted in interview by G.S. Viereck , October 26,1929. Reprinted in "Glimpses of the Great", 1930*

TIMETABLES

The trouble with our focus on phones and computers is that the art of paying attention has been lost. I am more than aware that while I am typing up my patients' notes, I am not paying full attention to their body language. We work with 'to do' lists and timetables, writing events in, scheduling appointments, and generally deciding what will happen before it does; thinking about future events while in a current meeting or scheduled event.

Thoughts and life are meant to be more like my ocean, droplets of consciousness spraying and crashing up onto the shore and falling back into the vastness of the ocean, which is like the universe. My late grandma would say to me: every drop counts, says the little mouse, who weed into the sea. That never inspired me to think I was making a big difference in the big scheme of things.

"Strenuous intellectual work and the study of God's Nature are the angels that will lead me through all the troubles of this life with consolation, strength, and uncompromising rigor."

—Albert Einstein, to Pauline Winteler - July 3,1897. AEA 29–453

Darwin (ol' Mr Evolution) – after stealing Wallace's work because he could, as he was a higher class –has a lot to answer for. Did you know Darwin was just on the boat to be an upper class companion to the captain? Rumour has it that he pissed off the ship's doctor/biologist, who left the ship, and then he created a role for himself with the aid of Wallace's research. Darwin bangs on about the survival of the fittest being the most successful, adaptable, and ruthless species. There are a lot of Darwinian humans at the top of their tree, after having stood on others – I know I've met a few, and interestingly, they often tend to be lonely and unhappy, after trying quick fixes of happiness and trying to find meaning. They become furious if illness and pain affect them, but money can't remove it. There are no pockets in shrouds – mind you, it is nice to be miserable in comfort.

The Ferrari of life runs in the heart: by being able to love, care, focus, and control emotions, and by being alive. The autopilot approach to 'to do' lists of boring jobs is death to imagination and happiness. We now know anger thins and ages the grey matter, and conversely, the sensory visceral centre linking brain to tum (anterior cingulate cortex) thickens in mindful mediators. Thanks to fMRI, we are able to identify how mind and body work together.

HOMEWORK:

Write down your daily 'to do' list, and think carefully about how much of it you are consciously enjoying, how much thrills you, and how much fills you with dreadful boredom and worry. Get my point?

THE LANGUAGE WE USE TO DESCRIBE ILLNESS AND PAIN

There is still a mystery surrounding lifestyle and pain. Let's just note first that pain and suffering are not the same. There is a stupid misconception that somehow our illness is someone else's responsibility and that someone else can cure it, and we practitioners have to talk responsibility because we are shaping a patient's perception about health and pain. Patients come to me with *déformation professionnelle*, which is the distorted way their professionals have deeply influenced and shaped their beliefs about themselves over the years. They bring not only their illness, but also this bag of tricks that you have to know how to field or prepare for attack. You have to sense, understand, and use their system of metaphors and meanings that dominate their lives not yours, then you must reframe any medical advice in terms that they can make sense of.

I recently started seeing a few big business-type patients at Harrogate and realised that my gentle, unpushy shamanic approach was as alien to them as a hot summer is to an eskimo. I initially found them nearly impossible to deal with, as they had led destructive and ruthless lives buying whatever and whoever they needed. The shaman in me felt repulsed, but the saint in me said regroup, use their language, and understand their values. I had to work my conscious brain hard, adapting my language to their needs. They were busy, intense, needy, and untrusting, and they inflicted upon me their values and expectations of practitioners, who in their eyes were ruthless moneymakers who would fail to cure them.

I read Cecil Helman's book, *Suburban Shaman* (Hammersmith Press Limited, 2006), and contacted my dear friend, Ken. I was told to change my language. Keeping ideas from these two sources in mind, I then talked to my patients about investing in a long-term bank of health; that there is a need to invest in your body to get a payoff of better health; and that it is profitable for the body to operate at a rich level of health. Communication is key to understanding, and awareness of how another individual sees the world is essential if you need someone to take your advice. If your values and beliefs are not aligned with the person you are trying to help, then rethink and change your language. That's what I did, and it worked. I found the gentleness and the trusting, caring nature in their soul beneath their brittle exterior.

PAIN AND MEDITATION

Here is a collection of brief summaries of a few of the studies Ruby Wax highlighted in her recent book, *Sane New World* (Hodder & Stoughton, 2013).

- In a study at Wake Forest University, a pain response was elicited with a laser. Doing an intense meditation programme of twenty minutes, four times a day, meditation beat morphine to reduce pain at a rate of 57%, using the brain's own opiates.
- Toronto and. Exeter University found that an eight week mindfulness programme improved happiness, and on scanning, was shown to activate the left prefrontal cortex.
- The immune system improved after eight weeks of mindfulness training at the University of Wisconsin. This was tested by injecting the flu virus.
- The University of California looked at longevity and mindfulness, and somehow showed an increase in our ticking clock – the telomere – which sits in our genes and determines life expectancy. It would be strange at Christmas if in a cracker you got your time of death rather than a crappy joke; if you don't change your life, this is your funeral date.
- Harvard University suggests we spend half our time daydreaming about lots of negative shit that could happen to us, and this occurs in the medial area of the cortex. Meditators showed that medial prefrontal cortex activity shifted to the lateral area, which brings focused attention back to a wandering mind. Wow, so meditating could give you a 50% shift in worrying about yourself. Also, there was an increase in hippocampus memory activity and the anterior cingulate cortex, which is known to put the brakes on stress.

Good old fMRI saves killing the subjects to find these things out.

Remember my terrible awareness experiences in Norfolk? Now, every time I run, I practice it, as otherwise I don't see cars. Have a picture or stopwatch or something, so that every time you see or hear it, you practice awareness. Or link your reminder to do this to an everyday task, like cleaning your teeth or cleaning the house.

Kabat-Zinn teaches us to focus in on the changing, malleable landscape of pain, so here's an exercise to help you switch from doing to being mode:

HOMEWORK:
Think about what you are hearing and from what direction the sound is coming. Ask yourself if it is annoying or comforting, and think about what you want to continue hearing. Reflect on your other senses: on what you can see and where it is; on how you are standing or sitting, and on how this position feels.

HOMEWORK:
For those of you who suffer from pain, feel the sensation rather than blocking it. Note what happens if you move and stretch: does the pain move, swirl, or travel in straight lines? Where did it come from and where does it go? What happens when you imagine breathing into it, breathing love and light and nurturing it, and feeling it melt like an ice cube in hot tea? Focus on what you were feeling and doing when the pain melted.

MENTAL GEAR SHIFT

Are you in doing or being gear? My fluffy cats teach me being mode. In the midst of writing, they cover my desk in wet paw prints and stamp on the keyboard. Their angelic blue eyes say, 'Hello, remember me? I am here too!' When I go out for my jogs, I chuckle at the zombie mindstate people walk in, blissfully unconscious, memory banks blank, with their telomere clocks speeding up.

Focus like a laser beam when it is necessary. Lay down memory, be in the moment, then at other times, float, drift, and daydream, but be in control and shift gear appropriately. All gearshifts are needed, and all have their use.

For me, painting, walking on my beach, scuba diving, and playing guitar badly all get my creative juices flowing and reduce my stress juices. It is like recharging my batteries, ready for 'doing mode' activities.

HOMEWORK:
Write down if you're in doing mode or being mode when you carry out certain tasks. Life expectancy is a fascinating topic, isn't it? Watch kids: they play in the moment, they don't ruminate about yesterday's play being better or tomorrow's play being boring. If you want to know how long their day is, get them to draw it, as well as their week. My point is that if you add 10 minutes of mindfulness to every day, you have lived another hour at the end of the week. If you doubled this time, you have doubled your perception of the length of your life. Being aware and conscious lays down memory.

I rarely get more than a day not working, and usually in that day I am writing because I enjoy it, so I practice visualisation and awareness when I remember; I am a willing student, but I need a lot more practice. I look at a clock and think about the power of manipulating time. Don't be asleep at the wheel of your life. I enjoy teaching as it turns subconscious techniques into conscious, it stops my 'to do' list of treatments, and it turns laziness, low energy, and low memory into innovative, inspiring twists on the same old threads.

HOMEWORK:
Stop! While you are reading this, take note of what is happening around you. If your answer is lots of stuff, then this book may be boring you.

Stress pushes our buttons, wanting us to find the well-trodden paths. Computers, tablet computers, and smart phones have inadvertently turned us into lazy zombies, letting technology think for us.

Lara has just jumped up onto my desk, whiskers twitching, ears back, sensing and tasting her world. She can sleep most of the day, as she's lived more than I have in that few moments in her cat world. My father's ninth decade is in only three years' time, but he still runs in the gym, swims, drives, cuts his own lawns, and says he doesn't want to hang out with old people. He can make his last years memorable, for as long as his conscious brain wants, and as long as life is pain-free and fun. Mother loves her healing, her crystal shop, and interacting with others, and again this fills her mind with purpose and interest, and extends her perception of life. We talk about the importance of the mind nearly every day. The brain waves alpha, beta, gamma, and theta allow healing, focus, and rest, all in good measure.

HOMEWORK:
Write with the other hand, drink from the other hand, prepare food, or eat consciously. Think about the tastes and textures, and ask your stomach to digest the food kindly. Drive with awareness of your surroundings and other drivers. Remember the route. Take snapshots on your phone – even if you delete them later – so that you can go through your day, identifying the highlights and considering any improvements you might make next time. Reinforce the happiness feeling. Water plants, think about what the water will do, think about if fertiliser is needed, and feel the leaves; if you close your eyes, can you remember what the plant looks like?

MOTIVATION

This driver is the difference between where we are and where we want to be. To achieve and grow is healthy; however, unrealistic goals cause stress. Drugging up the brain is not a healthy way to escape having your foot jammed down on the accelerator pedal.

UNRELENTING QUEST FOR ANSWERS

Humans are hardwired to seek answers. Some questions, however, have no answers, and we go round and round in circles getting more anxious, and being deluded into thinking that if we just get more information, we can work it out. Learning to let go and feel comfortable with saying 'I don't know' is important. Knowledge can be used as jousting by academics, and I have often been at the sharp end of that game. Only last week I was seen as a failure to another practitioner because I chose not to carry technical information in my head that I could look up in seconds.

Many years ago, I made a conscious choice to delegate a lot of skills and information to people I employ. If you are comfortable in your own skin, then you realise that none of us are here for hundreds of years, so thirty years of experience will give you only a tiny sliver of life. Connectivity and asking for help is a strength, not a weakness. At school we are wired to believe that we should remember academic facts and pass exams, or fail in life. In business, we do fail if we have a head full of useless academic facts but no knowledge of business experience.

SKYLA'S BRAIN AT 3 MONTHS

While I've been writing this book, my niece was nine months in the womb and three months outside. She has completed 12 out of the basic 24 months of brain development, and when she was born, she had a seriously undercooked brain. As babies, we poop and pee without control, and scream for ages, because we can – ha ha! But babies can't focus or communicate with language, and you can't get away with that behaviour as an adult.

In her first sixteen months, Skyla will develop her accent; if Auntie spends too much time with her, that will confuse the hell out of her language cells. By the time she is three years old, her ears, tongue, and mouth should be equipped to cope with any weird language. Skyla's emotional, attachment-bonding right brain grows fastest up until eighteen months. After this, the left brain fires up to grow more to accommodate cute baby language. Then the perception of I – of who I is and does and behaves – starts to kick in.

Babies will start crawling and interacting with the sensory environment; the motor and sensory parts of the brain will dance to paint a picture of Skyla's world for her and lay down the early belief systems of her world. Skyla studies my face closely, watching the facial muscles and looking to imprint emotion as the right and left hemispheres develop and link. Close bonding is important, so that a baby is able to imitate movement, facial expression, eye contact, emotion, and later on, words. All this wires into my niece's nervous system, cascading biological reactions deep in her brain, and growing it constantly.

My sister-in-law, Sara, often holds Skyla in her left arm or close to her tummy, with her left eye close to Skyla's right, and vice versa – this gazing is said to help link up the eyes, heart, brain, and emotion. Social and emotional learning are sculptured through every minute interaction, and loving looks build up an army of opioids and happy memories.

It makes me sad to think that so many children do not experience this, and that they rarely recover and find peace. Adults who find it difficult to have healthy relationships and keep friends may not have had a loving childhood. Adults who yearn for attention, to be needed, to act on stage, and to be comedians often honed their craft from despair and a lack of self-love stemming from childhood. The face of the carer is important, because the baby is processing fear, and understanding how to deal with it; a carer's expressionless face may lead the baby to suffer from depression as an adult. Michael Meaney's research showed that a mother's behaviour can switch off genes in the baby (Weaver et al., 2005).

Our future emotions are shaped by our parents, hardwiring our beliefs about ourselves and other humans. Just like robots, the brain assimilates bytes of information to build the big picture, and just like a jigsaw, the meaning maker within us chooses where to place the pieces. I often wonder whether, if I hypnotised my parents while they are doing a jigsaw, I could make the pieces invisible.

HYPNOSIS HOLDS THE KEY

There is only one brain, one mind. However, for training purposes we choose to say we have two, a subconscious and a conscious. I spent time learning trance, because it is proven to help with healing – I was taught as part of a NLP practitioners' course and then my dear spiritual gurus helped me further.

My trouble is staying here in the now, as I keep disappearing off into Snazzyland. It is said that if you can make your own limb go rigid (cataleptic... don't be rude, please) or relax a major muscle group, then you can help to induce healing in yourself. On many occasions when my mentor, Ken, led a meditation, and at times during June's reiki work, I could not move a muscle. I think they were grateful that I was still!

We would get June to hallucinate a Pac-Man going through her body, helping with all her pains. This is about linking up to the subconscious in order to attend to any healing issues. Erickson would write that patients are patients because they are out of rapport with their unconscious... once in rapport... [they] are in control of their destiny.

"Hope is both the earliest and the most indispensable virtue inherent in the state of being alive. If life is to be sustained hope must remain, even where confidence is wounded, trust impaired."

—*The Erik Erikson Reader, 2000*

"What was Freud's Galapagos, what species fluttered what kinds of wings before his searching eyes? It has often been pointed out derisively: his creative laboratory was the neurologist's office, the dominant species hysterical ladies."

—*The First Psychoanalyst, 1957*

There are different styles of hypnosis, many of which have funny names: Erickson, indirect-permissive, Estabrooks, authoritarian, and all sorts in between. I love the way some monks direct the management of subconsciously driven systems; it really does emphasise that what we think makes us well or ill. Deepak Chopra talks a lot about research into the mind and quantum physics, and the impact on every cell in the body: our immune system eavesdropping on our internal dialogue. The pictures and emotions that you select to pay attention to all affect the brain juices and neurochemistry throughout the body, constantly affecting the immune system.

What is real about this mind body link? Shamans would say that nothing is real, whereas Zen Buddhists would say that reality begins with the mind's perception. An example is people with multiple personalities: in one personality they feel pain and have high blood sugar, but not in another. Immediately, there is a measurable difference between the two personality states. This has been tested.

BRIEF SUMMARY OF THE HISTORY OF HYPNOSIS AND HEALING

The hypnotic trance for healing has been around for a very long time – since the early shamans, in fact. Egyptian papyrus scrolls show sleeping temples and the use of trance for healing, and India's healing temples have ancient Sanskrit writings about trance. Red Indian shamans also used trance.

I find it fascinating that magnets were also used, especially as magnetic resonance is now used for scanning and healing; Paracelsus, a Swiss doctor in the 1500s, used magnets in healing. Greatrakes, the great Irish stroker (steady, ladies) in the 1600s, used massage and magnets. In 1725, a man named Hell taught a chap called Mesmer how to wave a magnet over a bleeding cut to stop it. Later, it was shown that an ordinary stick would do the same thing, so Mesmer talked about the effect of the placebo response and 'magnetic energy' coming from the patient. Mesmer had excellent results with his trance work, but he upset the French authorities. Lavoisier, Benjamin Franklin, and Guillotine – on the French board of Inquiry – called him a fraud and denied that energy healing even existed, and this ban on healing and hypnotism went on from 1795 to 1985. In 1864, Braid did 500 operations using hypnotism. Bernheim and Liebert opened a school for hypnotism, Freud being one of the students.

Freud's use of cocaine caused all sorts of problems with the treatment of patients, and although at first he used touch, he became afraid that ladies would sue him for misconduct. Therefore, with Breuer, he invented no touch talking therapy, abandoning hypnosis in 1896. A few hypnotic sessions were exchanged for hundreds of talking sessions – for the rich only.
In Britain, Bramwell wrote in-depth about the history of hypnosis in 1903. Meanwhile, across the ocean, Americans were working on patients' susceptibility.

Twitmyer (1902) wrote about a knee jerk without a hammer touching the skin. Boris Sidis wrote the psychology of suggestion in 1903, and Russian scientist Pavlov experimented further with suggestion in 1904. Then later in 1943, Hull – an American – pushed for both hypnosis and suggestibility; he proposed that in a hypnotic trance, suggestion is much more powerful. A well known student of his was Milton Erickson.

Another leading light in hypnosis was Estabrooks, who had a more direct approach. Elman used a rapid inductions approach, and in 1957, Weitzenhoffer wrote about general hypnotic techniques. Le Cron in 1964 made ideomotor finger movements popular in NLP and hypnosis. I vaguely remember during an orthopaedics examination week, and feeling a little merry in a restaurant in London, being shown the hypnotic finger technique by Gordon, a clever, amusing, slightly drunk Scottish doctor. He said that this technique should be part of every doctor's repertoire, although I'm not sure his fingers should have been pointing in the way they were!

Zeig and Rossi wrote a lot about modern day workings of hypnotists, especially Erickson and Estabrook. It's crazy to think of all these names, with everyone standing on each other's shoulders, only to say what the shamans knew for thousands of years before them!

TRANCE: WHAT'S THAT?

We all spend a lot of time in a trance-like state without realising it. We do it while driving, watching television, and any time we become passive. Interestingly, the unconscious is actively storing lots of information at this time, and it can be a very useful relaxing state, uncritically absorbing information. Rapport between a healer and a patient opens the door to entering someone else's mind, and trance is a state we need to be in to be able to be hypnotised. This is very handy for hypnotherapists, because they can input lots useful data, like driving sheep through open pens.

I was put into trance on training courses in many different ways, with many involving awareness of my breath, then with true statements with hypnotic suggestions sandwiched in. Bandler, like Erickson, would talk us into trance using ambiguity in any representational system. This excites our subconscious and we open a direct channel to it. Ken, my old mentor and friend, would approach trance in this way at times, using sentences such as these: "I know that you are wondering... and it's a good thing to wonder... because that means you are relaxing... and relaxing all your body... all your body… you can learn… and you can… you know you can… and it's so much nicer than… you can learn everything now… or in the next few days…" Running one sentence into another, not finishing sentences, assuming knowledge, and assuming the client has expectations or feelings almost as if they have told you… and bam! You are shifting into trance.

Ken would tell us to weave everything the client says and does into the conversation, and affirm what they say and do with 'that's right' or a similar phrase. He very seriously told June and I one night, should one of us snore or trump, to weave it in. We couldn't stop laughing at this, much to his disgust. Pay close attention to everything the client does, he would say, and talk about it to them. It strengthens rapport.

We learned to sit opposite each other on courses and match our breathing rate, body language, and posture, and when the person was drifting into trance we would encourage them with, 'That's right'.

META MODEL OF QUESTIONING

With NLP, we were taught to dig a little with questioning, and to ask someone to give all the reasons why they felt they needed help. NLP stresses the importance of eliciting the client's strategy for having their problem or a diagnosis: to see if there was any trauma or anxiety attached to the first happening of the problem; to hear how it affects their lifestyle; to look into relationships and any influence, and very gently around childhood; and to seek out hidden truths and also gain trust as they slip into trance.

Once a client is in trance you can open a dialogue with the unconscious mind, to ask it to help in solving the problem. You are actively synchronising a dance together so that you can get to talk with the elusive subconscious. Skilled hypnotists can loosen your model of the world, challenging beliefs, ambiguities, implications, and puns, and activating new associations and mental mechanisms. I remember Bandler would tell stories in a similar way to Erickson, with hidden metaphors and imbedded commands and suggestions, with open loops at points of peak interest and with targeting the subconscious to dive into certain states.

Tony Robbins and Joseph McClendon were experts at putting the audience into trance, and their fire walk was an incredible example of this. I never failed to be amazed by them whilst watching the crowd. Except for Mr Grumpy, who came in after the trance work on a UPW event and said I am not walking on a f***ing fire.

HOMEWORK:
Finger Vice. Get your chum to clasp hands in front of you, then point up two forefingers an inch a part. Then discuss a vice around them, turning your hands in front of them. You can ask them to notice what is happening to your fingers.

HOMEWORK:
Helium Balloon and Book. Here is an exercise to show how our minds and bodies work with even the mildest of suggestions. Close your eyes and place your hands out in front of you. Imagine that on one is placed a heavy book, whereas to the other is attached a helium-filled balloon. Imagine what is happening to your hands because of the difference in weight: one hand being lifted up, while the other is being pulled down. Open your eyes and look at where your hands are.

If you get to be really good at this kind of practice – like Dr Esdaile's clients did in the 1800s – you could have an operation without anaesthetic. Some clients took 300 lessons to go deep, but that takes a lot of patience. Dr Esdaile could assist at the severest operation with the patient's pain relief being just 'mesmerism' hypnosis (Esdaile, 1846).

HOMEWORK:

Arm Levitation. I remember doing this for an examination. Match your breathing with a friend, speaking to them ideally on their in breath to get their arm to raise. That is, using words to describe the position of the arm on the lap and then lifting the arm. Then on every out breath, use suggestive relaxing words to deepen the relaxing trance. Keep matching their breath movements and either use matching out or in breath commands, suggestions, and ambiguous questions. We then asked questions connecting with finger movements or arm. You can get scripts for this in books or on courses.

My spiritual gurus would say we have in our head all the resources we need to heal. We would work with shamanic reiki or angelic healing, and converse with the subconscious mind to ask if it could heal a specific problem and how long it needed to do it, as it may have a pretty full agenda of more pressing issues. Erickson says it eloquently: "Can your unconscious mind get in touch with the blueprint of perfect health and healing that exists in the higher self and transfer it to the blueprint that the unconscious mind uses to create the body?" (James, Flores and Schober, 2000).

Dowsing is a tool I sometimes suggest to friends to open the connection, either using it ourselves or getting the client to use it. Holding the pendulum, with the elbow resting on a table, ask a direction for yes, no, and maybe, then ask some questions.

To avoid letting our unconscious mind get fixated on disease and negative dark thoughts driven by media exposure, my recommendation is that you work at all times with your unconscious mind and remind it of its highest purpose of preserving the carbon unit – the body – to achieve its greatest good.

Ray Kurzweil wrote an inspiring book, *The Singularity is Near: When Humans Transcend Biology* (Penguin Books, 2006). Kurzweil predicts that with the ever-accelerating rate of technological change, humanity is fast approaching an era in which our intelligence will become increasingly non-biological and millions of times more powerful. This will be the dawning of a new civilisation enabling us to transcend our biological limitations. In Kurzweil's post-biological world, boundaries blur between human and machine, real and virtual. This is already happening. In that case, how would we die? Would our consciousness sit in a machine that would house our soul? What meaning would life have?

"Only a life lived for others is a life worthwhile."

—Albert Einstein, quoted in the New York Times, June 20,1932 AEA 29-041

The Mind's Eye, picture by Snaz

SUMMARY

"The art of medicine consists in amusing the patient while nature cures the disease."

Voltaire

The old dogma of the unchangeable adult brain has been challenged with scientific proof, thanks mainly to scanning technology. My late great uncle raised enough funds to get one of the earliest scans into the Queen Elizabeth Hospital in Birmingham, and he had to suffer a lot of distrust from the medical profession while he did it. Now it is a mainstream diagnostic tool, and the brother to the technology I am endeavouring to get the UK to embrace.

I have discussed how outdated, long dormant, and disused brain networks will be ripped out/deleted, just like my friendly Zimbabwean electrician rips out disused cables and wires when he upgrades all my circuit boards at home and at the clinics. Contrary to older western medical beliefs, we now understand that the brain can and does repair damaged brain zones. Moreover, in contradiction to science dogma of years gone by, the brain can use areas previously delegated to another task to grow new neurones. Even more impressive, they can do all this into the 8th decade of a person's life.

Some of the early mind mapping wrongly believed that activity zones were carved in stone, and therefore unchangeable, and I discussed arguments for and against this. We are wired to keep exploring, to connect with others, and to deepen our understanding of the environment and our existence. We are meaning makers, driven by a sense of need and a lack of having stuff. We share our understanding and knowledge in stories to strengthen our wisdom, building on the shoulders of previous generations.

Evolution has always driven competition and a fight towards the most successful survivor. Be a leader; leaders create leaders, not followers. Just like the film *Groundhog Day*, we must not get complacent, as through constant improvements, we grow and feel more fulfilled. This was echoed in so many of Tony Robbins' and Joseph McClendon's seminars, and every time I presented on Z factor, I learnt how to do it better the next time.

At the time of writing, I have treated approximately 10,000 patients – just through the Wolseley practice alone – and every day I study a little more to see how I could do better. This knowledge is then ready to pass on in my teachings and in these books, distilling the best thoughts, advice and experiences to date, and understanding that misunderstandings are our most painful but greatest teachers.

One of the best pieces of advice I've ever been given was to never lose sight of the core of who you are and where you are going. I also remember the advice from a successful Hay House writer who asked, "If you were to write three minutes of a song about your life, what words would you put in?"

HOMEWORK:

Look at the above question. Would the words you used be what your heart or your head wanted to say? What would sum up the core essence of your soul, and what meaning do you put on yourself? Who are you? What have you changed through being here? I am known for saying: "What do you want people to say about you at your funeral?" How about how you touched the lives of others? How you made them feel? What epitaph will you leave behind? Do people get you, do they know who you are and were? Can others understand what you are about? Write your epitaph now, as if it were a eulogy being read out at your funeral by a close friend.

Woody Allen once said that 80% of success is showing up, and I would add that deciding what you want before you get there is also essential to a successful outcome. Life for me has been a heavy rush of meeting peoples' needs and wants as best I can within their values, beliefs, and time commitments. It is a never-ending driven need to explore humanity and healing, with a constant struggle to adjust the life balance – I want to let family and friends know how much I love and care for them, and I want to smell the roses along the way.

I find that I achieve the most when I can be on my own and when I can think through all my experiences. I share those that I feel will benefit others, both through writing and presenting, and of course, I internalise those that give me my personal meaning of existence. I often look back on my running footprints on my favourite beach, seeing how fast they disappear – it's always a sobering but realistic view of so many of our actions. For instance, the deeper ones take more waves to dissolve them. I look at the direction and stride length and realise how these physical actions sculpture my motor and sensory parts of my brain.

If I chose to make this a greater skill, I would laser focus and repeat and repeat. Then I would close my eyes and think through the running action. However, being an expert on sand running is not high on my agenda, so I slip into autopilot and give my memory banks a rest. With fMRI, we now know that just thinking about doing something will change electrical activity in the brain. One brain cell can fire 5 to 50 times a second, and our firing combinations consist of 10 to the millionth power, which is just mind boggling.

I looked in detail at how our brain works – where we hear, see, feel, and remember – and all within the reptilian, mammalian and human and computer bits. I touched on somatic mapping with fMRI, reducing the need to carve up brains to watch brain activity. Like the monkey experiments, you move a finger and the brain lights up in the area which is responsible. Lose the finger and another area swaps roles. Neuroplasticity is a modern discovery, telling us that we grow brain cells until we're in our eighties, and it has been proven that we can show less dementia if we are creative and enthusiastic about life.

Our thoughts are like splashes of waves on the beach, transient tides. Our neural networks connect via chemical synapses, allowing messages to pass between brain cells and to enter specialist areas of the brain. We are electrochemical beings, as our electrical signals hit a sea of chemistry and enter the next cell with a docking, lock and key mechanism. Fascinating.

I spoke about physical or mental repetition being linked to building survival skills, and being adapted for sporting expertise. Learning means repetition. My pain professor would say, "Repeat the skill a thousand times, then talk to me about needling." Nerves that work together fire together, and when we learn something new, the docking station at the end of the nerve receives an electrical signal and morphs in order to improve firing specificity and time. This means that your new skill is transmitted faster.

Alan was driving through Leeds the other day and could not remember the streets around his old university. I gently pointed out that he did his doctorate there 40 years ago, and the brain would have little recall. Like other things, it was a little dusty due to lack of use. I remember a back surgeon once saying to me that he liked his fellows to have done a thousand operations – not just one or two – and that he considered a robot an answer until human competence was safe enough. He actually built a robotic device to help, but this did not go down well in ego land – and no, I don't mean lego land!

There is no substitute for dedication and disciplined repetition of an activity, hence my stroke victims who repeatedly worked on moving and speaking in small baby steps, chunking the activities into manageable, bite-sized pieces.

Memory is not a DVD, it is fluid – it melts every time it's played and reshapes as it goes. Lawyers use memory techniques to manipulate witnesses, while therapists using the Havening technique can ease traumatic memories. We know our genes shape us to a certain extent, however, I discussed how early experience of emotional connections with parents can sculpture our future beliefs, our intellect, and our relationship skills. So, parents – love your kids!

People suffering with depression, anxiety and OCD can be taught how to bring awareness to unhelpful thoughts. I talked about physical pain being a diversion to mental, emotional pain (tension myositis syndrome), and how important it is that the therapist recognises the complexities of physical injuries layered on top of each other, and how touch can rewire traumatic memories. I also talked about how early memories are held in different parts of the brain, and embedded in sensory and emotional stimuli. This is the only type of memory we have before we're four years old, as the library – the hippocampus – is not built at this age. I touched on early parental separation, and the behaviour and emotional responses to this throughout life.

I looked at meditation, and about how Buddhist monks teach us the importance of practising compassion in meditation. Buddhists believe the mind has a formidable power of self-transforming the brain; a well-known scientific monk, Matthieu Ricard, stated that mental training through meditation allows us "to identify and to control emotions and mental events as they arise".

Meditation is all about this – and nurturing new qualities – until they become integral parts of the mind. We cannot control the outside world (for example, the weather), but we can control how we react to it, by how we transform that experience. I talked about meditation being a tool for the fusion of neuroscience and psychology, called 'cognitive science'. The Dalai Lama's Mind & Life Institute in California dedicates a lot of time and money to researching the brain/mind link, and as the Dalai Lama said, "Spirituality and science are different but complementary investigative approaches with the same greater goal of seeking the truth." He also added, "By gaining a deeper insight into the human psyche, we might find ways of transforming our thoughts, emotions and their underlying properties so that a more wholesome and fulfilling way can be found." Their research on the adaptable, irreversible wiring of the brain adds importance to knowledge of mindfulness techniques.

This relatively new science fascinates me; it's such an empowering feeling to know we can re-sculpture our brain's abilities and handicaps by changing our thoughts.

As you've been reading this book, I hope you have taken a look at my nutrition notes, and please always check with medics if combining supplements with prescribed drugs. Please eat healthily for your brain, especially good fats, omega oils and D3.

I hope you enjoyed the journey I shared with you on the mind, on how it was once thought to be hardwired, and that if damaged or poorly skilled, it was wrongly thought to be an unsolvable problem. We know now that it isn't unsolvable – it is a puzzle we can work out in order to better our health. I hope you smashed these dogmas, and any incorrect beliefs you previously held about your health, whilst you carried out your homework in this journal. It should empower you to have a healthier, happier life – something we all deserve.

I lost the physical presence of my spiritual guru and closest friend whilst writing this book, and the words spoken at her funeral – even though falling on only a few ears – were breathtaking. Her young carers were sobbing, as they'd witnessed a selfless, caring and strong soul – who had survived a crazy long time in a destroyed body – go through total organ failure. She would reach out to them to heal their needs, to hold their hands until she could not raise her own anymore, and I am hopeful they will carry that torch of humanity in their hearts for all of their future patients. She would say to me in the days before she died that she could not go if there was work to be done, and I told her to go as her body could not sustain any kind of quality of life. She promised that she'd find a way to work with me beyond the grave, and she does.

If you enjoyed *The Four Keys to Health* or the Mind volume of *The Human Garage*, keep an eye out for my second volume about my physical, practical techniques, embracing both old and new physical medicine – especially those I teach. The third volume, never before divulged, tells of my journey and experiences as a shaman.

FUTURE BRAIN

Right now, evolution is taking place outside a biological system, and an intelligence assistance is being developed to listen in on our conversations and access vast amounts of data to help us.

Ray Kurzweil, a major contributor to artificial intelligence who holds 19 honorary doctorates, has worked endlessly on the mystery of the human brain, and his latest brain model is pattern recognition, showing that we possess in the realm of 300 neuron modules in a hierarchical system wired to recognise specific patterns (Kurzweil, 2012).

His many lectures and books touch on some key subjects such as:

Right now, 3D printers are making the framework for human replacement organs, which stem cells infiltrate.

Synthetic cortices are being made that can connect through gateways to the brain, expanding the 300 million pattern recognition system in the neocortex to billions.

IBM is working with Nuance's Clinical Language Understanding to make master diagnostic and medical consultants.

Medical technology will be a million times more powerful in 10 years, so let's take a snapshot in my next book – all about the Body – on where physical medicine is in 2015, before it's so out of date.

In 2015, science and spirit have come together, and they now know that you hold the chisel to carve out your future, according to your thoughts and actions. It is up to you; it is in your hands.

HOMEWORK:
Go and create your future life.

ACKNOWLEDGEMENTS

I want to thank my parents for their enthusiasm and for encouraging me to fill my life with books.

For my husband Alan's patience at my stubborn persistence to write these books into the early hours after my clinics.

I want to thank Jessica, my friend and editor, for her patience at my last minute decisions to add bits and reframe and change right up to the last minute.

For Tanya for her typesetting craft to polish the look of the book.

Jessica Coleman's Editing Website: www.colemanediting.co.uk

Tanya Bäck's Typesetting/Design Website: www.tanyabackdesigns.com

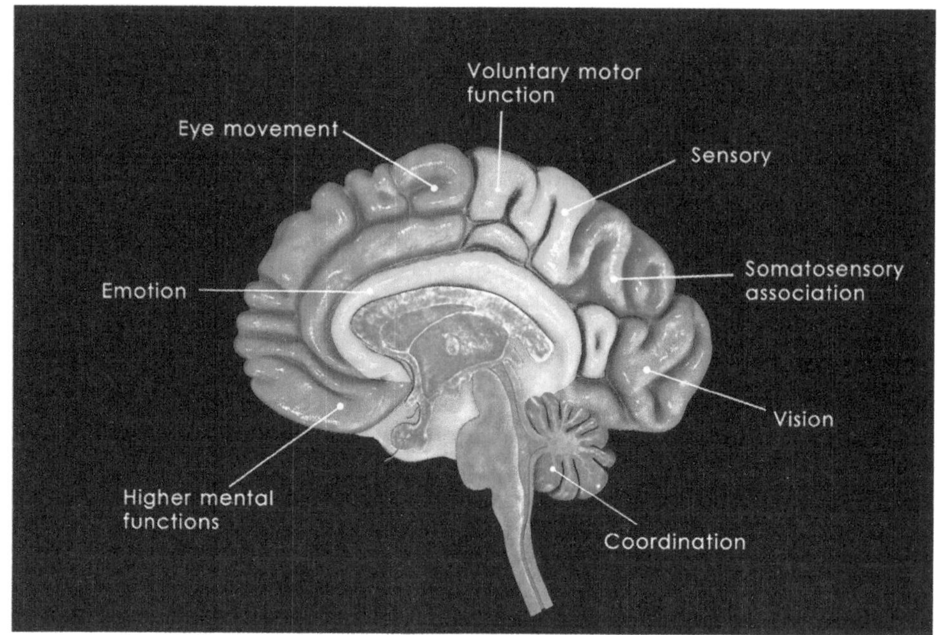

Brain functions

Median section of the brain

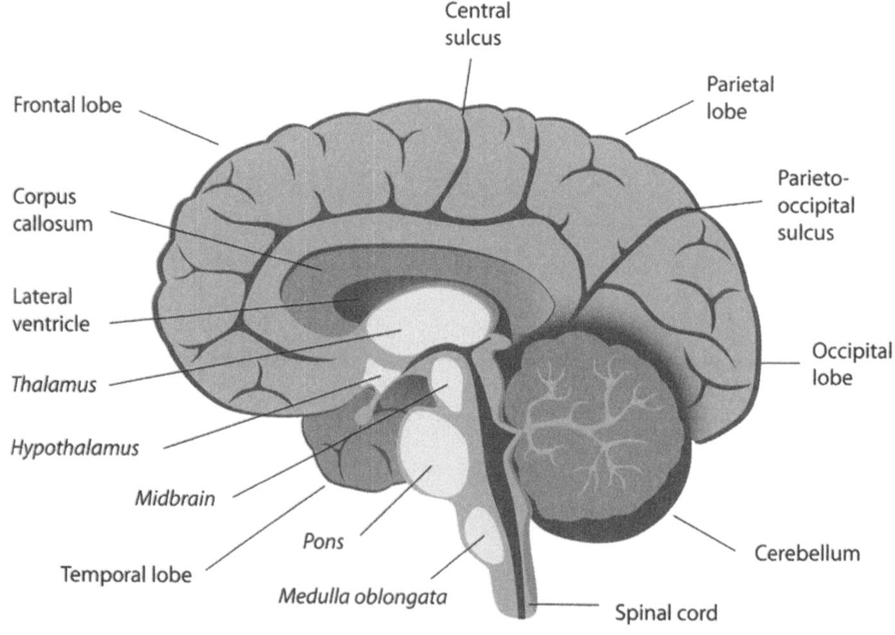

Mid-section anatomy

GLOSSARY

ACTION POTENTIAL: is a short-lasting event in which the electrical membrane potential of a cell rapidly rises and falls, following a consistent trajectory.

AXON: is a nerve fibre, a long slender projection of a nerve cell that conducts electrical impulses that are carried away from the cell body and translated into chemical ones to carry instructions across the synapse between the axon and dendrite of two adjacent neurones.

BASAL GANGLIA (OR BASAL NUCLEI): comprise multiple subcortical nuclei, which are situated at the base of the forebrain. Basal ganglia nuclei are strongly interconnected with the cerebral cortex, thalamus, and brainstem, as well as several other brain areas. The basal ganglia are associated with a variety of functions including: control of voluntary motor movements, procedural learning, routine habits, eye movements, cognition and emotion.

BDNF – BRAIN DERIVED NEUROTROPHIC FACTOR: a protein miracle growth for the brain, helps with new brain cell growth.

BRAINSTEM: is the posterior part of the brain, adjoining and structurally continuous with the spinal cord. In humans it is usually described as including the medulla oblongata (myelencephalon), pons (part of metencephalon), and midbrain (mesencephalon).

CELL: is the basic structural, functional, and biological unit of all known living organisms. Cells are the smallest unit of life that can replicate independently, and are often called the "building blocks of life".

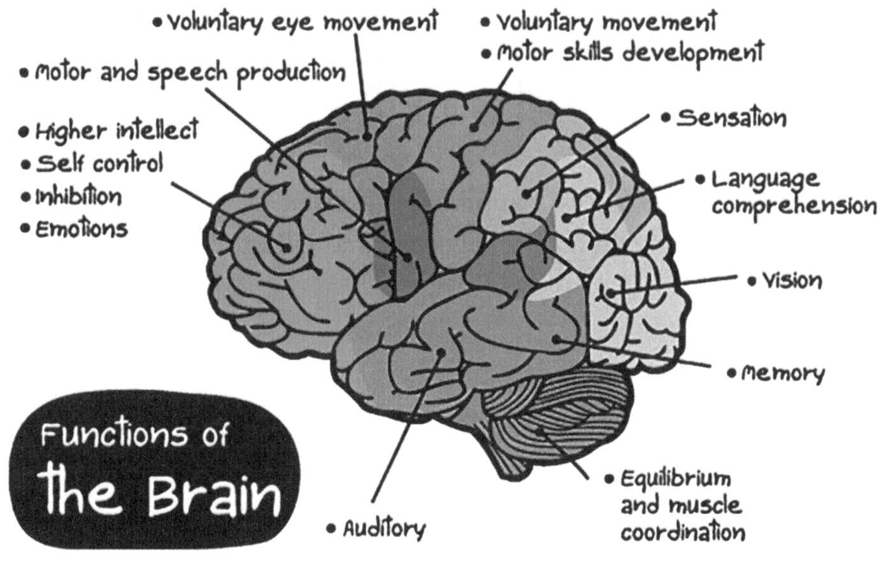

Brain functions

THE LIMBIC SYSTEM

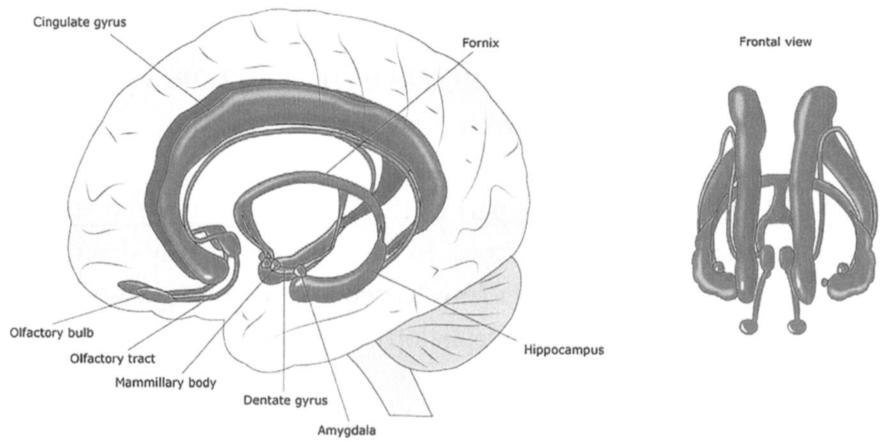

Limbic/monkey brain

CENTRAL NERVOUS SYSTEM: is the part of the nervous system consisting of the brain and spinal cord. The central nervous system is so named because it integrates information it receives from, and coordinates and influences the activity of, all parts of the bodies of bilaterally symmetric animals.

CEREBELLUM: a small, dense part of brain containing half of the brain cells, integrating sensory and autonomic motor function, rhythm and blues centre for movement, memory, language, and emotion.

CEREBRAL CORTEX: is the cerebrum's (brain) outer layer of neural tissue in humans and other mammals. It is divided into two cortices, along the sagittal plane: the left and right cerebral hemispheres divided by the medial longitudinal fissure. The cerebral cortex plays a key role in memory, attention, perception, awareness, thought, language, and consciousness. The human cerebral cortex is 2 to 4 millimetres (0.079 to 0.157 in) thick.

CEREBRUM (LATIN FOR *BRAIN*): refers to the parts of the brain containing the cerebral cortex (of the two cerebral hemispheres), as well as several subcortical structures, including the hippocampus, basal ganglia, and olfactory bulb.

CINGULATE GYRUS: also known as limbic cortex, this is a part of the brain situated in the medial aspect of the cerebral cortex. The cingulate cortex includes the entire cingulate gyrus, which lies above the corpus callosum, and continues in the cingulate sulcus. The cingulate cortex is part of the limbic lobe.

CONSCIOUSNESS: is the state or quality of awareness, or of being aware of an external object or something within oneself. Defined as: sentience, awareness, subjectivity, the ability to experience or to feel, wakefulness, having a sense of selfhood, and the executive control system of the mind.

CORTEX: six cells thick of outer grey matter, this is the highest evolved area of the brain and does rapid computing.

CORTISOL: the primary long-acting stress hormone helps mobilise sugar.

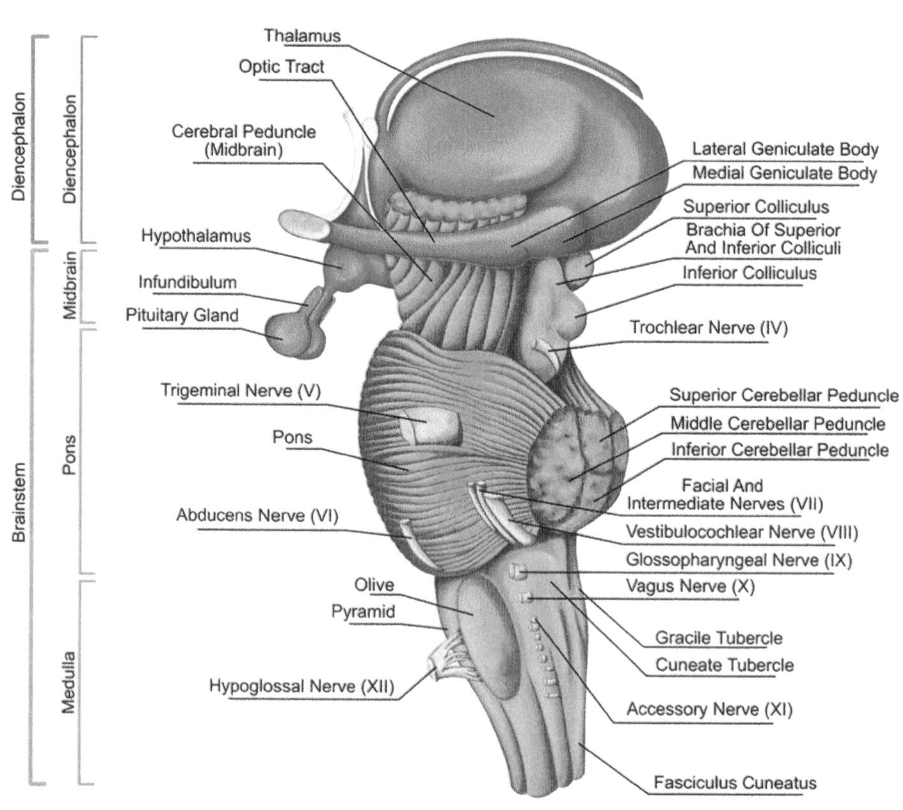

Brain stem/reptilian brain

High concentrations break down nerves and muscles.

DENDRITES: the branched projections of a neuron that act to propagate the electrochemical stimulation received from other neural cells to the cell body, of the neuron from which the dendrites project. Electrical stimulation is transmitted onto dendrites by upstream neurons along their axons via synapses which are located at various points throughout the dendritic tree. Dendrites play a critical role in integrating these synaptic inputs and in determining the extent to which action potentials are produced by the neuron.

DOPAMINE: a neurotransmitter key to moving, cognition, and pleasure.

ENDORPHINS: natural morphine-like hormones, they block pain signals.

EPINEPHRINE (ADRENALINE): released when stressed. Neurotransmitter in brain and hormone released from adrenal glands.

GAMMA AMINOBUTYRIC ACID (GABA): inhibits over activity of nerve cells.

GLUTAMATE: excitatory neurotransmitter of the brain.

HIPPOCAMPUS: one of two structures in the brain that produces its own cells. Like a librarian, it gathers data from everywhere, cross references new data with memory, and bundles it together, sending it to the prefrontal cortex for processing. It has a close relationship to cortisol and is easily damaged by stress.

HPA AXIS: stress control by signals between hypothalamus to pituitary to adrenal.

HUMAN GROWTH FACTOR: controls fuel allocation to brain cells vital to growth and anti-aging.

HYPOTHALAMUS: a small gland that signals the pituitary to release hormones to direct biological imperatives, i.e. sex drive.

LIMBIC BRAIN: a complex set of brain structures located on both sides of the thalamus, right under the cerebrum. It is not a separate system but a collection of structures from the telencephalon, diencephalon, and mesencephalon. It includes: the olfactory bulbs, hippocampus, amygdala, anterior thalamic nuclei, fornix, columns of fornix, mammillary body, septum pellucidum, habenular commissure, cingulate gyrus, parahippocampal gyrus, limbic cortex, and limbic midbrain areas.

MAXIMUM HEART RATE: the limit a heart can beat in a minute. Take your age from 220 for a rough idea of yours.

MEDULLA OBLONGATA (OR MEDULLA): is located in the hindbrain, in front of the cerebellum. The medulla oblongata is a cone-shaped neuronal mass responsible for multiple autonomic functions ranging from vomiting to involuntary functions such as sneezing. The medulla contains the cardiac, respiratory, vomiting, and vasomotor centers and therefore deals with the autonomic (involuntary) functions of breathing, heart rate, and blood pressure.

MIDBRAIN: is a portion of the central nervous system associated with vision, hearing, motor control, sleep/wake, arousal, alertness, and temperature regulation.

MOTOR NEURON (OR MOTONEURON): is a nerve cell (neuron) whose cell body is located in the spinal cord and whose fiber (axon) projects outside the spinal cord to directly or indirectly control muscles. Motor neurons are efferent nerves that carry signals from the spinal cord to the muscles to produce (effect) movement.

NANOROBOTICS: the emerging technology field creating machines or robots whose components are close to the scale of a nanometre (10^{-9} metres). More specifically, nanorobotics refers to the nanotechnology engineering discipline of designing and building nanorobots, with devices ranging in size from 0.1–10 micrometers and constructed of nanoscale or molecular components. The names nanobots, nanoids, nanites, nanomachines, and nanomites have also been used to describe these devices currently under research and development.

NANOTECHNOLOGY: engineering on an atomic scale.

NEUROEPINEPHRINE: a neurotransmitter that affects arousal, attention, and mood. It also sharpens the sympathetic nervous system to be alert.

NEUROGENESIS: the process of stem cells dividing and developing into new brain cells.

NEUROLINGUISTIC PROGRAMMING (NLP): is an approach to communication, personal development, and psychotherapy created by Richard Bandler and John Grinder in California.

NEURON: is an electrically excitable cell that processes and transmits information through electrical and chemical signals.

NUCLEUS: is a cluster of densely packed neurons, located deep within the cerebral hemispheres and brainstem. The neurons in one nucleus usually have roughly similar connections and functions.

PARASYMPATHETIC: one of two divisions of the autonomic nervous system, the other being the sympathetic nervous system. The autonomic nervous system is responsible for regulating the body's unconscious actions. The parasympathetic system is responsible for stimulation of "rest and digest" or "feed and breed" activities that occur when resting – especially after eating – including sexual arousal, tears, urination, digestion, and defecation. Its action is described as being complementary to that of the sympathetic nervous system, associated with the fight-or-flight response.

PITUITARY GLAND: sits under the hypothalamus and secretes controlling hormones.

PONS: is part of the brainstem, and lies between the midbrain (above) and the medulla oblongata (below), and in front of the cerebellum. This white matter includes tracts that conduct signals from the brain down to the cerebellum and medulla, and tracts that carry the sensory signals up into the thalamus.

PREFRONTAL CORTEX: this is the last to evolve and is what makes us human. It is concerned with working memory and decision-making.

ROBOT: is a mechanical or virtual artificial agent, usually an electro-mechanical machine that is guided by a computer program or electronic circuitry. Robots can be autonomous or semi-autonomous and range from humanoids such as industrial robots, medical operating robots, patent assist robots, dog therapy robots, collectively programmed *swarm* robots, UAV drones such as General Atomics MQ-1 Predator, and even microscopic nanorobots. By mimicking a lifelike appearance or automating movements, a robot may convey a sense of intelligence or thought of its own.

SENSORY NERVE CELLS: are nerve cells that transmit sensory information (sight, sound, feeling, etc.). They are activated by sensory input, and send projections to other elements of the nervous system, ultimately conveying sensory information to the brain or spinal cord.

SEROTONIN: a neurotransmitter, this is the policeman of out of control moods, calming us down.

SPINAL CORD: is a long, thin, tubular bundle of nervous tissue and support cells that extends from the medulla oblongata in the brainstem to the lumbar region of the spine.

STEM CELLS: undifferentiated cells that can develop into new cells. Fibroblast growth factor and vascular endothelial growth factor help this.

SYMPATHETIC NERVOUS SYSTEM: nerve cells that connect the brain to the body, activated by norepinephrine in stressful situations.

SYNAPSE: a structure that permits a nerve cell to pass an electrical or chemical signal to another neuron. It is the junction of the axon and the dendrite of the brain cell. Electrical signals turn to chemical across the synapse then back to electrical.

THALAMUS: is situated between the cerebral cortex and the midbrain. Some of its functions are the relaying of sensory and motor signals to the cerebral cortex and the regulation of consciousness, sleep, and alertness.

BIBLIOGRAPHY

CHAPTER ONE

Barrat, James. *Our Final Invention: Artificial Intelligence and the End of the Human Era.* Thomas Dunne, 2013.

Blackmore, Susan. *The Meme Machine.* Oxford University Press, 1999.

Crick, Francis. *The Astonishing Hypothesis: The Scientific Search for the Soul.* Simon & Schuster, 1994.

Damasio, Antonio. *Descartes' Error: Emotion, Reason and the Human Brain.* G.P. Putnam's Sons, 1994.

Damasio, A.R et al., 2000. 'Subcortical and Cortical Brain Activity During the Feeling of Self-generating Emotions' *Nature Neuroscience*, 3, 1049-56.

Dawkins, Richard. *The Selfish Gene.* Oxford University Press, 1999.

Dehaene, Stanislas, Sergent, Claire and Changeux, Jean Pierre, 2003. 'A Neuronal Network Model Linking Subjective Reports and Objective Physiological Data During Conscious Perception' *Proceedings of the National Academy of Sciences*, 100, 8520 – 8525.

Han and North in Hanson, Rick. *Buddha's Brain.* New Harbinger, 2008.

Judd, Lewis, 1990. *Peer To Peer*, vol 2, 10.

Kandel, E.R, 1998. 'A New Intellectual Framework for Psychiatry' *American Journal of Psychiatry*, no.4, 155.

Kocsis, B and Vertes, R.P, 1994. 'Characteristics of Neurons of the Supramammillary Nucleus and Mammillary Body that Discharge Rhythmically with the Hippocampal Theta Rhythm in the Rat' *Journal of Neuroscience*, 14, 7040-7052.

Kurzweil, Ray. *Are We Spiritual Machines?: Ray Kurzweil vs. the Critics of Strong A.I.* Discovery Institute, 2002.

Kurzweil, Ray. *How To Create A Mind*. Duckworth Overlook, 2012.

Kurzweil, Ray. *The Singularity Is Near*. Viking, 2005.

LeVay, Simon, 1991. 'A Difference in Hypothalamic Structure Between Heterosexual and Homosexual Men' *Science*, Nov 1.

Lewis, M.D, 2005. 'Self Organizing Individual Differences In Brain Development' *Developmental Review*, 25, 252-277.

Lewis, M.D and Todd, R.M, 2007. 'The Self Regulating Brain; Cortical-Subcortical Feedback and the Development of Intelligent Action' *Cognitive Development*, 22, 406-430.

Lutz, A.L, Greischar, N, Rawling, M, Ricard, and Davidson, R, 2004. Long-term Meditators Self-induce High-amplitude Gamma Synchrony during Mental Practice' *Proceedings of the National Academy of Sciences*, 101, 16369-16373.

Moravec, Hans, 2009. *Scientific American Journal*, March 23.

Newton, Michael. Journey of Souls: Case Studies of Life Between Lives. Llewellyn Publications, US, 2002.

Panksepp, Jaak. *Affective Neuroscience: The Foundations of Human and Animal Emotions*. Oxford University Press, 1998.

Pare, D.R and Pelletier, J.C, 2002. 'Amygdala Oscillations and the Consolidation of Emotional Memories' *Trends In Cognitive Sciences*, 6, 306-314.

Pease, Allan and Pease, Barbara. *Why Men Don't Listen and Women Can't Read Maps*. Orion, 2001.

Peters, Steve. *The Chimp Paradox: The Mind Management Programme to Help You Achieve Success*. Vermilion, 2012.

Rasia-Filho, A, Londero, R and Achaval, M, 2000. 'Functional Activities of the Amygdala; an Overview' *Journal of Psychiatry and Neuroscience*, 25, 14-23.

Robinson, M, Maletic, V, Oakes, S, Iyengar, S, Ball, G, and Russell, J, 2007. 'Neurobiology of Depression: An Integrated View Of Key Findings' *International Journal Of Clinical Practice*, 61, 2030-2040.

Savic et al., 2008. 'PET and MRI Show Differences In Cerebral Asymmetry and Functional Connectivity Between Homosexual and Heterosexual Subjects' *Proceedings of the National Academy of Sciences*, July 8, vol 105, 9403-9408.

Searle, John, 1995. 'The Mystery of Consciousness' *New York Review Of Books*, Nov 2, 60.

Thompson, E, Varela, F.J, 2003. 'Radical Embodiment; Neural Dynamics And Consciousness' *Trends In Cognitive Science*, 2001, Oct 1, 418-425.

Tucker, D.M, Derryberry, D and Luu, P, 2000. 'Anatomy and Physiology of Human Emotion: Vertical Integration of Brain Stem, Limbic and Cortical Systems' *Handbook of the Neuropsychology of Emotion,* Oxford University Press.

Wiener, M and Mehrabian, A. *Language within Language: Immediacy, a Channel in Verbal Communication.* New York: Appleton-Century-Crofts, 1968.

CHAPTER TWO

Abram, David. *The Spell Of The Sensuous: Perception And Language In a More-Than-Human World.* Vintage, 1997.

Allison, P.J et al., 2003. 'Dispositional Optimism Predicts Survival Status 1 Year After Diagnosis In Head And Neck Cancer Patients' *Journal Of Clinical Oncology*, vol. 21, no.3, 543-548.

Andrade, J and Feinstein, D, 2003. 'Preliminary Report on the First Large-Scale Study of Energy Psychology' *Emotional Freedom Techniques.*

Baron-Reid, Collette. *'Weight Loss for People Who Feel Too Much' Online Course.* Hay House, 2010.

Benson, Herbert. *The Relaxation Response.* Harper Paperbacks, 2000.

Brand, P, 1961. 'Rehabilitation In Leprosy' Video, *Medical Service Bureau.*

Brennan, Barbara. *Hands Of Light: A Guide To Healing Through The Human Energy Field.* Bantam, 1988.

Cousins, Norman. *Anatomy Of An Illness: As Perceived By The Patient.* W.W. Norton & Company, 1981.

Davidson, Richard, 2004. 'What Does the Prefrontal Cortex Do?' *Biological Psychology*, 67, 219-33.

Davidson, Richard. *The Emotional Life Of Your Brain.* Hudson Street Press, 2012.

Davidson, Richard and Kabat-Zinn, Jon. *The Mind's Own Physician: A Scientific Dialogue with the Dalai Lama on the Healing Power of Meditation.* New Harbinger Publications, 2001.

Davidson, R.J, Kabat-Zinn, J, Schumacher, J, Rosenkranz, M, Muller, D, Santorelli, S.F, Urbanowski, F, Harrington, A, Bonus, K and Sheridan, J.F, 2003. 'Alterations In Brain and Immune Function Produced By Mindfulness Meditation' *Psychosomatic Medicine*, 65, 567-70.

Deussen, Paul. *Sixty Upanishads of the Veda (2 Vols).* Motilal Banarsidass, 2010.

Doidge, Norman. *The Brain's Way Of Healing: Stories Of Remarkable Recoveries And Discoveries.* Viking, 2015.

Dusek, J.A, Otu, H.H, Wohlhueter, A.L, Bhasin, M, Zerbini, L.F, Joseph, M.G, Benson, H and Libermann, T.A, 2008. 'Genomic Counter Stress Changes Induced by the Relaxation Response' *PLOS ONE*, 3, 2576.

Easterlin, R.A, 1974. 'Does Economic Growth Improve The Human Lot?' *Proceedings Of The National Academy Of Sciences Of the USA.*

Edwards, Gill. *Conscious Medicine: A Radical New Approach To Creating Health And Well-being.* Piatkus, 2010.

Field, T, Diego, M and Hernandez-Reif, M, 2005. 'Massage Therapy Research' *Dev*, 27, 75-89.

Fiorillo, C.D, Tobler, P.N and Schultz, W. 'Discrete Coding of Reward Probability and Uncertainty by Dopamine Neurons' *Science*, 299, no. 5614, 1898-1902.

Fredrickson, B.L, Cohn, M.A, Coffre, K.A, Pek, J and Finkel, S.M, 2008. 'Open Hearts Build Lives; Positive Emotions, Induced Through Loving Kindness Meditation, Build Consequential Personal Resources' *Journal Of Personality And Psychology*, 95, 1045-62.

Galton, Francis. *Inquiries Into Human Faculty And Its Development.* Macmillan, 1883.

Gambarana, C, Masi, F, Tagliamonte, A et al., 1999. 'A Chronic Stress that Impairs Reactivity in Rats also Decreases Dopaminergic Transmission in the Nucleus Accumbens; a Microdialysis Study' *Journal of Neurochemistry*, 72, no. 5, 2039-2046.

Giltay, E.J et al., 2004. 'Dispositional Optimism And All-Cause And Cardiovascular Mortality In a Prospective Cohort Of Elderly Dutch Men And Women' *Archives Of General Psychiatry*, 61, 1126-1135.

Goldman, Connie and Mahler, Richard. *Tending The Earth, Mending The Spirit: The Healing Gifts Of Gardening*. Hazelden, 2000.

Harper M.L and Drozd, J.F, 2000. 'On the Neural Basis of EMDR Therapy; Insights From qEEG Studies' *Traumatology*, 15, 81-95.

Hausdorff, J.M et al., 1999. 'The Power of Physical Function of Older Persons; Reversibility of Age-related Gait Changes' *Journal of the American Geriatric Society*, 47, no. 11, 1346-49.

Helman, Cecil. *Suburban Shaman*. Hammersmith Press Limited, 2006.

Holzel, B.K, Gard, T, Hempel, H, Weygandt, M, Morgan, K, Vaitl, D, 2008. 'Investigation of Mindfulness Meditation Practitioners With Voxel Based Morphometry' *Social Cognition And Affective Neuroscience*, 3, 55-61.

Keown, Daniel. *The Spark In The Machine*. Singing Dragon, 2014.

Kirkley, Alexandra et al., 2008. 'A Randomised Controlled Trial Of Arthroscopic Surgery For Osteoarthritis Of The Knee' *New England Journal Of Medicine*, vol. 359, 1097-1107.

Kuyken, W, Byford, S, Taylor, R.S, Watkins, E, Holden, E, White, K, Teasdale, J.D, 2008. 'Mindfulness-based Cognitive Therapy To Prevent Relapse In Recurrent Depression' *Journal Of Consulting And Clinical Psychology*, 76, 966-978.

Langer, Ellen. *Mindfulness*. De Capo Press, 1989.

Langer, Ellen. *The Power Of Mindful Learning*. Addison-Wesley, 1997.

Layard, R. *Happiness: Has Social Science A Clue?* Lionel Robbins Memorial Lectures, London School Of Economics, 2003.

Lazar, S, Kerr, C, Wasserman, R, Gray, J, Greve, D, Treadway, M, McGarvey, M, Quinn, B, Dusek, J, Benson, H, Rauch, S, Moore, C and Fischl, B, 2005. 'Meditation Experience Is Associated With Increased Corticol Thickness' *Neuroreport*, 16, 1893-1897.

Levy, R et al., 2002. 'Longevity Increased by Positive Self Perceptions of Aging' *Journal of Personality and Social Psychology*, 83, no. 2, 261-70.

Lipton, Bruce. *The Biology Of Belief*. Hay House, 2008.

Lopez, Shane J and Snyder, C.R. *The Oxford Handbook Of Positive Psychology*. Oxford University Press, 2011.

Lutz, A.L, Greischar, N, Rawling, M, Ricard, and Davidson, R, 2004. Long-term Meditators Self-induce High-amplitude Gamma Synchrony during Mental Practice' *Proceedings of the National Academy of Sciences*, 101, 16369-16373.McEwen, Bruce and Lasley, Elizabeth. *The End Of Stress As We Know It*. Dana Press, 2002.

McLuhan, T.C. *The Message Of Sacred Places: Cathedrals Of The Spirit*. Harper Perennial, 1996.

Medina, John. *Brain Rules For Baby*. Pear Press, 2010.

Moseley, Bruce et al., 2008. 'A Controlled Trial of Arthroscopic Surgery For Osteoarthritis Of The Knee' *New England Journal Of Medicine*, vol. 359, 1097-1107.

Norfolk, Donald. *The Soul Garden: Creating Green Spaces for Inner Growth & Spiritual Renewal*. Overlook Press, 2002.

Rasolkhani-Kalhorn and Harper, M.L, 2006. 'EMDR and Low Frequency Stimulation Of The Brain' *Traumatology*, 12, 9-24.

Riley, Kathryn P et al., 2005. 'Early Life Linguistic Ability, Late Life Cognitive Function, and Neuropathology; Findings from the Nun Study' *Neurobiology of Aging*, 26, no. 3, 341-47.

Rohr, Richard. *Quest For The Grail: Soul Work And The Sacred Journey*. Crossroads Publishing Co, US, 1997.

Roszak, Thedore. *Ecopsychology: Restoring the Earth/Healing the Mind*. Sierra Club Books Publication, 1995.

Ruden, Ronald. *When The Past Is Always Present: Emotional Traumatization, Causes, And Cures*. Routledge, 2011.

Schneider, R.H et al., 2005. 'Longterm Effects Of Stress Reduction On Mortality In Persons Over 55 With Systemic Hypertension' *American Journal Of Cardiology*, 9, 1060-64.

Schwartz, Barry. *The Paradox Of Choice: Why More Is Less*. Harper Perennial, 2005.

Shroevers, M.J and Brandsma, R, 1995. 'Is Learning Mindfulness Associated With Improved Affect After Mindfulness Based Cognitive Therapy?' *British Journal Of Cardiology*, 9, 1960-64.

Stevenson, B and Wolfers, J, 2008. 'Economic Growth And Subjective Well-Being: Reassessing The Easterlin Paradox' *National Bureau Of Economic Research.*

Tomkins, S.S, 1982. 'Affect Theory' *Emotion In The Human Face.* Cambridge University Press.

Weiss, J, 1972. 'Psychological Factors in Stress and Disease' *Scientific American*, 226, 104-113.

Williams, Mark, Teasdale, John, Segal, Zindel and Kabat-Zinn, Jon. *The Mindful Way Through Depression: Freeing Yourself From Chronic Unhappiness.* Guildford Press, 2007.

CHAPTER THREE

Broman-Fulks, J.J, Berman, M.E, Rabian, B.A and Webster, M.J, 2004. 'Effects Of Aerobic Exercise On Anxiety Sensitivity' *Behaviour Research And Therapy*, 42, 125-136.

Broochs, Andreas, 2007. 'Comparison Of Aerobic Exercise, Clomiparime And Placebo Treatment Of Panic Disorder' American Journal Of Psychiatry, 155, 603-9.

Ciorciari, Joseph, 2002. 'EEG Coherence And Dissociative Identity Disorder' *Journal Of Trauma And Dissociation*, vol. 3, issue 1.

Colbert, Don. *Deadly Emotions: Understand The Mind-Body-Spirit Connection That Can Heal Or Destroy You.* Thomas Nelson, 2003.

De Moor, M.H, Beem, A.L, Stable, J.H, Boomsma, D.I, De Geus, E.J, 2006. 'Regular Exercise, Anxiety, Depression And Personality; a Population Based Study' *Prev Med*, Apr 42, 273-9.

Luria, A.R. *Higher Cortical Functions In Man.* Moscow University Press, 1966.

Luria, A.R. *The Man With A Shattered World: The History Of A Brain Wound.* Harvard University Press, 1972.

Ornstein, Robert. *Multimind: A New Way Of Looking At Human Behaviour.* Macmillan, 1986.

Rogers, Carl. *Client Centred Therapy: Its Current Practice, Implications And Theory.* The Riverside Press, 1951.

Sacks, Oliver. *The Man Who Mistook His Wife For A Hat*. Picador, 2011.

Sacks, Oliver. *The Mind's Eye*. Picador, 2010.

Tenberken, Sabriye. *My Path Leads To Tibet*. Arcade Publishing, 2003.

CHAPTER FOUR

Cotman C.W et al., 2007. 'Exercise Builds Brain Health: Key Roles Of Growth Factors Cascades And Inflammation' *Trends In Neuroscience*, 30, no.9.

Damasio, Antonio R et al., 2000. 'Subcortical and Cortical Brain Activity During The Feeling Of Self Generating Emotions' *Neuroscience*, 3, 1049-56.

Davidson, Richard, 2004. 'What Does the Prefrontal Cortex Do?' *Biological Psychology*, 67, 219-33.

Kee, N et al., 2007. 'Preferential Incorporation Of Adult-generated Granule Cells Into Spatial Memory Networks In The Dentate Gyrus' *Nature Neuroscience*, 10, no.3.

Lautenschlager, N.T et al., 2008. 'Effect Of Physical Activity On Cognitive Function In Older Adults At Risk From Alzheimer Disease: A Randomised Trial' *The Journal Of The American Medical Association*, 300, no. 9, 1027-37.

Maguire, E.A, Gadian, N.G, Johnsrude, I.S, Good, C.D, Ashburner, J, Frackowiak, R.S, Fith, C.D, 2000. 'Navigation Related Structural Changes In The Hippocampus Of Taxi Drivers' *Proceedings Of The National Academy Of Sciences Of The USA*.

Merzenich, M.M, Kaas, J.H, Wall, J.T, Nelson, R.J, Sur, M and Felleman, D.J, 1983. 'Progression Of Change Following Median Nerve Section In The Cortical Representation Of The Hand In Areas 3b And 1 In Adult Owl And Squirrel Monkeys' *Neuroscience*, 10, 639-665.

Merzenich, M.M, Nelson, R.J, Kaas, J.H, Stryker, M.P, Zook, W.M, Cynader, M.S and Schoppmann, A, 1987. 'Variability In Hand Surface Representation In Areas 3b and 1 in Adult Owl And Squirrel Monkeys' *Journal Of Comparative Neurology*, 258.

Nudo, R.J, Milliken, G.W, Jenkins, W.M and Merzenich, M.M, 1996. 'Use-Dependent Alterations Of Movement Representations In Primary Motor Cortex Of Adult Squirrel Monkeys' *Journal Of Neuroscience*, 16, 785-807.

O'Regan, J.K, 2001. 'A Sensorimotor Account Of Vision And Visual Consciousness' *Behavioural And Brain Sciences*, 24, 939-1031.

Pons, T.P, Garraghty, P.E, Ommaya, A.K, Kaas, J.H, Taub E and Mishkin, M, 1991. 'Massive Cortical Reorganization After Sensory Deafferentation In Adult Macaques' *Science*, 252.

Ratey, John J. *A User's Guide To The Brain: Perception, Attention, And The Four Theatres Of The Brain*. Vintage, 2001.

Ratey, Dr John J. *Spark!: The Revolutionary New Science Of Exercise And The Brain*. Quercus, 2008.

Sterr, A, Muller, M.M, Elbert, T, Rockstroh, B, Pantev, C and Taub, E, 1998. 'Perceptual Correlates Of Changes In Cortical Representation Of Fingers In Blind Multifinger Braille Readers' *Journal Of Neuroscience*, 18, 4417-4423.

Stryker, Michael P, Jenkins, William, M, Merzenich, Michael M, 1987. 'Anaesthetic State Does Not Affect The Map Of The Hand Representation Within Area 3b Somatosensory Cortex In Owl Monkey' *The Journal Of Comparative Neurology*, 258, 297-303.

Taub, E, Uswatte, G, King, D.K, Morris, D, Crago, J.E and Chatterjee, A, 2006. 'A Placebo Controlled Trial Of Constraint Induced Movement Therapy For Upper Extremity After Stroke' *Stroke*, 37, 1045-49.

CHAPTER FIVE

Behl, C, Davies, J et al.,1992. 'Vitamin E Protects Nerve Cells From Amyloid Beta Protein Toxicity' *Biochemical and Biophysical Research Communications*, 186.2, 944-950.

Brickman, A et al., 2014. 'Enhancing Dentate Gyrus Function With Dietary Flavanols Improves Cognition In Older Adults' *Nature Neuroscience*, 17, 1798-1803.

Gedgaudas, Nora T. *Beyond The Paleo Diet For Total Health And A Longer Life*. Healing Arts Press, 2011.

Moller-Levet et al., 2013. 'Effects Of Insufficient Sleep On Circadian Rhythmicity And Expression Amplitude Of The Human Blood Transcriptome' *Proceedings Of The National Academy Of Science*, 110, 12.

Saul, Andrew. *Doctor Yourself: Natural Healing That Works*. Basic Health Publications, 2012.

Siegel, D, 2015. 'This Is What Happens To Your Brain And Body When You Check Your Phone Before Going To Sleep' *Business Insider UK*, Feb 17.

Taheri, S et al., 2004. 'Short Sleep Duration Is Associated With Reduced Leptin, Elevated Ghrelin, And Increased Body Mass Index' *PLOS Medicine*, 1, no. 3.

CHAPTER SIX

Baer, R.A, Smith, G.T, Hopkins, J, Krietemeyer, J and Toney, L, 2006. 'Using Self Report Assessment Methods To Explore Facets Of Mindfulness' *Assessment*, 13, 27-45.

Begley, Sharon. *The Plastic Mind*. Constable, 2009.

Bird, G et al., 2010. 'Empathetic Brain Responses In Insula Are Modulated By Levels Of Alexithymia But Not Autism' *Brain*, 133, 1515-25.

Craig, A.D, 2002. 'How Do We Feel? Interoception: The Sense Of The Physiological Condition Of The Body' *Nature Reviews Neuroscience*, 3, 655-66.

Davidson, R.J, Kabat-Zinn, J, Schumacher, J, Rosenkranz, M, Muller, D, Santorelli, S.F, Urbanowski, F, Harrington, A, Bonus, K and Sheridan, J.F, 2003. 'Alterations In Brain and Immune Function Produced By Mindfulness Meditation' *Psychosomatic Medicine*, 65, 567-70.

Davidson, R.J and Kabat-Zinn, J. *The Mind's Own Physician: A Scientific Dialogue with the Dalai Lama on the Healing Power of Meditation*. New Harbinger Publications, 2001.

Dawkins, Richard. *The Selfish Gene*. Oxford University Press, 1999.

Dias-Ferreira, E et al., 2009. 'Chronic Stress Causes Frontostriatal Reorganization And Affects Decision-Making' *Science*, 325, no. 5940, 621-25.

Erikson, Erik H. *Young Man Luther: A Study In Psychoanalysis And History*. W. W. Norton & Company, 1958.

Esdaile, James. *Mesmerism In India, and Its Practical Application In Surgery And Medicine*. Forgotten Books, 2012.

Fredrickson, B.L and Tugade, M.M, 2004. 'Resilient Individuals Use Positive Emotions To Bounce Back From Negative Emotional Experiences' *Journal Of Personality And Social Psychology*, 86, 320-33.

Godden, D and Baddeley, A.D, 1980. 'When Does Context Influence Recognition Memory?' *British Journal Of Psychology*, 71, 99-104.

Helman, Cecil. *Suburban Shaman*. Hammersmith Press Limited, 2006.

Hillman, James and Christou, Evangelos. *The Logos Of The Soul*. New York Spring Publications, 2007.

Ivanowski, B and Malhi, G.S, 2007. 'The Psychological And Neuro-physiological Concomitants Of Mindfulness Forms Of Meditation' *Acta Neuropsychiatrica*, 19, 76-91.

James, Tad, Flores, Lorraine and Schober, Jack. *Hypnosis: A Comprehensive Guide*. Crown House Publishing, 2000.

Jha, A et al., 2007. 'Mindfulness Training Modifies Subsystems Of Attention' *Cognitive Affective And Behavioral Neuroscience*, 7, 109-19.

Kessler, R.C et al., 1995. 'Posttraumatic Stress Disorder In The National Comorbidity Survey' *Archives Of General Psychiatry*, 52, no.12, 1048-60.

Kurzweil, Ray. *The Singularity Is Near: When Humans Transcend Biology*. Penguin Books, 2006.

Kuyken, W, Byford, S, Taylor, R.S, Watkins, E, Holden, E, White, K, Teasdale, J.D, 2008. 'Mindfulness-based Cognitive Therapy To Prevent Relapse In Recurrent Depression' *Journal Of Consulting And Clinical Psychology*, 76, 966-978.

Levine, Peter. *Waking The Tiger: Healing Trauma – The Innate Capacity To Transform Overwhelming Experiences*. North Atlantic Books, 1997.

Low, C.A, Stanton, A.L and Bower, J.E, 2008. 'Effects Of Acceptance-Oriented Versus Evaluative Emotional Processing On Heart Rate Recovery And Habituation' *Emotion*, 8, 419-24.

Michalak, J, 2010. 'Embodied Effects Of Mindfulness-Based Cognitive Therapy' *Journal Of Psychosomatic Research*, 68, 311-14.

Peres, Julio F et al., 2007. 'Cerebral Blood Flow Changes During Retrieval Of Traumatic Memories Before And After Psychotherapy ASPECT Study' *Psychological Medicine*, 37, 1481-1491.

Perlmutter, David and Villoldo, Alberto. *Power Up Your Brain: The Neuroscience Of Enlightenment*. Hay House, 2011.

Sapolsky, R.M. *Stress: Aging Brain And The Mechanisms Of Neuron Death.* MIT Press, 1992.

Wax, Ruby. *Sane New World: Taming The Mind*. Hodder & Stoughton, 2013.

Weaver, I.C.G et al., 2005. 'Reversal Of Maternal Programming Of Stress Responses In Adult Offspring Through Methyl Supplementation: Altering Epigenetic Marking Later In Life' *The Journal Of Neuroscience*, 25(47), 11045-11054.

ALSO AVAILABLE FROM NICKY SNAZELL

The 4 Keys To Health

This book is a self-help manual of preventative health. It has four chapters – mind, food, fitness, and lifestyle – with questionnaires that score you red, amber, and green in terms of health; holding 4 green keys means you are in optimum health.

This book is a result of 30 years' study in the fields of biology, psychology, physiotherapy, and pain. It is my personal insight into health, shared with my patients and audiences internationally.

You can view a YouTube video of Nicky explaining the book at:
https://www.youtube.com/watch?v=sc_i1b979XA

COMING SOON FROM NICKY SNAZELL

The Body (The Human Garage Part 2)

Exercise is so needed by the body – it literally cries out for it – and the softer mind-body exercises are also so important when it comes to self-awareness and healing. The body is biological: you have to stress it for the muscles and bones to strengthen!

Throughout this series of books I am going to share with you my recipes of integrated medicine for physical health, and in this edition we focus on the body.

The Body is the second book in *The Human Garage* trilogy, and it will be available soon.

The Human Garage Part 3, The Soul, will also be available soon. This book will explore the science and spirituality of energy healing and the power of hands-on healing, as well as touching on the psychic side of things.

Lightning Source UK Ltd.
Milton Keynes UK
UKOW06f0803241115

263408UK00002B/7/P